127906.
(Gulf War
. etc ,

DARK VICTORY

DARK VICTORY

America's Second War Against Iraq

Jeffrey Record

Naval Institute Press
Annapolis, Maryland

Naval Institute Press
291 Wood Road
Annapolis, MD 21402

Library of Congress Cataloging-in-Publication Data
Record, Jeffrey.
     Dark victory: America's second war against Iraq / Jeffrey Record.
     p. cm.
     Includes bibliographical references and index.
     ISBN 1-59114-711-5 (alk. paper)
     1. Iraq War, 2003—Causes. 2. Iraq War, 2003—Influence. 3. Iraq War, 2003—Reconstruction. 4. United States—Politics and government—2001—5. National security—United States. I. Title.
     DS79.76.R43 2004
     956.7044'3—dc22
                    2003026154

Printed in the United States of America on acid-free paper ∞
11 10 09 08 07 06 05 04   9 8 7 6 5 4 3 2
First printing

Contents

Preface   vii

1   The Unfinished Business of 1991   1

2   The Neoconservative Vision and 9/11   17

3   The Bush Doctrine   30

4   Enemies: Osama's Al-Qaeda and Saddam's Iraq   45

5   War Aims   64

6   Analogies: Munich, Vietnam, and Postwar Japan   78

7   The War   90

8   The "Peace"   117

9   Dark Victory   141

Notes   157

Bibliography   173

Index   195

Preface

In the late spring of 2003, the United States concluded the so-called major combat phase of its second war against Iraq in just over twelve years. Both wars were relatively cheap in American blood, certainly when compared to twentieth-century U.S. conflicts against the Germans, Japanese, Chinese, and Vietnamese. Both wars were also short and militarily decisive; Iraqi forces were strategically isolated and hopelessly outclassed in almost every respect, especially leadership, training, manpower quality, and technology.

Yet politically—and wars are, after all, waged for political objectives—the results were less satisfying. The war of 1991 achieved its main declared political objectives of liberating Kuwait from Iraqi occupation and restoring its monarchy, and in so doing, thwarted Baghdad's bid for hegemony in the Persian Gulf. But Operation Desert Storm failed to topple Saddam Hussein, notwithstanding the George H. W. Bush administration's expectations that it would. The war erased the consequences of Saddam's aggression but left the perpetrator intact, albeit severely weakened. That failure, in turn, set the stage for the war of 2003, which did indeed remove the Iraqi dictator but which also saddled the United States with Iraq's political and economic reconstruction in circumstances of mounting insurgent violence. Rebuilding Iraq always was a tall order given not only the legacy of totalitarian rule and Iraqi society's deep ethnic and religious divisions but also the George W. Bush administration's indisposition toward "nation-building." Additionally, the second war, coming as it did in the wake of the Bush administration's de facto albeit temporary withdrawal from the Arab-Israeli peace process, excited profoundly negative reactions in the Islamic world. In so doing, it may have impeded America's war on terrorism by alienating Arab allies and expanding al-Qaeda's recruiting base. Indeed, U.S. failure to forestall the collapse of order and subsequent emergence of insurgent attacks on U.S. forces in postwar Iraq provided new opportunities for Islamic jihadists of all stripes who saw in Iraq an American analog to the Soviet experience in Afghanistan.

Though the two American wars against Iraq are historically linked, they were quite different in nature, objective, and legitimacy. The war of 1991 was a limited war dedicated to overturning a flagrant act of aggression and was waged by a grand global coalition operating under a United Nations' mandate. The legitimacy of Kuwait's forcible liberation was self-evident; the war's objective was to restore the status quo ante—that is, a Kuwait free of Iraqi control. The war of 2003, in contrast, was a preventive war to thwart Saddam Hussein's eventual acquisition of nuclear weapons, which the administration of George W. Bush believed would permit the Iraqi dictator to deter U.S. military action against his future transgressions. As such, it provoked substantial international opposition, even on the part of old friends and allies. There was no UN or other international institutional mandate.

The immediate aims of the second war were to remove Saddam Hussein and to strip Iraq of all its weapons of mass destruction. The war also demonstrated a willingness to act upon the precepts of the controversial use-of-force doctrine propounded by the Bush administration in the wake of the September 11, 2001, al-Qaeda attacks on the United States. The administration intended the war as a vivid warning to other hostile rogue states seeking to acquire weapons of mass destruction.

Beyond these objectives lay, at least in the eyes of the influential neoconservatives who provided the intellectual rationale for the war of 2003, the opportunity to transform Iraq into a model democracy whose very existence would undermine the autocratic regimes that dominate the Arab world, including such U.S. allies as Saudi Arabia and Egypt. In a speech at the neoconservative American Enterprise Institute in February 2002, the president himself declared: "A liberated Iraq can show the power of freedom to transform that vital [Middle East] region by bringing hope and progress into the lives of millions. . . . A new [democratic] regime in Iraq could serve as a dramatic and inspiring example of freedom for other nations in the region." The president went on to cite the success of the United States in transforming defeated postwar Germany and Japan into democratic states, noting that, at the time, "many said that the cultures of Japan and Germany were incapable of sustaining democratic values."[1]

The creation of an American client state in Iraq also would, it was believed, provide a substitute for a U.S.–Saudi security relationship compromised by Saudi promotion of Islamic extremism from which the September 11 attacks arose, as well as afford the United States a geographic base from which to intimidate Iran. In turn, a benign Iraq and a cowed Iran would redound to the immense strategic benefit of Israel, America's chief client state in the Middle East and a major focus of neoconservative security strategy in the Middle East and Persian Gulf.

It is, of course, still too early to judge the second war's lasting political and strategic consequences for Iraq, the Middle East, the war on terrorism, and the standing of the United States in the international community. But it is not too early to use the experience of the war and its immediate aftermath as a perspective from which to examine its origins, objectives, conduct, and unfolding strategic consequences. The historic and policy origins were manifest before hostilities commenced, as were declared and undeclared U.S. war aims. Moreover, an extensive body of informed prewar speculation about the war's conduct and consequences provided a context in which to judge actual military operations and political outcomes.

This book examines the origins, objectives, conduct, and consequences of the 2003 war against Iraq, just as did an earlier book of mine for the 1991 war. Indeed, if the second war against Iraq was essentially a continuation of the first, this book is no less a sequel to *Hollow Victory: A Contrary View of the Gulf War*. That book was so titled to underscore Saddam Hussein's political survival notwithstanding his forcible eviction from Kuwait and the destruction of much of his military power. That Saddam's overthrow was not an explicitly declared war aim cannot conceal the George H. W. Bush administration's obvious desire to remove him from power. President Bush's public comparison of Saddam Hussein to Adolf Hitler suggested no acceptable fate other than the dictator's extinction. U.S. forces, under the rubric of attacking "leadership" targets, bombed many places of his suspected whereabouts, and President Bush publicly called upon Iraqis to rid themselves of Saddam. There was, too, the declared U.S. war aim of restoring "the peace and stability of the Persian Gulf," which by definition could not be secured as long as Saddam remained in power; it was, after all, Saddam's invasion of Kuwait that had shattered the region's peace and stability in the first place. Bush himself conceded at the time of victory that he didn't share the "wonderfully euphoric feeling that many of the American people feel. . . . There was a definitive end to [World War II]," Bush said, but the Gulf War had ended "with Saddam Hussein still in power there—the man who wreaked this havoc upon his neighbors."[2]

But at the moment of military victory the administration was not prepared to assume responsibility for the political reconstruction of a post-Saddam Iraq, so it refused to order U.S. forces to advance on Baghdad. On the contrary, it declared a unilateral cease fire in the absence of any Iraqi request for terms, and it refused to support the Shiite and Kurdish rebellions, which may have come close to bringing Saddam down even without U.S. assistance. Subsequently, Dick Cheney, who was secretary of defense during the 1991 war and went on to become Pres. George W. Bush's vice president and a strong proponent of a second war on Iraq, explained U.S. inaction:

If you're going to go in and try to topple Saddam Hussein, you have to go to Baghdad. Once you've got Baghdad, it's not clear what you do with it. It's not clear what kind of government you would put in place of the one that's currently there now. Is it going to be a Shia regime, a Sunni regime or a Kurdish regime? Or one that tilts toward the Ba'athists, or one that tilts toward the Islamic fundamentalists? How much credibility is that government going to have if it's set up by the United States military when it's there? How long does the United States military have to stay to protect the people that sign on for that government, and what happens to it once we leave?[3]

Hollow Victory was highly critical of Desert Storm's disparity between military performance and political results:

While Desert Storm removed a symptom of the Iraqi "problem," . . . it failed to eliminate the problem's source. Saddam Hussein's continued governance of Iraq, and the survival of much of Iraq's latent capacity to threaten its neighbors, and to acquire usable ballistic missile and hyperlethal munitions capabilities, has voided Desert Storm's victory of much of its potential and intended political content. No satisfactory or enduring resolution of the Gulf crisis was possible without Saddam Hussein's removal from power, and his very survival is seen by some Arabs as an inspirational victory over a long-detested West. . . .

The very fact that one day in the coming years U.S. military forces might again have to return to the Persian Gulf to defend a helpless Kuwait and Saudi Arabia against a militarily resurgent Iraq, commanded by a Saddam Hussein now lusting for revenge, suggests that if Desert Storm was a crowning military achievement, it was also no less a politically bankrupt victory. While it temporarily wrecked much of the Iraqi army, it failed to eliminate an Iraqi leadership . . . that continues to pose, as it did before the Gulf War, the major threat to the Persian's Gulf "security and stability." That job remains unfinished.[4]

The war of 2003 corrected the mistake of 1991, but it was a preventive war against a hypothetical threat and may have created more problems than the one it solved. Translating military victory into an enduring, better peace is inherently difficult. The victors of World War I failed to so do in Europe, as did the George H. W. Bush administration in the Persian Gulf seven decades later. The task in the Gulf today is especially challenging, given the artificiality of the Iraqi state and the illegitimacy of the second U.S. war against Iraq in the eyes of the Arab and larger Muslim worlds. "Iraq is the Arab Yugoslavia," contended the journalist Thomas L. Friedman before the war. "It is a country congenitally divided among Kurds, Shiites and Sunnis, that was forged by British power and has never been held together by anything other than an iron fist. Transforming Iraq into a state with an accountable, consensual and decent government would be the biggest, most audacious war of choice any U.S. president has ever made— because it doesn't just involve getting rid of Saddam, but also building an integrated Iraq for the first time."[5]

In examining the origins, objectives, conduct, and consequences of America's second war against Iraq, this book focuses on the intersection of international politics, national foreign policy, and military action. It is policy analysis, not historical narrative; assessment, not description; informed judgment, not factual recitation. It examines the interaction of policy and war.

Chapter 1 examines the continuities of the first and second U.S. wars against Iraq. It focuses heavily on the manner in which the 1991 war was terminated and the quality of the "peace" it produced. It also assesses, in the context of U.S. and Iraqi war aims, the deterrent role of weapons of mass destruction during the war. The George W. Bush administration has declared that nuclear deterrence is no longer sufficient to assure U.S. security in the face of threats posed by rogue states like that of the recently deposed Saddam Hussein.

The failure of the first war to remove Saddam Hussein by no means made the second war inevitable; the terrorist attacks of 9/11 were pivotal in propelling the George W. Bush administration toward war on Iraq.[6] Saddam's very survival and his determination to overthrow the UN-mandated regime of weapons inspection and economic sanctions guaranteed an extremely hostile relationship between Washington and Baghdad. Moreover, if Saddam provided the central Iraqi continuity of the two wars, Pres. George W. Bush and his key foreign policy lieutenants provided it for the American side. The president's father waged the first war against Iraq, and the son brought key architects of that war into his administration, including Vice President Cheney (secretary of defense in 1991), Secretary of Defense Colin Powell (chairman of the Joint Chiefs of Staff in 1991), and Deputy Secretary of Defense Paul Wolfowitz (undersecretary of defense for policy in 1991). Pres. George W. Bush also selected as his national security adviser Condoleezza Rice, who had served his father on the National Security Council staff.

Chapter 2 examines the neoconservative "primacist" vision of America's role in the post–Cold War world and that vision's influence on President Bush's post-9/11 foreign, Middle East, and Iraq policies. Throughout the 1990s the neoconservatives, inspired by the foreign policies of Ronald Reagan, articulated their views on the role of the United States in the post–Cold War era, and they brought those ideas into the George W. Bush administration. Well-articulated ideas can have powerful policy consequences, and neoconservative thinking has not only provided the intellectual foundation of the administration's foreign policy but also accounts for the strong foreign policy unilateralism that has so dismayed allies and adversaries alike. Underlying the war and unilateralism is a foreign policy that seeks to enlist the offensive employment of U.S. military power on behalf of the globalization of American political values.

Chapter 3 documents and critically assesses the specific tenets of the use-of-force doctrine explicated by the George W. Bush White House after the 9/11 attacks and enshrined in the issuance in September 2002 of *The National Security Strategy of the United States of America*. Particular focus is accorded to the doctrine's controversial emphasis on preventive war as a means of assuring permanent U.S. military primacy. Other issues addressed include the doctrine's reassessment of deterrence and containment, its focus on regime change, its transformation of an implicit policy option—striking first— into a declaratory policy, and the precedent the doctrine offers for others to follow. Not since the proclamation of the Truman doctrine in 1947 has so sweeping a foreign policy shift been declared.

Chapter 4 addresses Saddam's prewar susceptibility to traditional policies of deterrence and containment and the relationship of the war against Iraq to the global U.S. war on terrorism. The Bush doctrine contends that deterrence and containment are inadequate means of dealing with terrorist organizations or with rogue states. In the case of Saddam Hussein, the Bush White House argued that only preventive war could eliminate the Iraqi threat. But that very war itself was intended to have a deterrent effect on others aspiring to challenge American military primacy. As for the relationship between the war on terrorism and Iraq, the Bush administration, in very much the same way that the Truman doctrine and NSC-68 postulated an undifferentiated, monolithic Communist threat, has lumped together Saddam Hussein and al-Qaeda, rogue states and international terrorist organizations. The Bush administration insisted before the war that Saddam and al-Qaeda, by virtue of having a common American enemy, had to be approached as a common enemy. This chapter assesses the validity, wisdom, and potential strategic consequences of doing so, using historical parallels where appropriate. Strategy is about discrimination and choice within an environment of limited resources, and the Bush administration's declared ambitions in the war on terrorism must be judged on that basis.

Chapter 5 examines declared and undeclared U.S. war aims, which range from a minimalist disarmament of Iraq to its democratization to the political transformation of the Middle East itself. The Bush administration has hitched its Middle East policy to an ambitious neoconservative agenda, which envisages regime change in Iraq as a vehicle for regional political revolution. During the 1991 war against Iraq and its aftermath, the George H. W. Bush administration hoped for a coup against Saddam that left intact military governance of Iraq; the alternative, it feared, was popular rebellion leading to the disintegration of central political authority and subsequent Iranian and other foreign intervention. That administration was dominated by realists who eschewed values in favor of interests as the basis for foreign policy. In contrast, the present administration has embraced an aggressive, values-based foreign policy that calls for preventive military action against potential threats to America's national security and the employment of force to create opportunities to spread democracy. The aims of the second war against Iraq flowed from this policy.

Analogies—Munich, Vietnam, and postwar Japan—are the subject of chapter 6, which draws upon my previous work *Making War, Thinking History*.[7] In using force, presidents have inevitably reasoned by historical analogy, and Pres. George W. Bush has been no exception. His administration justified preventive war against Iraq using the analogy of the democracies' failure to stop Hitler and other Axis aggressors in the 1930s; indeed, the president used the term "axis of evil" to describe the three target states of the Bush doctrine. If, however, proponents of the second war against Iraq invoked Munich, critics invoked the other dominant use-of-force analogy of the past three decades: the lost war in Vietnam. Their concern focused not on the military challenge of overthrowing Saddam Hussein (thought by hawks and most doves before the war to be quite feasible) but on the potential Iraqi political quagmire into which the United States would risk stumbling by virtue of a military victory. This was the same concern of the George H. W. Bush administration in 1991 and accounted for its swift military departure from Iraq at the conclusion of Operation Desert Storm and its refusal to assist popular uprisings against Saddam.

The chapter closes with an assessment of the validity of the Munich and Vietnam analogies as informants of the debate over the second war against Iraq and the analogy of direct U.S. military rule of Japan from 1945 to 1951 as an informant of the U.S. occupation of Iraq.

Chapter 7 assesses the interaction of policy and military operations. It examines the harmony of stated political aims and specific combat objectives as they were influenced by anticipated and unanticipated events that arose during the course of hostilities and their immediate aftermath. This chapter also assesses U.S. and Iraqi military performances in comparison to those of 1991. Before neither war was there any official doubt that Iraq could and would be defeated. In 2003, however, both sides pursued strategies quite different than those used in 1991—the United States because its war aims were more ambitious and Iraq because it had learned during the first war the futility of a territorial defense. Additionally, in the run-up to the 2003 war there was considerable division within the administration, roughly along civilian versus professional military lines, on the strength of anticipated Iraqi resistance. Optimists tended to believe that the Iraqi people, including those in the regular army, were eagerly awaiting liberation and that the certainty of a U.S. victory would demolish morale even inside the Republican Guard. Accordingly, they anticipated a quick Iraqi military collapse. In contrast were the more cautious military professionals, who did not assume the popularity inside Iraq of an American invasion and who anticipated the possibility of protracted urban warfare as the only means of bringing Saddam down.

Chapter 8 examines the difficulties, expected and unexpected, of transitioning from combat to stability and reconstruction operations. Clearly, the Bush administration expended much more time and energy on planning the war than it did on planning the peace. It is equally clear that the administration was surprised by the magnitude of civil disorder that erupted in the wake of the regime's collapse and that deep divisions within the administration impeded formulation and execution of a comprehensive and internally consistent program for Iraq's reconstruction. Matters were not helped by the administration's mistaken assumption that Iraqi gratitude for being liberated from Saddam Hussein would translate into welcome for an open-ended U.S. military occupation. Further complicating the challenges of restoring order and creating a new and democratic Iraqi society were the survival of significant Ba'athist Party remnants and the arrival of foreign jihadists looking to do battle with the American occupation.

Chapter 9 addresses the wisdom of the war and its likely political consequences. Specifically, it draws conclusions on the validity of the Bush doctrine as applied to Saddam Hussein's Iraq, rogue state motives for acquiring nuclear weapons, the strength and imminence of the Iraqi threat in 2003, the Bush administration's decision for war, the consequences of the war on Iraq for the war on terrorism, and the effects of the war on America's global leadership.

It is the central conclusion of this book that the U.S. war against Iraq in 2003 was not only unnecessary but also damaging to long-term U.S. political interests in the world. The war was unnecessary because Iraq posed no measure of danger to the United States that could justify war, and it was damaging because of the preventive, unilateralist nature of the war and because of the evident lack of preparedness of the United

States to deal with the predictable consequences of destroying the Saddam Hussein regime. Far from being a major victory in the Bush administration's declared war on terrorism, the war and its aftermath provided terrorists an expanded recruiting base and a new front of operations against Americans.

DARK
VICTORY

1

The Unfinished Business of 1991

The most immediate legacies of the 1991 Gulf War were the restoration of a sovereign Kuwait and of American military self-confidence. But given the events of 2003, by far the most strategically consequential legacy was the failure to topple Saddam Hussein, whose survival, defiance, lust for revenge, and suspected continuing efforts to acquire nuclear weapons occasioned the second American war with Iraq. In a sense, the intervening twelve years were a continuation of war by other means, including the U.S. establishment of no-fly zones over most of Iraqi territory, repeated punitive air and missile strikes, the imposition and enforcement of stringent military and economic sanctions, and sponsorship of potential coups to get rid of the Iraqi dictator. That said, there probably would have been no second war absent the terrorist attacks of 9/11. Those attacks and the Bush administration's reaction to them set the United States on the road to Operation Iraqi Freedom.

Ironically, it was only after the Gulf War that Saddam's removal became a declared objective of U.S. policy. Yet all measures short of invasion failed, leaving the policy choice that of continuing to pursue Saddam's containment and deterrence—even as the Gulf War coalition disintegrated—or resuming hostilities to destroy his regime. Until September 11, 2001, the administration seemed content with containment and deterrence, but the terrorist attacks on the United States produced a dramatic shift in policy.

Given the connection between the way in which the 1991 war was terminated and the perceived necessity to "finish the job" twelve years later—that is, given the likelihood that Saddam's destruction in 1991 would have voided the perceived need for a second riskier and more expensive war against Iraq—it is important to understand why the United States terminated the first war the way it did. Several facts contribute to this understanding.

First, though the George H. W. Bush administration, like virtually every one of its predecessors, cloaked its military interventions in the rhetoric of a moral crusade, the administration's foreign policy was predominately interest based. It used force in places like Panama and the Persian Gulf in situations where important, even vital, U.S. interests were threatened, and conspicuously resisted pressure for intervention in places, like the disintegrating Yugoslavia of the early 1990s, where such interests were believed to be absent, notwithstanding mushrooming Serbian atrocities that threatened to destabilize southeastern Europe. (The administration did send troops to Somalia for purely humanitarian reasons, but it did not anticipate either hostilities or a prolonged deployment.)

George H. W. Bush ultimately mobilized public opinion for war in 1991 on the basis not of appeals for a new world order free of acts of aggression but rather on the vivid postulation of a Saddam Hussein eventually armed with nuclear weapons.[1] Ironically, this was the core argument for war against Iraq in 2003 advanced by George W. Bush, although this argument was embedded in a larger ideological vision of America's moral mission in the world.

As "realists," those who formulated U.S. foreign policy from 1989 to 1993 focused on the international, not the internal, behavior of states. They rejected "do-goodism" for its own sake, including military intervention in circumstances where the United States had no concrete material interests, though they were certainly willing to drape American values over their realpolitik for the sake of mobilizing domestic public opinion. They went to war in the Gulf not for the sake of the Kuwaiti or the Iraqi people but to prevent the rise of a hostile hegemon in a region of incontestable strategic importance to the United States and its allies. For the George H. W. Bush administration, the Gulf War was first and foremost about oil and power, not about forging a "new world order" or ending tyranny in Baghdad. Indeed, the president had served for eight years as vice president in a Reagan administration that had strategically embraced Saddam Hussein as a de facto cobelligerent in Iraq's war against Iran.[2]

Second, the Bush administration of 1991 preferred a restoration of the status quo ante to regime change in Baghdad. The latter goal exceeded the UN mandate that the president had worked so hard to obtain. It also threatened to destabilize Iraq, for whose political and economic reconstruction the administration was not prepared to assume any responsibility. When the administration looked at Saddam Hussein, it saw an Arab Hitler, but when it looked at a march on Baghdad, it saw a desert Vietnam—an Arab quagmire in which disintegrated central political authority in Iraq mandated an open-ended U.S. occupation of the country as an alternative to Iranian intervention.

The administration would have welcomed a coup that removed the dictator, but it was not prepared to support the replacement of autocratic military rule in Iraq. It preferred stability over justice. In 1998 Brent Scowcroft, who had been the president's national security adviser in 1991, told ABC Television News, "I frankly wished [the Kurdish and Shiite uprising] hadn't happened. I envisioned a post-war government being a military government. . . . It's the colonel with the brigade patrolling the palace that's going to get [Saddam] if someone gets him." According to Richard Haass, who in 1991 was director for Middle East affairs on the National Security Council staff, U.S. policy was "to get rid of Saddam Hussein, not his regime."[3]

Third, the Bush administration of 1991 had good, perhaps even compelling, reasons for terminating the war the way it did; there was no international dissent, and no internal administration dissent, with the notable exception of Under Secretary of Defense Paul Wolfowitz.[4] In their joint memoir of the administration's major foreign policy accomplishments published in 1998, Bush and Scowcroft admit that "[t]he end of effective Iraqi resistance came with a rapidity which surprised us all, and we were perhaps psychologically unprepared for the sudden transition from fighting to peacemaking." With respect to Saddam's fate, they believed that "[t]rying to eliminate Saddam, extending the ground war into an occupation of Iraq, would have violated our guideline about changing objectives in midstream, engaging in 'mission creep,' and would have incurred incalculable human and political costs." Also: "Going in and occupying Iraq, thus unilaterally exceeding the United Nations' mandate, would have destroyed the precedent of international response to aggression that we hoped to establish. Had we gone the invasion route, the United States could conceivably still be an occupying power in a bitterly hostile land." Moreover, the idea of "forcing Saddam personally to accept the terms of Iraqi defeat at Safwan [the site of the cease-fire discussions] . . . and thus the responsibility and political consequences for the humiliation of such a devastating defeat" was in the end rejected because "we asked ourselves what we would do if he refused."[5] (Obviously, nothing.)

Secretary of State James A. Baker III recounted after the war that the administration's "overriding strategic concern . . . [was] to avoid what we often referred to as the Lebanonization of Iraq, which we believed would create a geopolitical nightmare." He also said that President Bush's unilateral cease-fire decision "was enthusiastically endorsed by the military, our coalition partners, the Congress, and American public opinion." He dismissed the "marching-to-Baghdad" option as a "canard," asserting that "the real objective was to eject Iraq from Kuwait in a manner that would destroy Saddam's offensive military capabilities and make his fall from power likely." Marching on Baghdad "would make a nationalist hero out of

Saddam" and transform the coalition war to liberate Kuwait into "a U.S. war of conquest." Baker also raised "the specter of a military occupation" and "ensuing urban warfare" that would create "a political firestorm at home" and prompt "the dissolution of the coalition." He concluded his discussion of war termination by declaring, "Saddam's departure was never a stated objective of our policy. We were always very careful to negate it as a war aim or a political objective."[6]

Colin Powell's memoirs display a particular sensitivity over the way the administration he served in 1991 handled war termination. "What tends to be forgotten is that while the United States led the way, we were heading an *international* coalition carrying out a clearly defined UN mission," he wrote. "Of course, we would have loved to see Saddam overthrown. . . . But that did not happen. And the President's demonizing of Saddam as the devil incarnate did not help the public understand why he was allowed to stay in power. It is naïve, however, to think that if Saddam had fallen, he would necessarily have been replaced by a Jeffersonian in some sort of desert democracy where people read *The Federalist Papers* along with the Koran." Powell concluded: "I stand by my role in the President's decision to end the war when and how he did. It is an accountability I carry with pride and without apology." Gen. H. Norman Schwarzkopf, who commanded Operation Desert Storm, declared in his memoirs that "at the time the war ended there was not a single head of state, diplomat, Middle East expert, or military leader who, as far as I am aware, advocated continuing the war and seizing Baghdad." Had the United States done so, "we would have been considered occupying powers and therefore would have been responsible for *all* the costs of maintaining or restoring government, education, and other services for the people of Iraq. . . . [W]e would have been like the dinosaur in the tar pit—we would still be there."[7]

Fourth, the Bush administration of 1991 made its decision to halt the war on the basis of an erroneous picture of the battlefield. President Bush gave the order to cease hostilities on the assumption that Iraq's Republican Guard, an indispensable pillar of Saddam's rule, had been destroyed in combat or trapped in southern Iraq. It thus believed the military victory to be of a greater strategic magnitude than was actually the case. Bush and Scowcroft admitted that, shortly after the cease-fire, "[w]e . . . discovered that more of the Republican Guard survived the war than we had believed or anticipated. Owing to the unexpected swiftness of the Marine advance into Kuwait, the Guard [operational] reserves were not drawn south into battle—and into the trap created by the western sweep around and behind Kuwait as we had planned." Powell also conceded that "more tanks and Republican Guard troops escaped from Kuwait than we expected," but that did not mean that "Saddam had pulled off some sort of Dunkirk at the end of Desert Storm."[8]

In fact, though crushing the Republican Guard had been one of six stated coalition military objectives, about half (four-plus out of eight divisions) of the Republican Guard in the Kuwaiti theater of operations escaped with most of their weapons and equipment.[9] The Marine Corps attack into Kuwait from the coalition right flank was expected to encounter tough resistance by frontline Iraqi regular army forces, thereby buying time for Republican Guard forces, withheld as an operational reserve, to move forward (southward) to reinforce the Iraqi line. At that point, Schwarzkopf would unleash the massive "left hook" that would encircle the Iraqis from the rear and "close the gate," thus bagging the entire lot, including the Republican Guard. Schwarzkopf, however, failed to adjust his battle plan to the unexpectedly swift collapse of the regular Iraqi army resistance to the marine advance into Kuwait. The "left hook" was not launched to "close the gate" in time to prevent a fighting withdrawal of many Republican Guard units back into Iraq.[10]

It was of course the escaped Republican Guard forces that crushed the Shiite and Kurdish rebellions. Because of this mistaken assumption about the guard, the administration had good reason to believe that Saddam would not survive the coalition victory. Baker conceded that "we never really expected him to survive a defeat of such magnitude." Thus, because of the coalition's misfire against the Republican Guard, wrote Bush and Scowcroft, "[w]e were disappointed that Saddam's defeat did not break his hold on power, as many of our Arab allies had predicted and we had come to expect."[11]

Fifth, even though enough of the Republican Guard got away to keep Saddam Hussein in power, the Bush administration, via the combination of the Gulf War and subsequent imposition of a tough sanctions and inspections regime, still managed to eliminate Iraq as a territorial aggressor state. Indeed, by the time Desert Storm was launched, Kuwait's liberation had become incidental to the larger strategic objective of taking down Iraq's conventional military power and war-making infrastructure. Operation Desert Storm thus contained a powerful element of prevention in the form of attacks on targets deep inside Iraq, such as nuclear, chemical, and biological weapons research and production facilities, that had no bearing on Iraq's ability to defend Kuwait. The administration "clearly placed great weight on the need to destroy Iraq's military machine, including its incipient capabilities in weapons of mass destruction," observed two critics of the administration's war termination behavior. "This barely disguised motive for the war recalled the classic justification for preventive war, which has always been that offensive war is an indispensable and justified means for dealing with future, though probable, threats to the vital interests of a state."[12]

Should the United States have marched to Baghdad and brought down Saddam and his regime? It is difficult to envisage the perceived necessity of a second war against Iraq absent Saddam Hussein's survival of the first. But at the time the arguments against doing so were convincing, at least for an administration riding the crest of a spectacular military win and determined to avoid stumbling into an Arab Vietnam. The Gulf War was fought for limited objectives, and the Bush administration was determined, as a matter of principle, to hold the line on pressures to escalate those objectives. Harry Truman had failed to do so in Korea and was punished by Chinese intervention and a bloody, stalemated war. So too, Saddam Hussein might escape capture or death indefinitely; the Bush administration had been embarrassed in its 1989 invasion of Panama by dictator Manuel Noriega's initial escape for two weeks.

Marching on Baghdad probably would have compromised Desert Storm's political legitimacy, which President Bush had assiduously cultivated by making the Gulf War a United Nations response to Iraq's flagrant violation of the UN charter. A unilateral American pursuit of Saddam Hussein would have raised regional fears of imperial motives. "Taking Baghdad," concludes the best political and diplomatic history of the war, Freedman and Karsh's *Gulf Conflict, 1990–1991,* "could have led to a political quagmire in that any imposed replacement for Saddam could well have been perceived as yet another brutal interference by 'Western imperialism' in their domestic affairs."[13]

Additionally, assuming responsibility for Iraq's political and economic reconstruction would have initially required costly U.S. occupation and governance of Iraq, a course of action favored by no member of the coalition, including the United States, whose political administration would be voted out of office just twenty months later by a majority of an electorate for which a struggling economy was always of greater concern than Kuwait's liberation. The Cold War had just ended and it was time to focus on domestic issues. There were also good reasons to believe that Saddam's days were numbered. He had suffered a humiliating defeat that had sparked major spontaneous uprisings by the Kurds. The threat to his rule was acute. As Freedman and Karsh recount: "These were undoubtedly the most difficult moments in Saddam's long and violent career. He had encountered stark challenges to his personal rule before, but never such a devastating combination of international indignity and domestic chaos. Fortunately for him, not only did the [Bush] Administration fail to provide military support for the Shi'ite and Kurdish uprisings, but the Western noose around Iraq seemed to loosen. The rebels were surprised. They had been encouraged by statements by coalition leaders urging the overthrow of Saddam . . . , but they failed to read the small print: the coalition was under no obligation to help."[14]

In a March 2003 interview with *Newsweek,* former president Bush, in response to a question about whether he believed at the time that the coalition's victory would provoke Saddam's internal overthrow, stated: "Absolutely. I thought he'd be dead, as did every single Arab leader, every leader in the Gulf felt he'd be gone. And Mubarak felt he'd be gone, the Brits, the French, everyone. So I miscalculated there, yes, but getting rid of him wasn't the objective."[15]

The Bush administration had what it believed were good reasons to stay within the UN mandate and a reasonable expectation (based in part on an erroneous picture of the Iraqi military situation) that Saddam would not survive his defeat in Kuwait. Who could have foreseen his continuation in power for another twelve years in the face of sanctions and inspections?

But the administration erred egregiously in its decision to cease hostilities unilaterally, in the absence of any Iraqi request for terms. An enemy army on the run should be pursued until destroyed or until enemy political authority requests terms for the cessation of hostilities. Indeed, there is no modern precedent for Bush's decision, except perhaps for Hitler's famous May 24, 1940, "halt" order to German forces that were on the verge of destroying Anglo-French forces falling back on Dunkirk. The decision, driven in part by White House concern over potential Arab perceptions that American forces were wantonly slaughtering Iraqis even though Kuwait's liberation had been secured (the misleadingly infamous "Highway of Death"), was embraced by Saddam Hussein, who feared an American march on Baghdad, as a heaven-sent reprieve, even a victory. Indeed, in a speech "celebrating" the first anniversary of the launching of Operation Desert Storm, Saddam pointedly remarked: "It was George Bush with his own will who decided to stop the fighting. Nobody had asked him to do so."[16]

The idea of voluntarily letting up on a fleeing enemy when in position to complete his destruction must have been incomprehensible to Saddam Hussein, who never gave quarter to any enemy. It is also contrary to post-eighteenth-century Western (including American) military doctrine, which emphasizes constant attacks to preclude the running enemy from regrouping and reestablishing his organizational and operational balance. As Lawrence E. Cline observed in a postwar assessment of Gulf War termination, "I can think of no significant occasions—certainly not in U.S.

military history—prior to the Gulf War in which retreating forces became 'off limits' as a matter of policy while in the military theater. When such incidents have occurred, they have been created from the bottom, soldiers have simply taken pity on an obviously beaten enemy."[17] Interestingly, Schwarzkopf himself, in his famous television interview with David Frost shortly after the cease-fire, claimed that he had recommended continuing the pursuit. "We had them in a rout and could have continued to wreak great destruction on them," he said. "We could have completely closed the door and made it in fact a battle of annihilation. . . . There were obviously a lot of people who escaped who wouldn't have escaped if the decision hadn't been made to stop where we were at that time."[18] (True, but that was not the general's advice at the time.)

Pursuing and continuing to destroy Iraqi forces until Baghdad requested terms for a cease-fire would not have been inconsistent with Desert Storm's declared political and military objectives. U.S. forces had already entered Iraqi territory in pursuit of those objectives, and a couple more days or even a week of fighting could have been used to force Saddam, via a request for terms, to publicly acknowledge defeat in a manner precluding his avoidance of responsibility for it. Thomas G. Mahnken, in his devastating indictment of the administration's war termination, reminds us that "[b]attlefield victories . . . do not themselves determine the outcome of wars; rather, they provide opportunities for the victor to translate battlefield results into political outcomes. Two things in particular must occur for military force to be decisive; the defeated power must accept defeat and the victor must formulate a settlement that accommodates the interests of all concerned, including the loser. In concrete terms, this means that either the incumbent government must accept responsibility for defeat while retaining its legitimacy, or it must be replaced by a cooperative yet credible successor."[19] By prematurely and unilaterally announcing an end to hostilities, the Bush administration failed to force the regime of Saddam Hussein to accept defeat or compel its replacement by a successor regime, which need not have been any less autocratic as long as it was cooperative.

Nor was the only alternative strategic choice a march to Baghdad, which might indeed have fractured the coalition and provoked the collapse of central political authority in Iraq, saddling the United States with the onerous task of Iraq's reconstruction. To coerce the regime into accepting defeat, the United States at the very least could have halted military operations without publicly declaring an end to the war. Beyond that, as Mahnken observes, the United States could have (1) continued the ground war until its forces had completely encircled the Republican Guard, (2) feinted toward Baghdad, or (3) occupied Iraqi oil fields as bargaining leverage.[20]

The fact of the matter is that the Bush administration paid little attention to war termination and had no plan for dealing with Iraq once Kuwait was liberated. The president, determined to avoid a repetition of what he viewed as excessive political management of the military in Vietnam, left the Gulf War's operational conduct almost exclusively to the military and even permitted Schwarzkopf to conduct cease-fire negotiations absent any political instructions from Washington. At Safwan, the site of those negotiations, Schwarzkopf not only allowed his Iraqi interlocutors to dupe him on post-cease-fire employment of helicopters but also went out of his way to assure them that U.S. forces would evacuate Iraqi territory as soon as possible and without any conditions.[21] The pledge to march out of Iraq was "an extraordinary assurance," observe Michael Gordon and Bernard Trainor. "The United States might have used its occupation of southern Iraq to press for further demands."[22] Saddam must have been dumbstruck.

Additionally, the Bush administration's failure to act in response to the Kurdish and Shiite uprisings was morally indefensible. "It is appalling that we stood aside in the uprisings," says Middle East expert William Quandt. "We even let one Iraqi division through our lines to get to Basra because the United States did not want the regime to collapse."[23] Washington and its Saudi allies still feared Islamic Iran more than they despised tyranny in Baghdad; indeed, who but Iran was better positioned and motivated to exploit the opportunities presented by the disintegration of central political authority in Iraq? Fear of chaos inside Iraq dictated inaction. Observes Kenneth Pollack: "[S]ince they [the president and his chief advisers] were convinced that Saddam would be overthrown in a nice, clean military coup, they saw no need to aid the rebels. In fact, they feared that doing so would preclude the military coup that they were hoping for by causing the officer corps (much of which was Sunni) to rally around Saddam as the only alternative to the Shi'ah and Kurds taking over."[24]

If, however, as a matter of policy, the United States was not prepared to intervene, then it should have refrained from publicly encouraging rebellion. Having promoted rebellion, it should have acted. This policy indifference to the fate of the Iraqi people, which effectively guaranteed Saddam's survival after the Gulf War, was extended after the war by the Bush and subsequent administrations in the form of continued economic sanctions that impoverished and sickened the Iraqi people. That indifference was captured in 1996 by the Clinton administration secretary of state Madeleine Albright in an interview with Lesley Stahl on CBS's *60 Minutes*. Stahl asked, "More than 500,000 Iraqi children are dead as a direct result of UN sanctions. Do you think the price is worth paying?" To which Albright replied: "It is a difficult question. But yes, we think the price is worth it."[25] For twelve years and across three administrations, the United States, *like Saddam Hussein,* subordinated the fate of an entire people to the fate of one man. Such was the price of policies, as characterized by former UN humanitarian aid coordinators Hans Von Sponeck and Denis Halliday, "that punish the Iraqi people for something they did not do, through economic sanctions that target them in the hope that those who survive will overthrow the regime."[26]

Though the Clinton administration claimed that sanctions served to keep Saddam Hussein "in his box," F. Gregory Gause noted in 1999 that "the only 'box' into which sanctions put Iraqis is coffins."[27] Various estimates, including a UNICEF study of the period 1991 to 1998, concluded that the impact of sanctions on Iraq's infant mortality rate during the 1990s accounted for as many as 500,000 excess deaths of children under the age of five.[28] Sanctions produced not only dead children but also malnourished children and adults. They also financially destroyed Iraq's once vibrant middle class. One analysis estimated that sanctions caused the deaths of more Iraqis than the sum total of dead inflicted by all the weapons of mass destruction ever employed, including the chemical weapons deaths of World War I and the atomic bombings of World War II.[29]

One recalls the pre–Gulf War debate over economic sanctions, which proponents claimed provided an alternative to war as a means of forcing Saddam out of Kuwait. Sanctions did not work then, and as a means of forcing Saddam out of power they did not work in the twelve years separating Operation Desert Storm and Operation Iraqi Freedom. On the contrary, economic sanctions, like the mindless no-fly zones, served as a cheap badge of toughness toward Saddam Hussein. They were designed less to unseat the Iraqi dictator (who used them to absolve himself of responsibility for Iraq's plight) than they were to protect the White House from the conservative domestic political backlash that would have erupted had the sanctions and zones been terminated. Instead of "ridding Iraq of its most noxious weapons," argued Sandra Mackey in 2002, "sanctions have been the playing field on which Saddam Hussein and the United States . . . have spent over a decade slowly slaughtering Iraqis and their frail society."[30]

Whatever the arguments against launching the second war against Iraq, its predicate cannot be gainsaid: war for regime change proved the only sure means of toppling Saddam. Sanctions succeeded only in inflicting misery upon the Iraqi people and isolating the United States from many of its friends and allies, especially in the Arab world. David Rieff, writing after the war of 2003, observed: "One may disagree with the policies the present [George W. Bush] administration has followed with regard to Iraq—

policies that have led to a brilliantly successful war and a staggeringly inept postwar occupation. But to its credit, at least it *had* a policy, one based on the understanding that Iraqi sanctions may have contained Saddam Hussein, but they had failed at weakening his grip on his country."[31]

The assumption that an embargo on the sale of oil would, at the very least, force Saddam to hand over what remained of his missiles and chemical and biological weapons and give up his pursuit of nuclear weapons was mistaken from the start because it ignored Saddam's conception of himself. "From Hussein's perspective," observed Sandra Mackey, "just the threat that he might someday unleash biological and chemical weaponry on his neighbors guaranteed that he remained a world figure, not just another tyrant presiding over what was in danger of becoming a starving Third World country. And weapons of terror provided his ultimate hold over his own people." There was also the promise that WMD, especially nuclear weapons, might deter a U.S. attack.[32]

Refusing to march on Baghdad, but having been the principal wrecker of Iraq's economy and infrastructure, the George H. W. Bush administration simply absolved itself of any responsibility for restoring it. Leaving the war "[c]ynically unfinished" (in the words of Iraqi exile dissident Kanan Makiya), the administration pocketed its military victory in the Gulf and abandoned Iraq to destitution and disease.[33] Power entails responsibility. Having defeated the Germans and Japanese in World War II, the United States moved in and engineered their political and economic reconstruction, transforming both countries from aggressor states into peaceful members of the international community. It did exactly the opposite in 1991; it used its irresistible military power without political accountability. As two critics of 1991 war termination put it, "having gone to war, we ought to have pursued a strategy that broke Baathist power decisively and created the conditions for the reconstruction and rehabilitation of the Iraqi state." Instead, "[w]e fastened upon a formula for going to war—in which American casualties are minimized and protracted engagements are avoided— that requires the massive use of American firepower and a speedy withdrawal from the scenes of destruction. . . . [The formula's] peculiar vice is that it enables us to go to war with far greater precipitancy than we otherwise might while simultaneously allowing us to walk away from the ruin we create without feeling a commensurate sense of political responsibility. It creates an anarchy and calls it peace. In the name of order it wreaks havoc. It allows us to assume an imperial role without discharging the classic duties of imperial rule."[34]

It is not without reason that the Gulf War "peace" of 1991 has been compared to the disastrous Versailles Treaty of 1919, most notably by

Donald and Frederick W. Kagan. Versailles was a punitive peace imposed upon a people who did not believe themselves to have been militarily defeated in 1918, and, like the Gulf War coalition, the coalition of states that defeated Germany disintegrated rapidly after the war. The problem was that even if the nature of the peace imposed was justified, it could not be sustained unless at least the British and French were prepared to enforce it indefinitely, which they were not. With the Nazis' rise to power, Germany began casting off one Versailles shackle after another, and Hitler succeeded in doing so in part because France would not go to war against Germany without Britain, yet British opinion had come to believe in the injustice of Versailles. Thus both Paris and London appeased Hitler's demands until March 1939, when Hitler gobbled up the rump of Czechoslovakia, his first conquest of a non-Germanic people.[35]

The Kagans believe "the peace the victorious coalition imposed on Iraq in 1991 bears a troubling similarity to the peace imposed on the Germans in 1919" because the terms "were harsh enough to engender resentment, hatred, and the desire for revenge in the hearts of the Iraqis without providing a satisfactory long-term defense against Iraq." The "fatal flaw" of both peaces "was less that [they were] too harsh, but that [they were] too difficult to enforce." The Kagans also note that in both 1919 and 1991, "the victorious forces had not overrun the defeated country, had not seized the capital, and had not destroyed the entire enemy army. In both cases, the key decision makers feared the 'chaos' that would follow such a total victory far more than the more remote danger of a revived threat emanating from the old enemy."[36]

Certainly in retrospect, the peace imposed on Iraq in 1991 was unsatisfactory. It failed to unseat Saddam Hussein or thwart his continued attempts to acquire nuclear weapons, although international sanctions and inspections may have placed such weapons beyond reach. It left the Iraqi people impoverished by economic sanctions and imprisoned inside an exceptionally vicious police state. And because the coalition of 1991, with the exception of the United States and Great Britain, subsequently disintegrated over the issue of postwar policy toward Iraq, the peace ultimately proved unenforceable.

This did not mean, however, that the United States failed to prevent a revived threat of Iraqi aggression. Aside from the impact of the 1991 war and persistent sanctions on Iraq's fighting power, credible American military primacy in the Persian Gulf deterred any further Iraqi attempts to acquire additional territory by force. In this respect, the comparison with Hitler was misleading. During the 1930s Hitler faced in Europe no equivalent to America's military dominance of the Gulf. Far from being dominated, Hitler sought domination with an army that by 1940 had no qualitative equal anywhere on the Continent. Moreover, for reasons of geography, national military posture, and domestic politics, neither French nor British military power was credible as a deterrent to Hitler's territorial acquisitions in central and eastern Europe—and Hitler knew it. In short, whereas deterrence of Iraqi conventional aggression worked from 1991 to 2003, it failed in Europe in the 1930s, at first because it was never attempted, and later because, though attempted, it was not credible.

The record of deterrence in 1990–91 deserves brief examination here because it was, like the unsatisfactory peace, a legacy of the Gulf War, and because the decision to launch a second war against Iraq twelve years later was driven in part by the George W. Bush administration's loss of confidence in deterrence. In the case of Saddam Hussein's invasion of Kuwait, deterrence failed because it was not seriously attempted and might not have worked even had it been.[37] In the summer of 1990 the Bush administration was understandably preoccupied by earthshaking events in Europe. Iran, not Iraq, was still the focus of American security concerns in the Gulf. A few weeks before the invasion, administration spokesmen publicly reiterated that the United States had no security commitment to Kuwait. The Bush administration was determined to sustain a cooperative relationship with Iraq, which it had inherited from a Reagan administration that had been a de facto cobelligerent in Iraq's war against Iran; it reassured Saddam Hussein that he was "a force for moderation" in the Gulf and that the "United States wish[ed] to broaden relations with Iraq."[38] Policy makers completely missed the depth of Saddam's economic desperation and misjudged Iraq's intentions toward Kuwait. A week before the invasion, the American ambassador to Iraq told Saddam Hussein: "[W]e have no opinion on Arab-Arab conflicts, like your border dispute with Kuwait."[39] A day earlier, the State Department's Margaret Tutwiler, when asked whether the United States had any commitment to defend Kuwait, declared, "we do not have any defense treaties with Kuwait, and there are no special defense or security commitments to Kuwait."[40]

Saddam, in short, had no convincing reason to believe the United States would go to war over Kuwait. The White House was distracted by momentous events in Europe and seemed indifferent to Kuwait. Nor was there reason for Saddam to believe the Saudis would court the domestic political dangers posed by inviting U.S. combat forces into the kingdom. Saddam also believed that America's experience in Vietnam had made the United States extremely war averse. Thus Pres. George H. W. Bush's decision to dispatch a half million U.S. troops to Saudi Arabia was a strategic surprise to the Iraqi dictator.[41]

Quite the reverse was true 2003. By the time Pres. George W. Bush launched the second U.S. war against Iraq, Saddam had the benefit of at least fourteen months of strategic warning, beginning no later than January 2002 when, in his state of the union address, President Bush declared Iraq a member of the "axis of evil" against which preventive war might be justified. Indeed, rarely has an attacking state so loudly telegraphed its strategic intent so far in advance, though it is far from clear that Saddam took this warning seriously until it was too late.

The United States failed to deter Iraq's invasion of Kuwait in 1990 because it did not attempt to do so. In contrast, the United States did attempt and apparently succeeded in deterring Iraq's wartime use of chemical and biological weapons—"apparently" because successful deterrence is measured by events that do not happen, and no one knows for sure why Saddam, though he threatened to use chemical weapons, did not do so. This success is especially noteworthy, given subsequent administration claims that deterrence was no longer a sufficient means of dealing with the threat of Saddam armed with weapons of mass destruction (see chap. 3). In 1991 Iraq had tens of thousands of chemical artillery shells and bombs, and a history of using them against Iranian forces as well as its own Kurdish inhabitants.[42]

That the United States sought to deter their use is a matter of record. Just six days after the Iraqi invasion, President Bush publicly warned that any use of chemical weapons against American troops would "be intolerable and . . . dealt with very, very severely."[43] Eight days before the launching of Operation Desert Storm, Secretary of State James Baker handed Iraqi foreign minister Tariq Aziz a letter from President Bush to Saddam which, among other things, declared: "Let me state too, that the United States will not tolerate the use of chemical or biological weapons, support of any kind of terrorist actions, or the destruction of Kuwait's oil fields and installations. The American people would demand the strongest possible response. You and your country will pay a terrible price if you order unconscionable actions of this sort."[44]

What Bush meant by "the strongest possible response" remains unclear, but many, probably including Saddam Hussein himself, took it to mean nuclear retaliation—against which he had no means of deterrence or defense. Husayn Kamil, Saddam's son-in-law and former chief of Iraq's WMD development, stated in 1995, after he defected to the West, that Iraqi officials were deterred from using chemical weapons for fear of U.S. nuclear retaliation.[45] "Saddam Hussein probably never had any intention of using chemical weapons because of his concern that severe and possibly nuclear retaliation would be forthcoming," concludes one expert. "With everything to lose and nothing to gain Saddam ultimately withheld the chemical card."[46]

In addition to successful deterrence there may have been some practical reasons for Iraqi nonuse of chemical weapons, including poor weather conditions that made effective use of such weapons difficult, deterioration of munitions stocks, and the early collapse of Iraqi command, control, and distribution capacity. Nonetheless, "[g]iven Iraq's past willingness to use chemical weapons against Iran and the Kurds," concludes the regional expert and military analyst Anthony Cordesman, "the deciding factor may have been the Coalition and Israel's ability to retaliate."[47]

If Saddam Hussein was not prepared to use chemical weapons to preserve his aggression in Kuwait, was he prepared to use them to save himself? Would he have used them had coalition forces advanced on Baghdad with the aim of unseating the Iraqi dictator? There is evidence, though hardly conclusive, that he would have. Several credible sources, including postwar UN inspectors on the ground, report that "Saddam had equipped a special force of al-Hussein [missiles] with WMD warheads and predelegated them launch authority to fire their missiles at Israel if communications with Baghdad were severed as a result of a nuclear attack or *a coalition drive on the capital*."[48] According to Khidir Hamza, a chief Iraqi nuclear scientist and adviser to Saddam Hussein who defected to the West in 1994, Saddam not only ordered the arming of missiles with chemical warheads "in the event allied troops stormed through the gates of Baghdad" but also gave orders "to bury thousands of chemical and biological weapons in southern Iraq, at Basra [and other sites along] the likely routes of Allied invasion." The dictator's "thinking was that the Allies, following U.S. tactical doctrine, would blow up the bunkers as they advanced, releasing plumes of invisible gas into the prevailing winds and ultimately onto themselves. Any depots the Allies missed would be blown up by retreating Republican Guard units. They literally wouldn't know what hit them, until it was too late—maybe weeks or months after the conflict ended. . . . A corollary benefit was that the chemical shower would decimate the despised Shia in the south, whom he concluded were of little concern to the Allies, given their potential role as troops for Iran."[49]

These plans were certainly consistent with Saddam's crash program, initiated in August 1990 when U.S. troops first began arriving in Saudi Arabia, to "produce enough fuel to build at least one nuclear device, a warhead that he could mount on a missile and hurl at the Israelis if the Allies invaded. It was his doomsday weapon. If his own demise were imminent, he planned to take everybody down with him." Fortunately for the rest of the world, the accelerated program was doomed from the start by lack of essential ingredients and engineering know-how.[50]

Though it failed to deliver, the crash program and, if true, plans to use chemical and biological weapons, seemingly spoke volumes about the limits of deterrence against Saddam Hussein. Deterrence worked as long as U.S. war aims remained limited to the recovery of Kuwait and did not include a march on Baghdad to overthrow the regime—that is, as long as Saddam believed he had a chance to survive. In circumstances where Saddam and his regime faced certain destruction, however, Saddam seemed to be prepared—at least in 1991—to lash out with everything he had since the consequences were no worse than not doing so. Interestingly, Charles Duelfer, a former UN inspector in Iraq, said that during his tour of Baghdad he found that "all Iraqis, from high government officials to the man on the street, were convinced that Iraq's chemical weapons had deterred coalition forces from advancing on Baghdad."[51]

The second American war against Iraq had many roots, the strongest among them being the Bush administration's strategic interpretation of the September 11, 2001, terrorist attacks on the United States. But a significant root was the failure of the first American war against Iraq to eliminate the source of the Iraqi threat. Operation Iraqi Freedom was inconceivable absent the haste and lack of foresight with which Operation Desert Storm was terminated in 1991. The victory of 1991 was neither militarily nor politically complete. The threat, though weakened, was left to fester. No one has summed up Desert Storm's limited accomplishments better than Colin S. Gray: "Undoubtedly, a decisive victory was secured in 1991 in terms of the explicit war aims of the Coalition. Victory decided that Kuwaiti oil, let alone Saudi oil, would not enrich Iraq. Also, the war and its consequences decided that the Iraqi path to achievement of deliverable weapons of mass destruction would be extraordinarily long, costly, and painful. Contrary to U.S. hopes and expectations, though, what the war did not decide was a political future for [an] Iraq innocent of Saddam Hussein and led by people committed to a regional order that would be judged constructive in Washington."[52]

2

The Neoconservative Vision and 9/11

The Clinton and pre-9/11 George W. Bush administrations sought regime change in Baghdad by measures short of war. The post-9/11 Bush administration used war to achieve regime change.

The 9/11 attacks had a profound impact on the Bush administration, triggering, among other things, the White House's promulgation of a new use-of-force doctrine that disconcerted allies and adversaries alike. The doctrine represented the most dramatic American foreign policy departure since the Truman administration adopted the policy of containment in the late 1940s. The intellectual foundations of that doctrine, however, had already been established during the 1990s by neoconservative ideologues who subsequently came to exert a powerful influence on the Bush White House.[1] Indeed, what became known as the Bush doctrine, as well as the Bush administration's grand strategy in the Middle East, reflects the neoconservatives' global and regional agendas. Anatol Lieven contends that

> [t]o understand the Administration's motivation [in pushing for war against Iraq], it is necessary to appreciate the breathtaking scope of the . . . global ambitions which the dominant neo-conservative nationalists hope to further by means of war, and which go way beyond their stated goals. There are of course different groups within this camp: some are more favorable to Israel, others less hostile to China; not all would support the most radical aspects of the program. However, the basic and generally agreed plan is unilateral world domination through absolute military superiority, and this has been consistently advocated and worked on by a group of intellectuals close to Dick Cheney and Richard Perle since the collapse of the Soviet Union in the early 1990s.[2]

The neoconservatives are committed to perpetuating American military primacy in the world via, if necessary, unilateral preventive military action against rising potential enemies, especially rogue states seeking to acquire nuclear weapons, and they believe that military action should be directed toward removing potentially threatening regimes. Neoconservative intellectuals, many of them Jewish and some of them sympathetic to the

Likud Party's security ambitions for Israel, have provided the core of the neoconservative construct of the world and the American role in it, though the neoconservative agenda commands support, in varying degrees, within the broader conservative community, including the Republican Party and its leader.[3] Indeed, the Bush administration is populated by prominent neoconservatives and other proponents of primacy, including the vice president and his staff, the secretary of defense, the deputy secretary of defense, and the former head and still member of the Defense Policy Board. These individuals, together with such influential neoconservative commentators as Robert Kagan, William Kristol, Charles Krauthammer, and Lawrence Kaplan, have provided both the intellectual and policy foundations of President Bush's post-9/11 foreign policy.

The neoconservative vision of America's present role in the world traces its origin to the collapse of the Soviet Union, which neoconservatives believe made the world safe for an ambitious, forward-leaning foreign policy reliant on force to rid the world of tyranny and promote the spread of democracy. The neoconservatives seek "nothing less than the transformation of world politics" via a "policy that proposes to use military supremacy aggressively, unilaterally and universally and, in such cases as Iraq, to attempt to impose [democratic] governance," observes Edward Rhodes. The policy's premise is that the security of the United States is assured in the long run only in a world of democracies—that is, a world rid of totalitarianism, autocracy, and terrorism. A democratic world would be a peaceful world because democracies do not fight each other. But a "democratic peace" is not inevitable. Getting to it requires an activist American internationalism based on military primacy and a willingness to use force to assure the ultimate triumph of American political values, to which, neoconservatives believe, people around the world aspire but which do not yet prevail everywhere because of persistent tyranny, especially in China and the Middle East. Pres. George W. Bush spoke to this vision in his June 2002 address to West Point's graduating class: "Wherever we carry it, the American flag will stand not only for our power, but for freedom. Our nation's cause has always been larger than our nation's defense. We fight, as we always fight, for a just peace—a peace that favors human liberty. We will defend the peace against threats from terrorists and tyrants. . . . And we will extend the peace by encouraging free and open societies on every continent. Building this peace is America's opportunity and America's duty."[4]

The president subsequently elaborated: "Freedom is the non-negotiable demand of human dignity; the birthright of every person—in every civilization. . . . Throughout history, freedom has been threatened by war and terror; it has been challenged by the clashing of wills of powerful states and the evil designs of tyrants; and it has been tested by widespread disease and poverty. Today, humanity holds in its hands the opportunity to further freedom's triumph over all these foes. The United States welcomes our responsibility to lead in this great mission."[5]

A pivotal neoconservative document was the 1992 Defense Planning Guidance, written for then Secretary of Defense Dick Cheney by then obscure Pentagon analysts Paul Wolfowitz (now deputy secretary of defense) and I. Lewis "Scooter" Libby (now Vice President Cheney's chief of staff). The guidance called for the establishment of American military primacy over Eurasia by preventing the rise of any potential hostile power capable of challenging that primacy. It also endorsed a policy of preventive disarmament of rogue states seeking to acquire weapons of mass destruction. The document, leaked excepts of which provoked sharp condemnations on Capitol Hill, was never translated into policy because Pres. George H. W. Bush was not reelected.

During the 1990s, however, the neoconservative vision remained very much alive in such conservative think tanks as the Hudson Institute, the Center for Security Policy, and especially the American Enterprise Institute. The *Weekly Standard,* the neoconservative magazine edited by William Kristol, became a major vehicle for the exposition of the neoconservative vision, as did the *National Interest, Commentary,* and the *New Republic.* The neoconservatives, also known as "democratic imperialists" for their emphasis on coercing others to adopt liberal political values, were united in their condemnation of the George H. W. Bush and Clinton administrations' foreign policies. Bush's was criticized for its "narrow realism," Clinton's for its toothless idealism, and both for their failure to take advantage of U.S. military primacy in the post-Soviet world.[6] Both, especially Clinton, were also pummeled for deference toward and reliance on the United Nations, NATO, and other formal multilateral institutions that traditionally served to legitimize U.S. use of force. Neoconservatives believe that America's power is inherently and self-evidently legitimate by virtue of America's political values and that the United States should not hesitate to exercise its power unilaterally, if necessary. For neoconservatives, the mission defines the coalition, not vice versa. In the words of one observer, "America's global power must not be challenged. The US reserves for itself the right to decide who might be its enemies and how they are to be dealt with. No other nation can be permitted to challenge its primacy."[7]

In 1997 leading neoconservative intellectuals and their past and future allies in government, including Cheney, Wolfowitz, and Donald Rumsfeld, founded the Project for a New American Century (PNAC) dedicated to the following goals: increased defense spending; challenge to "regimes hostile to our interests and values"; promotion of political and economic freedom abroad; and acceptance of "responsibility for America's unique role in preserving and extending an international order friendly to our security, our prosperity, and our principles." In its "statement of principles," PNAC noted that "the United States stands as the world's preeminent power," but asked: "Does [it] have the vision to build upon the achievements of past decades? Does [it] have the resolve to shape a new century favorable to American principles and interests?" The statement bemoaned that "we seem to have forgotten the essential elements of the Reagan Administration's success: a [strong] military . . . a foreign policy that boldly and purposefully promotes American principles abroad; and national leadership that accepts the United States' global responsibilities." The statement concluded: "Such a Reaganite policy of military strength and moral clarity may not be fashionable today. But it is necessary if the United States is to build on the successes of this past century and to ensure our security and our greatness in the next."[8]

The neoconservatives' agenda and critique of the George H. W. Bush and Clinton administrations appeared in a seminal 2000 book, *Present Dangers, Crisis and Opportunity in American Foreign and Defense Policy*, edited by Robert Kagan and William Kristol, and containing essays by such neoconservative luminaries as Reuel Marc Gerecht, William Schneider, William J. Bennet, Donald Kagan, Paul Wolfowitz, and Richard Perle (whose essay "Iraq: Saddam Unbound," attacked Clinton's policy toward Baghdad and called for Saddam's forcible removal). In their introductory essay, "National Interest and Global Responsibility," Kagan and Kristol summarized the case for a foreign policy based on America's global military primacy. The "present danger," in their view, is that "the United States, the world's dominant power on whom the maintenance of international peace and the support of liberal democratic principles depends, will shrink from its responsibilities and—in a fit of absent-mindedness, or parsimony, or indifference—allow the international order that it created and sustained to collapse. Our present danger is one of declining military strength, flagging will and confusion about our role in the world."[9]

With the demise of the Soviet Union, America's global task "ought to have been obvious. It was to prolong this extraordinary moment and to guard the international system from any threats that might challenge it. This meant, above all, preserving and reinforcing America's benevolent global hegemony." Instead, the 1990s witnessed America's failure to finish off Saddam Hussein after the Gulf War; to check the growth of Chinese military power and imperial ambitions ("The American response to China's

aggressive behavior at home and abroad has . . . been one of appeasement."); to shun "confronting the moral and strategic challenges" of dealing with "evil regimes" (instead, "the United States tried to do business
with them in pursuit of the illusion of stability.")[10]

In Kagan and Kristol's view, "a fundamental change in the way our
leaders and the public think about America's role in the world" was required. Specifically, what was needed was "a foreign policy based on
American hegemony, and on the blending of principle with material interest," which in the long run would "mean fewer, not more, overseas interventions than under the 'vital interest' standard" because a "forward-leaning conception of the national interest would emphasize early action before
crises erupt." The tool of such a forward-leaning foreign policy would be
an "America capable of projecting force quickly and with devastating effect to important regions of the world," which would enable the United
States to "set about making trouble for hostile and potentially hostile nations, rather than waiting for them to make trouble for us." Sustaining this
capacity for preemptive attack and preventive war against "smaller powers
seeking to acquire weapons of mass destruction and missiles to launch
them at American forces, at our allies and at the American homeland"
would require robust antimissile defenses. Thus antimissile defenses would
serve not only to protect Americans but also to prohibit target states from
deterring American military action against *them.*[11]

Kagan and Kristol then proceeded to denounce the "idea, common to
many foreign policy minimalists and commerce-oriented liberals alike, that
the United States can 'do business' with any regime, no matter how odious
and hostile to our basic principles." Such regimes, in their view, deserved
removal by one means of another. It was "absurd" and "self-defeating" not
to have finished off Saddam Hussein in 1991, and those "who caution
against the difficulties of occupying and reforming such [defeated tyran-
nical] countries . . . may wish to reflect on the American experiences in
Germany and Japan—or even the Dominican Republic and Panama."[12]

"National Interest and Global Responsibility" closed by condemning
restrictive use-of-force doctrines and American foreign policy thinkers who
defined "the 'national interest' as consisting of a grid of ground, sea lanes,
industrial centers, strategic choke-points and the like." This narrow, mate-
rialistic definition of interest was "foisted upon our foreign policy establishment by 'realists' in the middle of the century," and it should be sup-
planted by a foreign policy based on "[h]onor and greatness in the service
of liberal principles."[13]

For Wolfowitz, in his essay "Statesmanship in the New Century," "the
core of American foreign policy is . . . the universalization of American

principles." "[N]othing could be less realistic," he wrote, "than the version of 'realism' that dismisses human rights as an important tool of foreign policy." In his view, citing the triumph of democracy in the Philippines, "[d]emocratic change is not only a way to weaken one's enemies, it is also a way to strengthen our friends."[14]

The election of George W. Bush in 2000 ushered the neoconservatives into power. Of the twenty-five founding members of the Project for a New American Century, ten entered the new administration: Dick Cheney (vice president), Donald Rumsfeld (secretary of defense), Paul Wolfowitz (deputy secretary of defense), Richard Perle (chairman of the Defense Policy Board), Paula Dobriansky (under secretary of state for global affairs), I. Lewis Libby (Vice President Cheney's chief of staff), Peter Rodman (assistant secretary of defense for international security affairs), Zalmay Khalilzad (special envoy to the Middle East), Eliot Abrams (NSC staffer responsible for Middle East policy), and Eliot Cohen (member of the Defense Policy Board).[15] Other neoconservatives who were not PNAC founders, such as Douglas Feith and John Bolton, also assumed key positions within the administration. Their direct influence on policy, along with the continuing indirect influence of neoconservatives outside the administration, is evident in the president's controversial use-of-force doctrine and policy toward Iraq.

Before turning to that doctrine and policy, however, it is necessary to examine the neoconservative view of America's role in the Middle East and the relationship of that role to Operation Iraqi Freedom. The best vehicle for doing so is a book published on the eve of the war by Lawrence F. Kaplan and William Kristol, *The War over Iraq: Saddam's Tyranny and America's Mission*. Kaplan and Kristol predictably condemned the George H. W. Bush and Clinton administrations' policies toward Iraq:

> [T]he first Bush and Clinton administrations opted for a combination of incomplete military operations and diplomatic accommodation. Rather than press hard for a change of regime, President Bush halted the U.S. war against Iraq prematurely and turned a blind eye as Saddam slaughtered the insurgents whom the United States had encouraged to revolt. For its part, the Clinton administration avoided confronting the moral and strategic challenge presented by Saddam, hoping instead that an increasingly weak policy of containment, punctuated by the occasional fusillade of cruise missiles, would suffice to keep Saddam in his box.[16]

They denounced the "narrow realism" of Bush's foreign policy as the product of "a brand of *realpolitik* which counsels that American foreign policy should be grounded in self-interest, narrowly understood," and the Clinton administration's "wishful liberalism that, in the case of Iraq, meant following the United Nations, employing American power fitfully and apologetically, often ignoring Saddam's challenges, and eventually presiding over the erosion of sanctions and weapons inspections." They then called for a "distinctly American internationalism" based on "American exceptionalism—a belief in the uniqueness and the virtue of the American political system that, when translated into foreign policy terms, offers the United States as a model for the world." Such an internationalism rejects the liberals' argument "that peace and political liberty can best be fostered within international organizations and through international cooperation."[17]

With respect to Iraq, Kaplan and Kristol contended that the "realist argument for deterrence is weak" because "Saddam has revealed himself to be a pathological risk-taker." The combination of a pathological Saddam and his continued search for nuclear weapons to support his ambition "to dominate his region and deter the United States" mandates a preventive war to stop him. "Today we may attack Iraq with minimal risk because Saddam has yet to acquire a nuclear bomb. Once he does, the equation changes. Then it is we who will be deterred." But the objective of a war against Iraq would not be confined to Saddam's removal. As in the case of the defeated Axis states of World War II, the United States would impose democracy on Iraq and in so doing provoke "powerful reverberations in the Arab world." Specifically, "Iraq's experience of liberal democratic rule . . . could increase pressure already being felt by Teheran's mullahs to open that society. Iraq's model will be eyed warily by Saudi Arabia's theocrats to the south . . . . Meanwhile, Iraq could even replace Saudi Arabia as the key American ally and source of oil in the region. A democratic Iraq would also encourage the region's already liberalizing regimes— such as those in Qatar, Morocco and Jordan—to continue on their paths to democracy."[18]

Paul Wolfowitz, perhaps the most influential neoconservative at the White House (President Bush is said to call him "Wolfie"), clearly believed that war with Iraq offered the key to the Middle East's transformation. In September 2002 he told the *New York Times*'s Bill Keller: "You hear people mock [the idea of a democratic Iraq] by saying that Iraq isn't ready for Jeffersonian democracy. Well, Japan isn't Jeffersonian democracy either. I think the more we are committed to influencing the outcome, the more chance there could be that it would be something quite significant for Iraq. And I think if it's significant for Iraq, it's going to cast a very large shadow, starting with Syria and Iraq, but across the whole Arab world."[19]

Neoconservatives are quite hostile to the autocracies that continue to dominate the Middle East and to U.S. support of many of them. (Here, ironically, the neoconservatives share common ground with Osama bin

Laden.) In their view, the absence of democratic rule has promoted political and religious extremism of the kind that delivered the 9/11 terrorist attacks on the United States. And neoconservatives—with good reason—include the Saudi theocracy on their list of guilty regimes.[20] As Philip Gordon has observed, 9/11 rendered the Middle Eastern status quo no longer acceptable to the United States: "It was not lost on Americans that the majority of the 11 September hijackers came from Saudi Arabia and Egypt, U.S. allies where the combination of repressive regimes and American support for them (and for Israel) led to alienation, resentment and hatred for the West. The practice of these and other states to protect their legitimacy, by couching themselves in Islamic rhetoric, permitting and even encouraging anti-American and anti-Israel expression as an outlet for populations not allowed to protest in other ways, and allowing the financing of Islamist terrorist networks, has now come to be seen—perhaps belatedly—as a threat to Western security."[21]

Richard Perle, in an interview given shortly after U.S. troops entered Baghdad, declared, "[w]e have a serious problem with the Saudis and that is they have been funding extremist institutions and actual terrorists around the world, and this isn't just wealthy Saudi individuals. It includes the government." This Saudi-inspired terrorism "poses such an obvious threat to the United States that it is intolerable that they continue to do this." Perle went on to warn: "I hope they are reconsidering and will take the appropriate action to stop that and stop it immediately."[22]

A U.S. takeover of Iraq would hopefully start a chain reaction in the Middle East, with autocratic dominoes falling to democratic change. "Would Saddam's removal set the region aflame?" asked Perle before the war. "Fear that the Arab world will unite in opposition to Saddam's removal lures even thoughtful critics into opposition. It seems at least as likely that Saddam's replacement by a decent regime would open the way to a far more stable and peaceful region." Perle continued: "A democratic Iraq would be a powerful refutation of the patronizing view that Arabs are incapable of democracy. And an end to Saddam's incitement of Palestinian terror would surely help the search for peace." In an August 2003 editorial for the *Washington Post,* National Security Adviser Condoleezza Rice argued that the United States must commit itself to the transformation of the Middle East just as it had committed itself to the transformation of Europe after World War II. "Much as a new democratic Germany became a linchpin of a new Europe, so a transformed Iraq can become a key element of a very different Middle East in which the ideologies of hate will not flourish."[23] George Packer has succinctly captured the neoconservatives' regional story line:

The Arab world is hopelessly sunk in corruption and popular discontent. Misrule and a culture of victimhood have left Arabs economically stagnant and prone to seeing their problems in delusional terms. The United States has contributed to that pathology by cynically shoring up dictatorships; Sept. 11 was one result. Both the Arab world and official American attitudes toward it need to be jolted out of their rut. An invasion of Iraq would provide the necessary shock, and a democratic Iraq would become an example of change for the rest of the region. Political Islam would lose its hold on the imagination of young Arabs as they watched a more successful model rise up in their midst. The Middle East's center of political gravity would shift from the region's theocracies and autocracies to its new, oil-rich democracy. And finally, the deadlock in which Israel and Palestine are trapped would end as Palestinians, realizing that their own backers were now tending their own gardens, would accept compromise. By this way of thinking, the road to Damascus, Tehran, Riyadh and Jerusalem goes through Baghdad.[24]

For moral and strategic reasons, neoconservatives are committed to a values-based foreign policy. They believe that America's liberal political ideals of individual freedom, democratic governance, and rule of law are universally desired and applicable, and that because America's political virtue is self-evident, others need not fear our power. They believe that the end of the Cold War has freed America to promote the spread of its liberal political values more forcefully and purposefully than ever before. Only in a world where those values prevail will American security truly be assured; democracy thus equals security.

But achieving this goal means, among other things, that the United States cannot accept permanent coexistence with "evil" regimes that oppose American power and values. On the contrary, when opportunity permits, the United States, forcibly if necessary, should unseat tyrannical governments and help install democratic replacements—this is the great lesson of the Gulf War. Moreover, the United States should not permit incipient threats to mature into deadly, undeterrable menaces—this is the great lesson of the democracies' appeasement of Hitler in the 1930s. The United States should be prepared to strike early and strike first. Thus the neoconservatives would make the world safe for democracy. They would succeed where Woodrow Wilson failed.

The sine qua non of such an ambitious foreign policy is, of course, the perpetuation of global American military primacy against all challengers and a willingness to use force unilaterally. Neoconservatives are united on this issue, even if they differ on how best to ensure primacy. Some focus on near-term military solutions to foreign challenges to U.S. global military primacy and display less enthusiasm for follow-up nation-building efforts to eliminate the political roots of those challenges, whereas others see military intervention as the necessary first step in a much larger enterprise aimed at political transformation. To use two of Walter Russell Mead's four categorizations of the sources of U.S. foreign policy, the "Wilsonians" believe that "the United States has both a moral obligation and an important national interest in spreading American democratic and social values throughout the world," whereas the "Jacksonians" believe that the foremost goal of U.S. foreign policy "should be the physical security and economic well-being of the American people."[25]

The neoconservatives' pre-9/11 focus was on hostile and threatening states, not terrorist organizations. References to terrorist and other nonstate threats were notable for their scarcity. Neoconservatives were obsessed with Iraq, Iran, and North Korea, and above all with China, which they regarded as America's long-term strategic rival. They were hard-liners on China, rejecting the assumption, which underpinned the Clinton administration's China policy, that the combination of internal Chinese economic liberalization and growing dependence on the international capitalist trading order would eventually spur movement toward political democracy at home.

As for Pres. George W. Bush, he was not a subscriber to the neoconservative vision when he took office in January 2001. On the contrary, he came into office as a self-avowed realist critical of Clinton's interventions in Haiti and the Balkans. In a November 1999 speech, he declared that "a President much be a clear-eyed realist," a statement that, as Nicholas Lemann noted, reflected "exactly the foreign-policy doctrine that Cheney's Pentagon team rejected, partly because it posits the impossibility of any one country's ever dominating world affairs for any length of time."[26] Until 9/11 the president displayed much less interest in foreign policy than he did in such domestic issues as tax cuts, deregulation, expanded oil drilling, government support of faith-based charities, and blocking stem cell research. Nor did he support significant increases in defense spending—certainly not of the magnitude the service chiefs and the neoconservatives were calling for. (During the 2000 election campaign Al Gore had called for a significantly larger five-year defense spending plan than Bush had proposed.) He moreover registered no significant departure from his predecessor's policies toward Iraq, Iran, and North Korea; indeed, Kaplan and Kristol complained that he "proceeded to water down even the demands that the Clinton team had imposed on Iraq."[27]

Then came 9/11, which immediately transformed Bush into a foreign policy president and prompted him, over the following year, to embrace the neoconservative vision of the world and America's role in it. As Kaplan and Kristol approvingly recounted, "Bush transformed himself from a realist following in his father's footsteps to an internationalist touting America's ideals as sincerely and forcefully as Harry Truman, John Kennedy and Ronald Reagan before him."[28] The blunt assessment of the prestigious London-based International Institute for Strategic Studies is that "[t]he events of 11 September 2001 provided hawks, including those of 'utopian' persuasion, with the opportunity to push Iraq to the top of the agenda. They successfully exploited the belief in the upper tier of the government immediately after the attacks that there was a better than even chance that Iraq had been involved, and the more broadly held concern that Baghdad might in future supply WMD to terrorists. In bureaucratic terms, this resulted in the insertion of a single provision, at the end of a presidential guidance document otherwise dedicated to the government's response to 11 September, instructing the military to prepare for war with Iraq."[29]

Neoconservative White House speechwriter David Frum, in his 2003 memoir of the impact of 9/11 on President Bush, traced the transformation of Bush's thinking from realism to idealism with respect to the war on terrorism, a transformation reflected in Bush's broadening conception of the source of the terrorist challenge to include the absence of democracy in the Middle East. Traditional U.S. policy had favored stability over justice, but the "pursuit of stability in the Middle East had brought chaos and slaughter to New York and Washington. Bush decided that the United States was no longer a status quo power in the Middle East."[30]

Iraq quickly began moving to center stage in the Bush White House, with Rumsfeld and Wolfowitz pushing hard. Kenneth Pollack, an Iraqi expert formerly with the CIA and National Security Council (NSC) staff identified the Iraq "hawks" within the administration as a "group led by Deputy Secretary of Defense Paul Wolfowitz and a number of others in the offices of the Secretary of Defense and Vice President. This band had an almost obsessive fixation on getting rid of Saddam's regime. . . . From day one, they urged an aggressive regime change strategy relying on [Iraqi exiles] and U.S. air power to topple Saddam. Their dogma was that the Iraqi regime was the root cause of nearly every evil to befall the United States (from Arab-Israeli violence to international terrorism), while the Iraqi people were waiting to rise up against Saddam and would do so if the United States demonstrated it was serious about overthrowing him." Indeed, even though al-Qaeda was immediately and correctly suspected as the source of the attacks, both Secretary of Defense Donald Rumsfeld and Deputy Secretary of Defense Wolfowitz wanted to focus U.S. military action on Iraq.[31]

According to the legendary journalist Bob Woodward's account of the administration's first reactions to the attacks (which remains undisputed by President Bush, who gave Woodward cooperative interviews), at a National Security Council meeting immediately after the terrorist attacks, both Rumsfeld and Wolfowitz argued unsuccessfully for an American military response that included an assault on Iraq. "Rumsfeld raised the question of Iraq. Why shouldn't we go against Iraq, not just al-Qaeda? he asked. Rumsfeld was speaking not only for himself when he raised the question. His deputy, Paul D. Wolfowitz, was committed to a policy that would make Iraq a principal target of the first round in the war on terrorism. . . . Rumsfeld was raising the possibility that they could take advantage of the opportunity offered by the terrorist attacks to go after Saddam immediately."[32] Thus from the start, neoconservatives inside the upper reaches of the Bush administration were prepared to lump together Iraq and al-Qaeda into an undifferentiated "terrorism" threat and to use the al-Qaeda attacks as a fulcrum for a war on Iraq that would finish the unfinished business of 1991.

Secretary of State Colin Powell opposed the Rumsfeld-Wolfowitz option and persuaded the president to focus on al-Qaeda first. "Any action needs public support," he argued. "It's not just what the international coalition supports; it's what the American people want to support. The American people want us to do something about al-Qaeda."[33] There was also no evidence of an Iraqi hand in the September 11 attacks.

At another NSC meeting at Camp David on September 15, by which time the focus was on coercing the Taliban to turn over the al-Qaeda leadership or face forcible regime change in Afghanistan, Wolfowitz again raised the issue of Iraq. When National Security Adviser Condoleezza Rice asked whether those at the meeting

> could envision a successful military operation beyond Afghanistan . . . Wolfowitz seized the opportunity. Attacking Afghanistan would be uncertain. He worried about 100,000 American troops bogged down in mountain fighting in Afghanistan six months from then. In contrast, Iraq was a brittle, oppressive regime that might break easily. It was doable. He estimated that there was a 10 to 50 percent chance Saddam was involved in the September 11 terrorist attacks. The U.S. would have to go after Saddam at some time if the war on terrorism was to be taken seriously. . . .
>
> [But] Bush had strong reservations about attacking Iraq. . . . He was concerned about two things, he said later. "My theory is you've got to do something and do it well and that . . . if we could prove that we could be successful in [the Afghanistan] theater, then the rest of the task would be easier. If we tried to do too many things—two things, for example, or three things—militarily, then . . . the lack of focus would have been a huge risk."

Bush's other concern was one he did not express to his war cabinet but that he would say later was part of his thinking. He knew that around the table were advisers—Powell, Cheney, Wolfowitz—who had been with his father during the Gulf War deliberations. "And one of the things I wasn't going to allow to happen is, that we weren't going to let their previous experience in this theater dictate a rational course for a new war." In others words, he didn't want them to use the war on terror as an excuse to settle an old score."[34]

Exactly when President Bush decided on war with Iraq is not clear. In March 2003 *Time* published a long account tracing the post-9/11 evolution of his thinking on Iraq as influenced increasingly by neoconservative argumentation. This account has the president declaring to startled senators meeting with Rice in March 2002—six months after 9/11: "F——k Saddam. We're taking him out." The president had poked his head into Rice's office and heard the senators discussing the possibilities of dealing with Iraq through the United Nations or a coalition of U.S. allies in the Middle East. A postwar *Financial Times* account concluded that Bush had decided on war no later than December 2002, when he was confronted with Saddam Hussein's twelve-thousand-page declaration regarding charges that Iraq still possessed WMD. The declaration seemed to be nothing more than a tedious obfuscation, leading the president to conclude that Saddam Hussein had made a strategic decision not to cooperate. "There was a feeling that the White House was being mocked," according to one National Security Council source. "A tinpot dictator was mocking the president. It provoked . . . anger inside the White House. At that point, there was no prospect of a diplomatic solution."[35]

But the decision for war with Iraq, whenever it was made, was not simply a product of presidential anger and neoconservative determination to settle accounts with Saddam Hussein. It was no less an implementation of a controversial use-of-force doctrine formulated and declared in the year following 9/11.

3

The Bush Doctrine

During the year following the September 11 attacks, the Bush administration, with the help of surrogate anti-Taliban ground forces, bombed the Taliban regime from power and disrupted al-Qaeda operations in Afghanistan. It also began to turn its attention increasingly toward Iraq as the next target state in its war on terrorism, in large part because Bush, according to White House speechwriter David Frum, had come to see regime change in Baghdad as the key to something much greater. "If the United States overthrew Saddam next [after overthrowing the Taliban in Afghanistan, Bush reasoned], it could create a reliable American ally in the potential superpower of the Arab world. With American troops so close, the Iranian people would be emboldened to rise against the mullahs. And as Iran and Iraq built moderate, representative, pro-Western regimes, the pressure on the Saudis and the other Arab states to liberalize and modernize would intensify. It was quite a gamble—but also quite a prize."[1]

Perhaps most significantly, the administration proclaimed a new doctrine governing American use of force that departed radically from traditional approaches and provoked strong international opposition. The doctrine reflected Pres. George W. Bush's adoption of the neoconservative vision of the world and of America's role in it.

The historian Walter LaFeber has summarized the neoconservative foreign policy philosophy in the following formula: "American exceptionalism plus the nature of U.S. power equals the efficacy of its unilateralism." The specifics of what became known in the year following 9/11 as the Bush doctrine consist of a series of presidential pronouncements culminating in the administration's issuance, in September 2002, of *The National Security Strategy of the United States of America*. In addition to *The National Security Strategy,* the key declarations are President Bush's speeches before a joint session of Congress on September 20, 2001, before the Warsaw Conference on Combating Terrorism on November 6, 2001, his state of the union address on January 29, 2002, his remarks before the student body of the Virginia Military Institute on April 17, 2002, and his address to the graduating class at the U.S. Military Academy at West Point on June 1, 2002. By the fall of 2002 the administration had in place a clear, declaratory use-of-force policy whose objective was stated in the title of chapter 5 in *The National Security Strategy:* "Prevent Our Enemies from Threatening Us, Our Allies, and Our Friends with Weapons of Mass Destruction."[2]

What are the tenets, strengths, weaknesses, and implications of the Bush doctrine?

The National Security Strategy declares that the "U.S. national security strategy will be based on a distinctly American internationalism that reflects the union of our values and our national interests. The aim of this strategy is to help make the world not just safer but better." President Bush's cover letter to the document states: "The greatest danger our Nation faces lies at the crossroads of radicalism and technology. Our enemies have openly declared that they are seeking weapons of mass destruction, and evidence indicates that they are doing so with determination. The United States will not allow those efforts to succeed . . . .America will act against such emerging threats before they are fully formed."[3] However, as John Lewis Gaddis has observed, "Preemption . . . requires hegemony." Thus, in his West Point speech, Bush declared: "America has, and intends to keep, military strengths beyond challenge." *The National Security Strategy* states: "Our forces will be strong enough to dissuade potential adversaries from pursuing a military buildup in the hopes of surpassing, or equaling, the power of the United States" and then proceeds to chide China for "pursuing advanced military capabilities that can threaten its neighbors in the Asia-Pacific region," [which is] "an outdated path that, in the end, will hamper its own national greatness."[4]

Thus the Bush doctrine defines the threat as political and religious extremism joined by the availability of weapons of mass destruction. "When the spread of chemical and biological and nuclear weapons, along with ballistic missile technology—when that occurs," said Bush at West Point, "even weak states and small groups could attain a catastrophic power to strike great nations."[5] Secretary of Defense Rumsfeld subsequently spoke of a "nexus between terrorist networks, terrorist states, and weapons of mass destruction . . . that can make mighty adversaries of small or impoverished states and even relatively small groups of individuals."[6]

The Bush doctrine identifies three threat agents: terrorist organizations with global reach, weak states that harbor and assist such terrorist organizations, and rogue states. Al-Qaeda and the Taliban's Afghanistan embody the first two agents, respectively. Rogue states are defined as states that

> brutalize their own people and squander their national resources for the personal gain of their rulers;

display no regard for international law, threaten their neighbors, and callously violate international treaties to which they are party;

are determined to acquire weapons of mass destruction, along with other advanced military technology, to be used as threats or offensively to achieve the aggressive designs of these regimes;

sponsor terrorism around the globe;

and reject human values and hate the United States and everything it stands for.[7]

The two most threatening attributes of rogue states are inherent regime aggressiveness and the search for WMD, especially nuclear weapons, which are far more status-enhancing and efficient engines of mass slaughter than chemical and biological weapons. (Indeed, nuclear weapons are in a class by themselves and should not be lumped together with chemical and biological weapons, whose relative destructiveness is small and contingent on a host of natural conditions and enemy defenses over which the user has little control. Only nuclear weapons can produce instantaneous physical destruction on a truly massive scale.)[8]

Rogue states, according to *The National Security Strategy,* seek WMD to threaten us. Indeed, in 2002 Deputy Secretary of State Richard Armitage asserted that rogue states' "unrelenting drive to possess weapons of mass destruction brings about the *inevitability* that they will be used against us or our interests."[9] President Bush in his 2003 state of the union address declared that "Saddam Hussein has gone to elaborate lengths, spent enormous sums, taken great risks to build and keep weapons of mass destruction. But why? The only possible explanation, the only possible use he could have for those weapons, is to intimidate, or attack."[10] By implication, rogue states could not possibly be interested in WMD for defensive or deterrent purposes.

A key feature of the Bush doctrine's postulation of the threat is its conclusion that Cold War concepts of deterrence and containment are insufficient to deal with WMD-seeking rogue states and are irrelevant against terrorist organizations. "In the Cold War," states *The National Security Strategy,* "we faced a generally status-quo, risk-averse adversary. . . . But deterrence based only on a threat of retaliation is less likely to work against leaders of rogue states more willing to take risks, gambling with the lives of their people, and wealth of their nation. . . . Traditional concepts of deterrence will not work against a terrorist enemy." This judgment echoed President Bush's earlier remarks in his West Point speech: "Deterrence, the promise of massive retaliation against nations, means nothing against shadowy terrorist networks with no nation or citizens to defend." And:

"Containment is not possible when unbalanced dictators with weapons of mass destruction can deliver those weapons on missiles or secretly provide them to terrorist allies."[11] (In contrast to containment of Communism, which was aimed at its territorial expansion, containment of Iraq from 1991 to 2003 targeted Saddam's territorial *and* nuclear ambitions. It was therefore "vertical" as well as "horizontal" containment.) Thus, according to the Bush doctrine, rogue states are a double threat; they seek not only to acquire WMD for themselves but also could transfer them to terrorist "allies."

Making matters worse, argued the Bush White House, the threat is not just undeterrable—it is also imminent, requiring urgent responses. Less than two months after the 9/11 attacks, President Bush declared, "We will not wait for the authors of mass murder to gain weapons of mass destruction."[12] In his subsequent state of the union address, he further stated that "time is not on our side. I will not wait on events, while dangers gather. I will not stand by, as peril draws close and closer." At West Point, he warned, "If we wait for security threats to materialize, we will have waited too long." *The National Security Strategy* declares simply: "We cannot let our enemies strike first."[13] National Security Adviser Condoleezza Rice underscored the administration's sense of danger, telling CNN on September 8, 2002, that the risk of waiting for conclusive proof of Saddam Hussein's determination to acquire nuclear weapons was too great because "we don't want the smoking gun to become a mushroom cloud," a metaphor President Bush subsequently repeated.[14] Three months later Deputy Secretary of Defense Paul Wolfowitz warned an international audience: "The notion that we can wait to prepare assumes that we know when the threat is imminent. . . . When were the attacks of September 11 imminent? Certainly they were imminent on September 10, although we didn't know it. . . . Anyone who believes that we can wait until we have certain knowledge that attacks are imminent has failed to connect the dots that led to September 11."[15]

The Bush doctrine postulates an imminent, multifaceted, undeterrable, and potentially calamitous threat to the United States—a threat that, by virtue of the combination of its destructiveness and invulnerability to deterrence, has no precedent in American history. By implication, such a threat demands an unprecedented response.

The judgment that we are dealing with enemies who are prepared to "strike first," "to threaten or use weapons of mass destruction against the United States,"[16]and "who would [not] hesitate to use weapons of mass destruction if they believed it would serve their purposes" inevitably dictates a policy of what the Bush administration has chosen to call "anticipatory self-defense."[17] The administration bills the policy as a strategy of preemption. In his West Point speech, President Bush announced that the "war on terror will not be won on the defensive. We must take the battle to the enemy, disrupt his plans and confront the worst threats before they emerge. In the world we have entered the only path to safety is the path of action. And this nation will act." *The National Security Strategy* declares that the "United States has long maintained the option of preemptive actions to counter a sufficient threat to our national security," and given the risk of inaction against enemies prepared to strike first, "the United States will, if necessary, act preemptively." The document goes on to say, "Legal scholars and international jurists often conditioned the legitimacy of preemption on the existence of an imminent threat—most often a visible mobilization of armies, navies, air forces preparing for attack." However, "[w]e must adapt the concept of imminent threat to the capabilities and objectives of today's adversaries." Because rogue states know they cannot win with conventional weapons, "they [will] rely on acts of terror and, potentially, the use of weapons of mass destruction—weapons that can be easily concealed, delivered covertly, and used without warning."[18]

The Bush administration does not regard preemption as a substitute for nonmilitary measures. Preemption is a supplement tailored to deal with the new, nondeterrable threat. But the question does arise as to whether preemption best characterizes the new policy. The Pentagon's official definition of preemption is "an attack initiated on the basis of incontrovertible evidence that an enemy attack is imminent." In contrast, preventive war is "a war initiated in the belief that military conflict, while not imminent, is inevitable, and that to delay would involve greater risk."[19] Harvard's Graham Allison has captured the logic of preventive war: "I may some day have a war with you, and right now I'm strong and you're not. So I'm going to have the war now." Allison went on to point out that this logic was very much behind the Japanese attack on Pearl Harbor, adding that "in candid moments some Japanese scholars say—off the record—that [Japan's] big mistake was waiting too long."[20] Or as Lawrence Freedman, sympathetic to the Bush doctrine, put it: "Prevention is cold-blooded: it intends to deal with a problem before it becomes a crisis, while preemption is a more desperate strategy employed in the heat of crisis. Prevention can be seen as preemption in slow motion, more anticipatory or forward thinking, perhaps even looking beyond the target's current intentions to those that might develop along with greatly enhanced capabilities."[21]

Preventive war rests on long-range calculations about power relationships and is attractive to states that feel themselves in irreversible decline relative to potential adversaries. This would include militarily dominant states determined to thwart the emergence of peer competitors. Observes Jack S. Levy: "The preventive motivation for war arises from the perception that one's military power and potential are declining relative to that of a rising adversary, and from fear of the consequences of that decline."[22]

It is important to understand the distinction between preemptive attacks, which are rare, and preventive wars, which are not.[23] As defined above, preemptive attack is justifiable if it meets Secretary of State Daniel Webster's strict criteria, enunciated in 1837 and still the legal standard, that the threat be "instant, overwhelming, leaving no choice of means and no moment of deliberation." Preemptive war has legal sanction in exceptional circumstances because, as Chris Brown points out, the "right to preempt is . . . an extension of the right of self-defense." Preventive war, on the other hand, has none, because the threat is neither certain nor imminent. This makes preventive war indistinguishable from outright aggression, which may explain why the Bush administration has insisted that its strategy is preemptive, although *The National Security Strategy*'s chapter 5, which summarizes the case for striking first, is titled "*Prevent* Our Enemies from Threatening Us" (emphasis added). Administration officials have been wont to dismiss the distinction between preemptive attack and preventive war, and have at times used the terms interchangeably. As the foreign policy analyst David C. Hendrickson notes, however, preventive war "is directly contrary to the principle that so often was the rallying cry of American internationalism in the twentieth century," and that in "the epoch of the world wars, doctrines of preventive war were closely identified with the German and Japanese strategic traditions."[24]

Webster, of course, could not have been expected to anticipate the emergence of international nonstate actors capable of launching devastating attacks with no visible preparation. On the other hand, Iraq in 2003 posed no credible, much less imminent, threat to the United States. There was no case for preemption as traditionally defined. Indeed, if anyone had a case for preemption it was Saddam Hussein. By mid-March he faced hostile forces massing in Kuwait and elsewhere in the region, forces dispatched there for the avowed purpose of attacking Iraq and overthrowing his regime. Saddam could justifiably have invoked Daniel Webster.

If the U.S. attack on Iraq did not qualify as preemption, was it in fact a preventive war based on assumption of the inevitability of hostilities and the desire to strike before the military balance became less favorable to the United States—that is, before Saddam Hussein acquired deliverable nuclear weapons? The Bush administration's statements during the year before its attack pointed strongly to a conviction that war was inevitable, which became virtually a self-fulfilling prophecy given its declared willingness to start a war with Iraq based on the stated judgment that time was not on the American side. In his address to the nation from Cincinnati on October 7,

2002, Bush asked the question, "If we know Saddam has dangerous weapons today, and we do, does it make any sense for the world to wait to confront him as he grows stronger and develops even more dangerous weapons?" The president went on to assert that Iraq could be "less than a year" away from building a nuclear weapon, and that if allowed to do so, "a terrible line would be crossed. Saddam Hussein would be in a position to blackmail anyone who opposes his aggression . . . to dominate the Middle East . . . [and] to threaten America" by "pass[ing] nuclear technology to terrorists."[25]

There may indeed have been a case for starting a preventive war against Iraq in March 2003, but we should be clear that it *was* a preventive war not a preemptive attack. On the other hand, *The National Security Strategy* is certainly right in insisting on the need to revisit the traditional distinction between preemption and prevention in the face of undeterrable nonstate enemies armed with WMD, and perhaps even rogue states. "Perhaps the gulf between preemption and prevention," observes Michael Waltzer, "has now narrowed so that there is little strategic (and therefore little moral) difference between them." Moreover, against Iraq, at least, the United States had an established record of preventive military operations even before the launching of Operation Iraqi Freedom. As noted in 1994 by Richard Haass, who later served the Bush administration as head of the State Department's Policy Planning Staff, the "Desert Storm coalition's attacks against Iraqi unconventional warfare capabilities inside Iraq involved preventive employment of force; the capabilities targeted were not yet in a state of development to affect the course of [the Gulf War]."[26] Indeed, by the time Desert Storm was launched, Kuwait's liberation—a certainty—had become incidental to the larger aim of preventing future Iraqi aggression by destroying Iraqi WMD capacity and gutting Iraq's conventional military capabilities. Kuwait could have been liberated without striking targets in Iraq, albeit probably at significantly greater cost.

Yet preventive strikes *during* a war are not to be equated with strikes that *initiate* war. A wartime belligerent can legitimately target the enemy's future potential as well as extant military capabilities, whereas invading a state with which one is not at war and which displays no evidence of preparation for imminent war-initiation is something quite different.

The Bush doctrine has sparked worldwide controversy. Its postulation of an undifferentiated terrorism/rogue state threat, demotion of deterrence, focus on regime change, elevation of preventive war—always an implicit policy option—into a declaratory doctrine, and the precedent it sets for others to act have attracted enormous commentary.[27] Chapter 4, "Enemies," addresses the issues of threat definition and post-9/11 perspectives on deterrence. The remainder of this chapter examines the issues of regime change, war initiation, and precedent.

With respect to regime change, it is clearly the most effective means of defeating threats posed by rogue and terrorist-hosting weak states. But actual regime change can entail considerable, even unacceptable, military and political risk, depending on local, regional, and international circumstances. Doctrinal prescription, if insensitive to the uniqueness and dominance of circumstance, is a recipe for disaster. "I deplore doctrines," George F. Kennan once observed. "They purport to define one's behavior in future situations where it may or may not be suitable."[28]

The issue is not the desirability of regime change, but rather, in each specific case, its feasibility, costs, risks, and potentially unintended consequences as weighed against the magnitude and imminence of the threat. Preceding administrations were content to treat symptoms of aggression; offenders were driven back to their own borders or subjected to coercive diplomacy, but they were left intact, free to fight another day. The George H. W. Bush administration restricted its main declared Gulf War objective to the expulsion of Iraqi forces from Kuwait. The Clinton administration recoiled from initiating a decisive use of force in the Balkans against the Bosnian Serbs and later Serbia, and countered al-Qaeda attacks on American interests in Africa, the Middle East, and the Persian Gulf with ineffectual punitive missile strikes.

The present Bush administration, in contrast, has adopted regime change as an explicit policy objective with respect to rogue states. Indeed, it was emphasizing regime change even before 9/11. In its September 2001 *Report of the Quadrennial Defense Review,* the main text of which was written and approved before the terrorist attacks, the Rumsfeld Defense Department declared that possible instances of failed deterrence in the future mandated a capacity to "decisively defeat any adversary." Specifically, "U.S. forces must maintain the capability at the direction of the President to impose the will of the United States and its coalition partners on any adversaries, including states and non-state entities. Such a decisive defeat could include changing the regime of an adversary state or occupation of foreign territory until U.S. strategic objectives are met."[29] This pre-9/11 hint of things to come materialized in the administration's toppling of both the Taliban in Afghanistan and Saddam Hussein in Iraq. In so doing, the Bush White House extended into the twenty-first century an established American practice of the twentieth, in which the United States repeatedly overthrew regimes it did not like in its own hemisphere and sometimes elsewhere.

But Iran, North Korea, and other potential rogue state targets of the Bush doctrine are not banana republic weaklings. Iran is reportedly well along the way to acquiring the capacity to build nuclear weapons, and North Korea is believed already to have them. Even without nuclear weapons, both countries would be much more difficult to subdue than was Iraq—North Korea by virtue of its Communist discipline and ability to hold Seoul hostage via massed long-range artillery, and Iran because of its historic xenophobia and relatively large territory and population. (Iran has almost four times the space of Iraq and three times its population.)

Even if all rogue states were military pushovers, the postwar task of creating a new, enduring, and nonthreatening political order remains. Terminating wars in a manner that produces a better and enduring peace is an inherently difficult task.[30] Before Operation Iraqi Freedom, there was certainly no encouragement in the Bush administration's visceral aversion to participation in "nation-building," an aversion whose price was evident in the deterioration of the security situation in Afghanistan in 2003. Yet regime change imposes postregime military, political, and economic responsibilities, and failure to step up to those responsibilities not only betrays those liberated by regime change but also invites a "worse peace" that incubates future threats.

With respect to the Bush doctrine's embrace of preventive war, it is important to recognize that striking first is an implicit policy option in any foreign policy crisis. "Preemption has always been available as a tool of foreign policy or military doctrine," observed Secretary of State Colin Powell in September 2002. "When you see something coming at you, when it is such a clear and present danger, and you know what is going to happen, and you believe that you can make the case that it is going to happen, it is an option that is available to a president or to a leader."[31]

The United States has moreover a modest history of anticipatory military action. Before the War of 1812, James Madison authorized military operations in Spanish Florida in an attempt to preempt the British from using it as a base from which to attack the United States. Indeed, the subsequently proclaimed Monroe doctrine was aimed at preempting renewed European military intervention in the Western Hemisphere following the overthrow of Spanish rule in most of Latin America. The post–Civil War winter campaigns against the western Indians were preventive in nature. In 1898 the United States launched a preemptive attack on the Spanish fleet in the Philippines even though that target had nothing to do with the origins of the Spanish-American War. NSC-68, the 1950 document that spelled out the Truman administration's Cold War strategy of containment, explicitly accepted the idea of a preemptive nuclear strike if a Soviet attack was known to be on its way or about to be launched.[32] During the Cold War the United States engineered the covert and overt overthrow of regimes it believed were precursors to the establishment of expanded Soviet power and influence (e.g., in Iran in 1953, Guatemala in 1954, and Grenada in 1983). U.S. intervention in Vietnam was justified as a means of preventing other Asian "dominoes" from falling to Communism.

U.S. action during the Cuban Missile Crisis of 1962 was preemptive to the extent that the U.S. naval "quarantine" (i.e., blockade) and threat of nuclear retaliation against the Soviet Union were aimed at forestalling the establishment on the island of a permanent force of Soviet medium-range nuclear ballistic missiles. Pres. John F. Kennedy found a way out of the crisis without resorting to war, in part because he regarded a preemptive strike (air or ground invasion or both) against Cuba as contrary to America's tradition as an opponent, not a perpetrator, of aggression. Undersecretary of State George Ball argued that a preemptive strike was "contrary to our traditions, . . . a course of action that would cut directly athwart everything we have stood for during our national history, and condemn us as hypocrites in the opinion of the world." The president's influential brother and attorney general, Robert F. Kennedy, opposed a military strike because "it would be a Pearl Harbor type of attack."[33] At one point, while listening to those arguing for an invasion, he passed a handwritten note to presidential speechwriter Theodore Sorenson: "I know how Tojo felt when he was planning Pearl Harbor."[34] Indeed, by the sixth day of the crisis President Kennedy himself was pejoratively referring to the massive air strike/invasion option as "this particular Pearl Harbor recommendation."[35] In the wake of the crisis, however, President Kennedy did warn that "we no longer live in a world where only the actual firing of weapons represents a sufficient challenge to a nation's security to constitute maximum peril."[36]

The twin issues are the wisdom of preventive war and its transformation from an implicit policy option into a declaratory doctrine. Both, together with the U.S. invasion of Iraq in defiance of the United Nations, have reinforced an image of America, widely held among friends and adversaries alike, of a unilateralist, overbearing "hyperpower" insensitive to the concerns of others. "At no time in the last 50 years has the United States stood in such antagonism to both the primary norms and the central institutions of international society," contends David C. Hendrickson. "The reason is not difficult to find. These rules and institutions convey a simple message to the Bush administration: by right you should not do what you want to do (invade Iraq, wage preventive wars, etc.)."[37]

At the root of the problem is the failure of the neoconservatives who have provided the intellectual and doctrinal foundation for the Bush administration's foreign policy to grasp the fact that others do not see us as we see ourselves—that is, as a benign and historically exceptional force whose moral and political values are universally appealing. We may be what the neoconservatives think we are, but that does not automatically make us so in the eyes of others. The neoconservative view is that America is not just virtuous but self-evidently virtuous, and that its power therefore should not be feared but welcomed. This extraordinary naivete led, among many other things, to confident prewar predictions that the war against Iraq would be a "cakewalk," that all Iraqis other than Saddam and his henchmen were dying to be liberated and occupied by an invading American army (the analogy was made to France's liberation in 1944), and that Saddam's regime would collapse like a house of cards at the first knock of American military power. The neoconservatives inside the Bush administration know they are right; they have no self-doubt; and they believe the United States can mold the world in its own values and interests.

Interestingly, during the 2000 presidential campaign, George W. Bush declared, "Our nation stands alone right now in the world in terms of power. And that's why we've got to be humble and project strength in a way that promotes freedom. . . . If we are an arrogant nation, they'll view us that way, but if we're a humble nation, they'll respect us." Preventive war, however, has never been associated with humility; on the contrary, it is indistinguishable from aggression. As a doctrine, preventive war rests on speculative, worst-case scenarios of what *might* happen at some distant point in the future; it postulates hypothetical threats before they materialize, if in fact they do. The doctrine also reflects pursuit of the inherently unattainable goal of absolute security, and as such it is a prescription for endless conflict. "The fact that a state might pose a threat in the foreseeable future should be seen as a reason to construct defenses against it, to pursue a containment strategy," argues Chris Brown, "because to attempt instead to eliminate all such threats is to commit to an endless series of wars to end all wars."[38] As such, preventive war against another state is both strategically and morally the wrong choice in almost every conceivable set of circumstances. Preventive war also assumes that the hostile regime's behavior is impervious to change, when in fact most, though not all, regimes do change over time. The Soviet Union of Nikita Khrushchev, to say nothing of Mikhail Gorbachev, was not the Soviet Union of Stalin. Nor was the China of Jiang Zemin the China of Mao Zedong.

The international legal expert Richard Falk has judged the Bush doctrine to be "a doctrine without limits, without accountability to the U.N. or international law, without any dependence on a collective judgment of responsible governments and, what is worse, without any convincing demonstration of practical necessity."[39] With respect to the last point, others have noted that in the late 1940s and early 1950s preventive warriors in the United States, including a secretary of the navy and several senior air force generals, convinced that war with the Soviet Union was inevitable, called for an attack on that country before it acquired deliverable nuclear weapons, and that subsequent events vindicated Pres. Harry Truman's rejection of calls for preventive war.[40] Truman himself recounted that "I have always been opposed even to the thought of such a war. There is nothing more foolish than to think that war can be stopped by war. You don't prevent anything by [starting a] war except peace."[41] Indeed, at the time, Truman felt compelled to publicly denounce calls for preventive war. "We do not believe in aggression or preventive war," he declared in a radio broadcast in 1950. "Such a war is the weapon of dictators, not [of] free democratic countries like the United States."[42]

Pursuit of permanent American primacy via perpetual military supremacy and, as a matter of doctrine, an aggressive willingness to use force preemptively, even preventively, to dispatch threatening regimes and promote the spread of American political values and economic institutions is imperialism pure and simple and invites perpetual isolation and enmity. Such a course also undermines the very international order the United States created after World War II, which has served America's security so well. As John Ikenberry comments: "America's nascent neoimperial grand strategy threatens to rend the fabric of the international community and political partnerships precisely at a time when that community and those partnerships are urgently needed [to wage war on terrorist threats]. It is an approach fraught with peril and likely to fail. It is not only politically unsustainable but diplomatically harmful. And if history is any guide, it will trigger antagonism and resistance that will leave America in a more hostile and divided world."[43]

We have "a special obligation to rest our policies on principles that transcend the assertions of preponderant power," wrote Henry Kissinger in September 2002. "World leadership requires the acceptance of some restraint even on one's actions to ensure that others exercise comparable restraint. It cannot be in either our national or the world's interest to develop principles that grant every nation an unfettered right of preemption against its own definition of threats to its security."[44] Even more troubled by the Bush administration's unilateralism and endorsement of preventive war was Brent Scowcroft, Pres. George H. W. Bush's national security adviser.

> Part of the Bush administration believes that as a superpower we must take advantage of this opportunity to change the world for the better, and we don't need to go out of our way to accommodate alliances, partnerships, or friends in the process, because that would be too constraining. [But relying almost solely on ad hoc] coalitions of the willing is fundamentally,

fatally flawed. As we've seen in the debate about Iraq, it's already given us an image of arrogance and unilateralism, and we're paying a very high price for that image. If we get to the point where everyone secretly hopes the United States gets a black eye because we're so obnoxious, then we'll be totally hamstrung in the war on terror. We'll be like Gulliver with the Lilliputians.[45]

In the British historian Sir Michael Howard's view:

An explicit American hegemony may appear [to the administration] preferable to the messy compromises of the existing order, but if it is nakedly based on . . . military power it will lack all legitimacy. Terror will continue, and worse, widespread sympathy with terror. But American power placed at the service of an international community legitimized by representative institutions and the rule of law, accepting its constraints and inadequacies but continually working to improve them: that is a very different matter. . . . [The United States] must cease to think of itself as a heroic lone protagonist in a cosmic war against "evil," and reconcile itself to a less spectacular and more humdrum role: that of the leading participant in a flawed but still indispensable system of cooperative global governance.[46]

If the Bush doctrine is unsettling to the rest of the world, it also invites abuse and establishes a dangerous precedent for others to follow. For the United States, the risk is doctrinal degeneration into an excuse for attacking regimes we simply do not like versus regimes that pose a clear and present danger. The doctrine invites abuse because it offers no criteria by which to judge a threat justifying preventive war. A rogue state is not automatically a target; if it were, attacks on Iran and North Korea would have automatically followed the subjugation of Iraq. Indeed, what justifies an attack on Iraq but not on Iran and North Korea? Had the Bush doctrine been in place after World War II, it could have been invoked against the Soviet Union and China, both of which met the new *National Security Strategy* definition of a rogue state and were pursuing acquisition of nuclear weapons until 1949 and 1964, respectively. "Because the doctrine sets no bounds," argues an analysis of *The National Security Strategy,* "might the U.S. again choose preemption even though deterrence would this time be appropriate? And knowing this, might others be more likely to strike even earlier—requiring the U.S. to improve its first-strike capabilities in return? The logic of offense and defense could make a world of unbounded preemption very ugly indeed."[47]

A Brookings Institution critique concludes that the Bush doctrine's "silence on the circumstances that justify preemption" raises the danger that other countries "will embrace the preemption argument as a cover for settling their own national security scores. . . . [U]ntil the Administration can define the line separating justifiable preemption from unlawful aggression in ways that will gain widespread adherence abroad, it risks seeing its words used to justify ends it opposes." In the fall of 2002 Russia invoked American endorsement of preemption as justifying military action against Georgia, from which Chechen separatists conduct operations. India could attack Pakistan, happily invoking the Bush doctrine on the charge of Pakistan's sponsorship of terrorism in Kashmir. And China, notwithstanding *The National Security Strategy* s advice to Beijing not to pursue advanced military capabilities, could justify a preventive war against Taiwan as a means of forestalling its threatened independence or unfavorable (to China) alteration of the military balance across the Taiwan Strait. Or, observes Ken Jowitt, China "might very well use the Bush security doctrine's logic to launch an anticipatory attack on Japan and/or a united Korea before they . . . 'go nuclear.'"[48]

The Bush doctrine could also be invoked on behalf of suppressing any and all insurgencies. "One of the worst spillover effects of the manner in which the US government has orchestrated its response to September 11 has been the hunting license issued to states around the world to intensify violence against their opponents, and to validate such actions by claiming to be fighting against terrorism, helping the American-led global war on terror," observes Richard Falk. The American policy reaction to 9/11 "has been read . . . as an unconditional authorization for state violence. . . . If terrorists are equated with evil, and their governmental opponents are regarded as inherently good, then it is obvious that violence by the latter against the former is never excessive or wrong."[49]

The Bush doctrine could not only excuse preventive war and domestic terrorism by other states but also stimulate nuclear proliferation among potential targets of U.S. preventive attack. Before Operation Iraqi Freedom, the Bush administration made it quite plain that it believed a nuclear-armed Iraq would be an out-of-control, undeterrable Iraq—an Arab North Korea that could be attacked only at great risk. Francois Heisbourg contends that the Bush doctrine is likely to spark "precautionary proliferation" on the part of states "that fear finding themselves on the list of targets for U.S. preventive action," and he includes a Saudi Arabia terrified by the prospect of U.S.–sponsored regime change in Riyadh. "Under certain circumstances, [acquiring nuclear weapons] might prove tempting for a country such as Saudi Arabia, which already possesses large medium-range Chinese CSS-2 rockets," he speculates. "[S]uch a scenario could be prompted by warfare aimed at regime change throughout the Middle East—in the wake of intervention in Iraq, for instance. Neoconservative discourse on democratizing the Middle East helps fuel such fears," and it is worthwhile recalling that "two years elapsed between the sale of the sizable Chinese CSS-2 missiles to Saudi Arabia and its detection by U.S. intelligence."[50]

In the earliest years after the Cold War, before the Soviet Union exploded its first atomic bomb, there were calls in the United States for preventive war against another evil dictator. The calls continued even after the Soviets detonated their first bomb in 1949 because throughout the 1950s the United States still enjoyed an enormous nuclear first-strike advantage over Russia. In 1950 the commandant of the air force's new Air War College in Montgomery, Alabama, publicly asked to be given the order to conduct a nuclear strike against fledgling Soviet atomic capabilities. "And when I went to Christ," said the commandant, "I think I could explain to Him why I wanted to do it now before it's too late. I think I could explain to Him that I had saved civilization. With it [the A-bomb] used in time, we can immobilize a foe [and] reduce his crime before it happened."[51]

President Truman fired the commandant.

4

Enemies: Osama's Al-Qaeda and Saddam's Iraq

The great Prussian war theorist Carl von Clausewitz believed that the "first, the supreme, the most far-reaching act of judgment that the statesman and the commander have to make is to establish . . . the kind of war on which they are embarking, neither mistaking it for, nor trying to turn it into, something that is alien to its true nature. This is the first of all strategic questions and the most comprehensive."[1]

In the wake of the 9/11 attacks, Pres. George W. Bush declared a "war against terrorism of global reach."[2] Subsequently and repeatedly, he and other administration spokesmen used the more general terms, "global war on terrorism," "war on terror," and "battle against terrorism."

The nature and parameters of this war, however, remain frustratingly unclear. The Bush administration has postulated a multiplicity of enemies, including rogue states, WMD proliferators, terrorist organizations, and terrorism itself. It has also, at least for the purposes of mobilizing and sustaining domestic political support for the war on Iraq and potential other preventive military actions, conflated them as a general, undifferentiated threat. In so doing, it has arguably sacrificed strategic clarity for the sake of the moral clarity it so prizes in foreign policy and may have set the United States on a path of open-ended and unnecessary conflict with states and nonstate entities that pose no direct or imminent threat to the United States.

Discussion of the war on terrorism is bedeviled by the absence of any commonly accepted definition of terrorism. Even inside the U.S. government, different departments and agencies use different definitions reflecting different professional perspectives on the subject.[3] A 1988 study counted 109 definitions of terrorism that covered a total of 22 definitional elements.[4] Walter Laqueur has also counted more than 100 definitions and concludes that the "only characteristic generally agreed upon is that terrorism involves violence or the threat of violence."[5] Yet terrorism is hardly the only enterprise involving violence and the threat of violence. So do war, coercive diplomacy, and barroom brawls.

The National Security Strategy defines "terrorism" as "premeditated, politically motivated violence perpetrated against innocents."[6] This definition, however, begs the question of who's innocent and by what standards is innocence determined? The indiscriminate U.S. firebombing of Japanese cities in 1945 certainly terrified their civilian inhabitants, many of whom were women and children who had nothing to do with Japan's war effort. The distinction between soldiers and civilians as legitimate targets tends to disappear in total wars, and the United States and al-Qaeda are locked in total war. And what about *threatened* as opposed to actual violence? Is not the inducement of fear a major object of terrorism, and isn't threatened action a way of generating fear?

Consider the Pentagon's official definition of terrorism: "The calculated use of unlawful violence to inculcate fear; intended to coerce or to intimidate governments or societies in the pursuit of goals that are generally political, religious, or ideological."[7] The difficulty with this definition is that it confines terrorism to nonstate actors at war with governments or societies. Would this not include those who stormed the Bastille in 1789 and the Hungarian Freedom Fighters of 1956? The definition, moreover, excludes governmental terrorism (e.g., Stalin's Russia, Mao's China, Pol Pot's Cambodia), which has accounted for many more victims than have the likes of al-Qaeda, the Jewish Irgun and Stern Gang, and the Tamil Tigers.

The Bush administration's rhetoric on terrorism perversely invites any state facing violent internal threats to label them as "terrorist" threats and to employ whatever means necessary to combat them, including the kind of terrorism of counterterrorist operations practiced by Israeli security forces in the West Bank and Gaza. Perhaps inadvertently, the White House's language has become, as Conor Gearty puts it, "the rhetorical servant of the established order, wherever it might be and however heinous its own activities are." Because the Bush administration has cast terrorism and terrorists as always the most evil of evils, what the terrorists do "is always wrong [and] what the counter-terrorist has to do to defeat them is therefore invariably, necessarily right. The nature of [established] regime, the kind of action that is possible against it, the moral situation in which the violence occurs—none of these complicating elements matters a jot against the contemporary power of the terrorist label."[8] Thus Palestinian terrorism is condemned, while brutal Israeli responses are accepted. Yasir Arafat is denounced as a perpetrator of terrorism and Ariel Sharon hailed as a man of peace. Richard Falk observes: "'Terrorism' as a word and concept became associated in U.S. and Israeli discourse with antistate forms of violence that were so criminal that any method of enforcement and retaliation was viewed as acceptable, and not subject to criticism. By so appropriating the meaning of this inflammatory term in such a self-serving manner, terrorism became detached from its primary historical association dating back to the French Revolution. In that formative setting, the state's own political violence against its citizens, violence calculated to induce widespread fear and achieve political goals, was labeled as terrorism."[9]

Even if a satisfactory definition of terrorism were available, there is the issue of whether terrorism, which includes political assassination, is always morally unacceptable regardless of circumstances. Are there morally imperative ends that justify employment of terrorism as a means? Was Jewish terrorism against British rule in Palestine, such as the 1947 Irgun attack (led by Menachem Begin) on the King David Hotel in Jerusalem (killing ninety-three people, including seventeen Jews), justified as a means of securing an independent Jewish state?[10] "Terrorism may be the only feasible means of overthrowing a cruel dictatorship, the last resort of free men and women facing intolerable persecution," argues Laqueur. "In such conditions, terrorism could be a moral imperative rather than a crime—the killing of a Hitler or Stalin early on in his career would have saved the lives of millions of people."[11] In short, in circumstances where the choice is between one of two evils, might selection of the lesser evil be justified? The United States chose to fight alongside Stalin to defeat Hitler, and it effectively became a cobelligerent with Saddam Hussein in Iraq's war with the Ayatollah Khomeini's Iran.

Can one man's terrorist be another man's patriot? "Is an armed Kurd a freedom fighter in Iraq but a terrorist in Turkey?" asks Tony Judt. "Were al-Qaeda volunteers terrorists when they joined the U.S. financed war [against the Soviets] in Afghanistan?" What of the U.S. Phoenix Program and free-fire zones in Vietnam? Were they justified as means to defeat the "evil" of Communism? And what about the Nicaraguan Contras? Paul L. Atwood reminds us that Pres. Ronald Reagan declared them to be the moral equivalent of the founding fathers even though the U.S.–trained forces "systematically attacked schools and hospitals built by their political opponents, the Sandinistas, killing and injuring women and children in clear attempts to sow terror."[12]

A second problem with the Bush administration's proclaimed war against terrorism with global reach is the term "global reach." Does global mean an al-Qaeda-like capacity to strike the United States and overseas American targets and interests, or does it mean simply an ability to sponsor and conduct terrorist activities across someone else's border? The Provisional Wing of the Irish Republican Army does not threaten the United States.

This problem is compounded by the subsequent and more common official use of the term "war on terrorism," which taken literally, would commit the United States to combat all terrorist organizations everywhere regardless of whether they posed a threat to U.S. interests. And in fact the administration's *National Strategy for Combating Terrorism,* issued in February 2003, links together terrorist groups that operate within a single country, those that operate regionally across at least one international border, and those that are truly global into a single "transnational network structure, enabled by modern technology and characterized by loose interconnectivity both within and between groups." Because of interconnectivity and operational cooperation among all three geographical tiers of terrorist organizations, defeating the global-reach organizations requires defeating their regional and national analogs.[13] "Defining it as a broad war on terrorism was a tremendous mistake," the highly respected strategist Stephen Van Evera says of the Bush administration's response to the 9/11 attacks. "It should have been a war on Al Qaeda. Don't take your eye off the ball. Subordinate every other policy to it, including the policies toward Russia, the Arab-Israeli conflict, and Iraq. Instead," he continues, "the Administration defined it as a broad war on terror, including groups that have never taken a swing at the United States and never will. It leads to a loss of focus. . . . And you make enemies of the people you need against Al Qaeda."[14]

A third problem is that terrorism, however defined, is not a proper noun; like guerrilla warfare, it is a *method* of violence, a *way* of waging war. As such it is no more defeatable than guerrilla warfare. How do you defeat a technique, as opposed to a flesh and blood enemy? You can kill terrorists, infiltrate their organizations, and attack their state sponsors, but terrorism as a method of violence will persist as long as the politically desperate and the militarily impotent are with us. A generic war on terrorism "fails to make the distinction between the differing objectives of those who practice terrorism and the context surrounding its use," observes D. Robert Worley. "Failing to make the necessary distinctions invites a single, homogenous policy and strategy"—a dangerous, one-size-fits-all approach.[15]

By ballooning a justifiable war on a specific terrorist organization into a general war on terrorism around the world—indeed, into a "responsibility to . . . rid the world of evil," the Bush administration has sought moral clarity but has unintentionally done so at the expense of intellectual and strategic clarity.[16] Such a broad objective is not a useful informant of strategy, and given the fact that key allies in the war on terrorism, such as Pakistan and Saudi Arabia, remain in the business of sponsoring or inciting terrorism, even moral clarity takes a beating.

In its war on terrorism the Bush administration also has lumped together not just terrorist organizations with different agendas and threat levels to the United States; it has further stapled together terrorist organizations (e.g., al-Qaeda) and rogue states (e.g., Iraq, Iran, and North Korea). As former senator and cochairman of the U.S. Commission on National Security for the Twenty-first Century Gary Hart put it, after 9/11 "[Saddam] Hussein mysteriously morphed into Osama bin Laden, or vice-versa."[17]

Both terrorist organizations and rogue states, of course, embrace violence and are hostile to the existing international order and, more specifically, to the presence of U.S. power in their respective regions. They share a common enemy in the United States and, for rogue states and terrorist organizations in the Middle East, a common enemy in Israel. As international pariahs they are often in contact with one another and at times even cooperate with one another. But the scope and endurance of such cooperation is highly contingent on local circumstances. Rogue states and terrorist organizations are fundamentally different in character and vulnerability. Al-Qaeda is a secret, transnational organization present in an estimated sixty countries.[18] Rogue states are sovereign entities defined by specific territories and populations; as such, they are much more exposed to decisive military attack than terrorist organizations.

Moreover, al-Qaeda remains a far more deadly and immediate threat than was Saddam's Iraq. As the former National Security Council counterterrorism experts Daniel Benjamin and Steven Simon wrote in 2002:

> There are very good reasons to end Saddam Hussein's brutal reign over Iraq, but terrorism is not one of them. There is little or no history of cooperation between Iraq and al-Qaeda, and, as demonstrated by the U.S. warning to Baghdad against using a weapon of mass destruction during the Gulf War, Saddam Hussein can be deterred and will not court the destruction of his regime. Al-Qaeda, on the other hand, cannot be deterred and must be destroyed. The confusion about these matters and the ease with which the war on al-Qaeda has blurred into a move against Iraq suggest that America's leaders may not yet have taken al-Qaeda's full measure.[19]

Benjamin went on to predict that

> [t]he greatest terrorist dangers will likely come not with Hussein's cooperation with al Qaeda before the United States topples him but from the fact that his removal would present jihadists with rich new opportunities. Even if Iraqis greet GIs as liberators . . . the lesson of the past decade is that important parts of the Islamic world will not see it that way. [The Gulf War of 1991] stoked the radicals' belief that Washington was

seeking to dominate the Arab world and destroy Islam. For al Qaeda, this was a catalytic event. . . . Now, thousands of recruits later, al Qaeda and its affiliates would find American forces in a post-Hussein Iraq to be an irresistible target. . . . .Those who today blow up French tankers off Yemen or bars in Bali will soon be picking off GIs in Basra.[20]

Additionally, no two rogue states or two terrorist organizations have identical agendas. Far from it. The longest and one of the bloodiest conventional wars since 1945 was waged between two "axis of evil" states, and the persistence of Iraqi-Iranian enmity was evident in the absence from Tehran of vocal opposition to the Bush administration's invasion of Iraq. Tyrannical states quarrel as much, even more, with each other than they do with democracies.

In this regard, the Bush administration's very use of the term "axis" is misleading because it implies an operational solidarity that never existed between any of its member states. The term presumably was intended to imply an analogy between Iraq, Iran, and North Korea and that of the Axis powers of World War II. The new "axis" states have as little in common with each other as did the old Axis powers. In the case of the latter, there was no strategic coordination, much less operational cooperation, between Germany and Japan. Even in Europe, differing German and Italian imperial agendas became the source of great tension between Berlin and Rome, and Italian military incompetence compelled Hitler time and again to divert German forces into such secondary (for the Germans) theaters of operations as North Africa and the Balkans. Mussolini ended up as a German puppet.

There are also inherent limits to cooperation between religious fanatics and secular tyrants. In the case of al-Qaeda, the very idea of the modern state is anathema. Al-Qaeda regards nationalism as an apostate threat, a divider of Muslims from one another. Osama bin Laden's goal is the establishment of a politically indivisible Muslim community, and he regarded Saddam and all other secular Arab leaders as infidels. For Saddam, who spent eight years waging war against the existential threat to his regime posed by the Ayatollah Khomeini, Osama could never have been a trustworthy ally. Saddam, whose role models were Saladin and Stalin, not Mohammed, killed far more Islamic clerics than Americans. It is noteworthy that bin Laden remained silent during the first three weeks of Operation Iraqi Freedom; only on April 8, as U.S. forces entered Baghdad, did he issue a taped message calling on Muslims to mount suicide attacks against the United States and its allies in response to the U.S. invasion of Iraq.[21] Did bin Laden wait until he knew his chief secular opponent in Iraq was finished? Robert Harvey contends that "bracket[ing] al-Qaeda with Saddam is on par with equating Nazism and Soviet communism during the inter-war period as examples of European extremism, and represents the kind of quasi-racist dismissal by Washington of differences between Arab countries and political movement that most irks people in the region."[22]

But the greatest difference between Osama bin Laden and Saddam Hussein is that Osama *attacked the United States,* killing three thousand people, whereas Saddam never attacked the United States or its allies. (Kuwait was not an ally in 1990.) In so doing Osama forced a war of necessity on the United States—the first enemy to do so since the Japanese attacked Pearl Harbor sixty years earlier. The United States was thus already at war with al-Qaeda when it made a war-of-choice decision to attack Iraq eighteen months after the 9/11 attacks.

The prewar Bush administration nonetheless strove mightily to define Saddam Hussein and Osama bin Laden as an undifferentiated threat. In September 2002 President Bush declared, "you can't distinguish between al Qaeda and Saddam when you talk about the war on terrorism. They're both equally as bad, and equally as evil, and equally as destructive." He added that "the danger is that al Qaeda becomes an extension of Saddam's madness and his hatred and his capacity to extend weapons of mass destruction around the world."[23] Administration officials were convinced that Iraq had had a hand in the 9/11 attacks, and they sought to postulate a hearty operational relationship between Iraq and al-Qaeda. They also raised the specter of Saddam's transference of WMD to al-Qaeda.

The war did not change the administration argument. On May 1, 2002, President Bush, in declaring an end to major military operations in Iraq, stated that the "battle of Iraq is one victory in the war on terror that began on September 11, 2001—and still goes on. That terrible morning, 19 evil men—the shock troops of a hateful ideology—gave America and the civilized world a glimpse of their ambitions." Bush later added: "The liberation of Iraq is a crucial advance in the campaign against terror. We've removed an ally of al Qaeda, and cut off a source of terrorist funding. And this much is certain: No terrorist network will gain weapons of mass destruction from the Iraqi regime, because the regime is no more. In [these] 19 months [since the 9/11 attacks] that changed the world, our actions have been focused and deliberate and proportionate to the offense. . . . With those attacks, the terrorists and their supporters declared war on the United States. And war is what they got."[24]

In fact, there is no convincing evidence of Iraqi complicity in 9/11 or of a functioning alliance between Iraq and al-Qaeda or of Saddam's willingness to share his WMD with anyone. Baghdad simply never had the kind of symbiotic relationship with al-Qaeda that al-Qaeda enjoyed with the Taliban. And though Iraq had sponsored terrorism, it was far from the top of the list of states that did—and that continue to do so. "Terrorism is the least of the threats posed by Iraq to the interests of the United States," contended the Iraqi expert Kenneth Pollack in 2002. "If the only problem the United States had with Saddam Hussein's regime were its involvement with terrorism, our problems would be relatively mild. On the grand list of state sponsors of terrorism, Iraq is pretty far down—well below Iran, Syria, Pakistan, and others. Similarly, if one were to make a list of all of Saddam Hussein's crimes against humanity, his support for international terrorism would be far down the list, almost beside the point when compared to his mass murders, horrific torture, use of WMD against civilians, and other atrocities."[25]

Why, then, the administration's insistence on a monolithic threat in the absence of any persuasive evidence? Did it reflect an attempt to use the 9/11 attacks as an excuse to start a war with Iraq, or did it reflect instead a genuine inability (or refusal) to recognize the great differences between Saddam Hussein and his secular, Stalinist state and Osama bin Laden and his religiously fanatical transnational terrorist network? Saddam's regime was certainly easier to destroy militarily than al-Qaeda; he was much more vulnerable to decisive military defeat than the unknown number of secret al-Qaeda cells scattered around the world. One commentator has suggested that the war on Iraq was "a substitute for the war against terrorism," while another contends that "the march on Baghdad" was designed "to make us *forget* about Al Qaeda," whose continued attacks after 9/11 in Afghanistan, Pakistan, and elsewhere underscored what appeared to be the war on terrorism's very limited success.[26]

The record shows that Secretary of Defense Rumsfeld and his deputy Paul Wolfowitz raised the issue of attacking Iraq immediately after 9/11 and returned to that issue in subsequent National Security Council meetings, and they did so in the absence of any evidence linking Saddam to 9/11. Sometime between then and President Bush's state of the union address on January 28, 2002, in which he declared Iraq, Iran, and North Korea to be an "axis of evil," they and other neoconservatives inside and outside the administration seem to have persuaded the president that the war on terrorism required regime change in those three states, a goal neoconservatives had been promoting for a decade. Indeed, regime change as a U.S. military mission was for the first time explicitly identified in the September 2001 *Report of the Quadrennial Defense Review,* which called for the "decisive defeat" of future enemies, including "changing the regime of an adversary state or occupation of foreign territory until U.S. strategic objectives are met."[27]

In the months that followed the state of the union address, President Bush, in formal statements as well as informal remarks to the press, used the term "war on terrorism" to include everything from continuing operations in Afghanistan, the ongoing hunt for the al-Qaeda leadership, and the increasingly probable U.S. assault on Iraq. By the fall of 2002, the administration, to the growing dismay of friends and foes alike overseas, had become obsessed with Saddam Hussein to the point where, gauging from public presidential references to Saddam and Osama bin Laden, the destruction of the latter and the rest of the al-Qaeda leadership seemed distinctly secondary to the removal of Saddam. (Gary Hart likened the administration's preoccupation to Captain Ahab's obsession with Moby Dick; another analogy would be the obsession of Pres. John F. Kennedy and his brother Robert with Fidel Castro.)[28]

Indeed, in a rare formal news conference on March 6, 2003, President Bush linked the case for war against Iraq to the 9/11 attacks, implying that Saddam would replicate them once he got nuclear weapons. "Saddam is a threat. And we're not going to wait until he does attack," he declared. "Saddam Hussein and his weapons [of mass destruction] are a direct threat to this country," he reiterated. "If the world fails to confront the threat posed by the Iraqi regime . . . free nations would assume immense and unacceptable risks. The attacks of September the 11th, 2001, showed what enemies of American did with four airplanes. We will not wait to see what . . . terrorist states could do with weapons of mass destruction." Later on, he stated: "Saddam Hussein is a threat to our nation. September the 11th changed the—the strategic thinking, at least as far as I was concerned, for how to protect our country. . . . Used to be that we could think that you could contain a person like Saddam Hussein, that oceans would protect us from his type of terror. September the 11th should say to the American people that we're now a battlefield, that weapons of mass destruction in the hands of a terrorist organization could be deployed here at home." When asked about the possible human and financial cost of a war with Iraq, Bush declared, "The price of doing nothing exceeds the price of taking action. . . . The price of the attacks on America . . . on September the 11th were [*sic*] enormous. . . . And I'm not willing to take that chance again. . . . The lesson of September the 11th . . . is that we're vulnerable to attack . . . and we must take threats which gather overseas very seriously."[29]

Opponents of a preventive war against Iraq, including former national security advisers Brent Scowcroft and Zbigniew Brzezinski, made a clear distinction between the character, aims, and vulnerabilities of al-Qaeda and Iraq. In their view, the al-Qaeda threat was much more immediate, dangerous, and difficult to defeat. They feared that a war of choice against

Iraq would weaken a war of necessity against al-Qaeda by distracting America's strategic attention to Iraq, by consuming money and resources much better spent on homeland defense, and because the war on Iraq was profoundly unpopular around the world, especially among Muslims, by weakening the willingness of key countries to share intelligence information so vital to winning the war against al-Qaeda.

In August 2002 Scowcroft wrote a pointed op-ed in the *Wall Street Journal* in which he declared, "Our pre-eminent security policy . . . is the war on terrorism." An attack on Iraq "would seriously jeopardize, if not destroy, the global counterterrorist campaign we have undertaken," in part because the international unpopularity of a U.S. attack on Iraq would result in a "serious degradation in international cooperation with us against terrorism." Others argued that Saddam was a fading threat compared to that posed by the younger fanatics of terrorism and that the two should not be confused. "Saddam Hussein is 65 years old . . . and represents the threat of yesterday," argued the *Wall Street Journal*'s Gerald F. Seib. "These young terrorists [of al-Qaeda] are the threat of today and tomorrow. And we shouldn't fool ourselves: By itself, taking out the Iraqi leader will do little to eliminate them as a threat. In the short term, going after Iraq may stir them up further." Former secretary of state Madeleine Albright concurred: "It makes little sense now to focus the world's attention and our own military, intelligence, diplomatic, and financial resources on a plan to invade Iraq instead of on al Qaeda's ongoing plans to murder innocent people. We cannot fight a second monumental struggle without distracting from the first one."[30] Robert Baer, CIA veteran and best-selling author, also argued that Iraq was a distraction from the war on terrorism: "Aside from Zacarias Moussaoui, every single major arrest has been done by a foreign government. You're going to get less and less support from . . . these governments" once there is a war with Iraq.[31]

The strategic dangers of assuming an undifferentiated threat when none exists were evident during the first two decades of the Cold War. U.S. intervention in Vietnam rested upon the judgment that Vietnamese Communism was little more than an extension of Chinese Communism, which in turn was little more than an Asian extension of Soviet Communism. Four successive American political administrations failed to see that Vietnamese Communism, far from being an export from Moscow or Beijing, was the product of a unique set of local circumstances, including a fiercely xenophobic people who had legitimate political and social grievances against the corrupt American client state in Saigon. They failed to see that it was Vietnamese *nationalism,* as much and perhaps more than Marx and Lenin, that inspired the Vietnamese Communists, who saw the Americans in South Vietnam as the successors of the hated French colonial regime. Indeed the greatest American strategic deficiency of the first half of the Cold War was a policy blindness both to sharp nationalist antagonisms within the so-called Communist Bloc and to the overwhelmingly nationalist content of anticolonial and most postcolonial insurgencies. In the end, nationalism proved to be a far more potent and enduring force than Communism.

With respect to Iraq, prewar U.S. strategic myopia fixated on Baghdad's perceived invulnerability to deterrence. In his March 6, 2003, press conference, President Bush in essence said that Saddam Hussein was just itching to attack the United States and that it was therefore imperative to remove him from power before he acquired nuclear weapons, the mother of all WMD. Opponents of the war with Iraq still claim that Saddam was deterrable—indeed, was being deterred since 1991—as long as the United States did not attack him and place him in the equivalent of a "Hitler's bunker in Baghdad." Unlike ephemeral terrorist organizations, Saddam, they contended, presided over a state with attackable assets, including his own personage. Interestingly, in January 2000 Condoleezza Rice wrote an article in *Foreign Affairs* in which she declared, with respect to Iraq, that "the first line of defense should be a clear and classical statement of deterrence—if they do acquire WMD, their weapons will be unusable because any attempt to use them will bring national obliteration." She also said that rogue states "were living on borrowed time" and that "there should be no sense of panic about them."[32]

The case for "Saddam the Undeterrable" rested essentially on four claims. First, Saddam was evil, and evil people enjoy doing evil things. Bush repeatedly used the term "evil" with respect to both al-Qaeda and Saddam and made the case for war against Iraq as a means of preventing an Iraqi repetition of the 9/11 attacks. Yet Saddam's role model, Stalin, was if anything, more evil than his Iraqi mimic, but his remarkably cautious Cold War statecraft reflected a healthy respect for American power and will.

Second, Saddam was "unbalanced," "mad," "a madman"—terms the president used with respect to the Iraqi dictator. Yet can Saddam really be compared to the suicide bombers of al-Qaeda? Was Saddam eager to throw away his own life and regime for the sake of attacking the United States? Whatever the Iraqi dictator was or was not, was he not above all a survivor who valued his own life and position to the point of willingness to massacre suspected internal enemies and to personally murder his own colleagues? Saddam "is a rational and political calculator who can reverse himself on a dime if his regime is threatened," said Jerrold Post, former CIA profiler of Saddam Hussein, before the war. "But he can become extremely dangerous when he is backed into a corner."[33]

Third, Saddam had already used chemical weapons against his own people as well as Iranian forces during the Iraq-Iran War of 1980–88. This claim is certainly true, but it begs the question of why he did not use them during the Gulf War or Operation Iraqi Freedom. The fact that he used chemical weapons against the Kurds and the Iranians, enemies who were in no position to retaliate effectively, and later refrained from using them against enemies—Israel and the United States—who *were* in a position to launch devastating retaliation strongly suggests that credible threats of retaliation did in fact deter him. He had vast stocks of chemical munitions on hand in 1991 and did not use them, and although he had none in 2003, U.S. military planners clearly expected Iraqi chemical attacks. In 1991 questions arose as to the possibility of other explanations for Iraqi nonuse of WMD, including breakdown of command and control, munitions deterioration, and inability to marry munitions to functioning delivery systems. In 2003 there was also speculative evidence that the Iraqis got rid of their WMD sometime in the 1990s for reasons that remain as yet unclear (see chap. 7).

The fact nevertheless remains that, with respect to the use of WMD, there is no evidence that Saddam Hussein was unconstrained by the logic and reality of traditional deterrence. He was as deterred as was Stalin before him. This fact is consistent with the behavior of other rogue states. How, for example, is the absence of war on the Korean Peninsula for the last fifty years to be explained except by the presence of credible U.S. and South Korean deterrence? The North Korean "axis of evil" state is the longest-running rogue state in the world today, and it is far better armed with WMD and means of delivering them than was Saddam's Iraq.

Philip Bobbitt, in his magisterial *Shield of Achilles,* has questioned the argument that rogue states are not deterrable. Discussing the wisdom of ballistic missile defenses, which have been sold, like preventive war, on the grounds of rogue state undeterrability, Bobbitt asks: "Is it really sensible to think that providing the great states of the West with ballistic missile defenses would actually discourage a 'rogue state' to a greater degree than the assurance of nuclear annihilation that would surely follow such an attack[, which] already deters them today? To believe this assumes a psychological hypersensitivity to the mere possibility of failure on the part of the leaderships of Iraq, Iran, and North Korea that seems incompatible with their characters . . . and an indifference to survival that these leaders, though they may seek it in their recruits, do not prominently display themselves."[34]

Bobbitt, however, does not discern the neoconservatives' real objective for ballistic missile defenses: to prevent rogue states from deterring

U.S. military action against *them*. As stated by Kaplan and Kristol in *The War over Iraq:* "The real rationale for missile defense is that without it, an adversary armed with long-range ballistic missiles can, as Robert Joseph, President Bush's counterproliferation specialist at the National Security Council argues, 'hold American cities hostage and thereby deter us from intervention.' In other words, missile defense is about preserving America's ability to wield power abroad."[35]

Fourth, Saddam had a demonstrated capacity for catastrophic miscalculation.[36] He had plunged his country into three disastrous wars (the Second Kurdish War of 1974–75, the Iraq-Iran War of 1980–88, and the Gulf War of 1991), completely misjudging the strength and will of his adversaries. And there was strong evidence that the Gulf War convinced him that the acquisition of nuclear weapons would provide him immunity from American military responses to future Iraqi aggression. (Certainly, the Bush administration believes that a nuclear-armed Saddam would have attempted to "blackmail" his neighbors as well as Israel and the United States.)

Personality cult dictatorships are prone to strategic misjudgment. "Mr. Hussein is often unintentionally suicidal," wrote Kenneth Pollack before the war. He "is a risk-taker who plays dangerous games without realizing how dangerous they truly are," because he "is deeply ignorant of the outside world and surrounded by sycophants who tell him what he wants to hear."[37] As such, he was quite unlike Stalin, to whom he had been compared by believers in the efficacy of traditional deterrence against Saddam. Though cruel and ruthless, Stalin was also cautious and patient. "That Saddam [is] an admirer [of Stalin] and perhaps an intentional imitator, I do not doubt" observed George F. Kennan in late 2002. "But the streak of adventurism that has marked Saddam's behavior was quite foreign to Stalin."[38]

Richard K. Betts argued that "reckless as [Saddam] has been, he has never yet done anything Washington told him would be suicidal."[39] To be sure, his invasion of Kuwait turned out to be a disastrous miscalculation, but in August 1990 Saddam was financially desperate and had little reason to believe the United States would react the way it did; indeed, far from attempting deterrence, the George H. W. Bush administration unwittingly gave the Iraqi dictator a green light. And there is no question that Saddam's invasion of Iran ten years earlier (which the United States welcomed) also was an act of profound misjudgment. But it too was strategically understandable if morally unjustifiable: the Ayatollah Khomeini was attempting to overthrow Saddam's regime by fomenting Shiite unrest in southern Iraq. John J. Mearsheimer and Stephen M. Walt, highly regarded experts on international politics and opponents of war on Iraq, contended:

Saddam has dominated Iraqi politics for more than 30 years. During that period, he started two wars against his neighbors—Iran in 1980 and Kuwait in 1990. Saddam's record in this regard is no worse than that of neighboring states such as Egypt or Israel, each of which played a role in starting several wars since 1948. Furthermore, a careful look at Saddam's two wars shows that his behavior was far from reckless. Both times, he attacked because Iraq was vulnerable and because he believed his targets were weak and isolated. In each case, his goal was to rectify Iraq's strategic dilemma with a limited military victory. Such reasoning does not excuse Saddam's aggression, but his willingness to use force on these occasions hardly demonstrates that he cannot be deterred.[40]

Ironically, some neoconservatives favored preventive war against Iraq because they believed it would deter other rogue states from acquiring WMD. The war on Iraq, wrote Charles Krauthammer in December 2002, "will serve as a higher form of deterrence. The idea is to deter states not from using weapons of mass destruction but from acquiring them in the first place." Removing Saddam Hussein will provide "a clear demonstration to other tyrants that to acquire WMD is a losing proposition. Not only do they not purchase you immunity [from attack] (as in classical deterrence). They purchase you extinction."[41]

None of the aforesaid in this chapter is to argue that Saddam Hussein was anything less than an exceptionally thuggish tyrant who had committed aggression against his neighbors and his own people. His removal from power was always desirable, and there was never any doubt that the United States had the military power to remove him. But the Bush administration's claim of a direct Iraqi threat to the United States in the form of surprise 9/11-like attacks with WMD lacked credibility from the start. Such a threat was inconsistent with Saddam's secular state and his behavior during the Gulf War. Then and after, Iraq was vulnerable to devastating American retaliation, and Saddam never placed the goal of damaging U.S. interests above that of his own survival. He always loved himself more than he hated the United States.

As for the administration's asserted threat of a revenge-motivated Saddam's transfer of WMD to al-Qaeda, there is no evidence that such a transfer was ever made, even though Saddam was in possession of chemical and biological weapons at least some of the time during the period separating the first and second American wars against Iraq. Moreover, the administration never addressed the question of whether the Iraqi dictator could ever have been certain that he could make such a transfer without a trace of evidence. And even if he could have been certain on that score, would he not also have had to worry that the Bush administration would consider an al-Qaeda WMD attack to be prima facie evidence that such a transfer had been made?

There was also the issue of control. Saddam Hussein and his regime were always about political control because control meant survival. How likely was it, therefore, that Saddam, a Stalin-like paranoid and megalomaniac, would have transferred his hard-earned WMD—the very capacity that elevated him on the world stage as "threatener" of America and Israel—to an Islamist terrorist group beyond his control? As Benjamin and Simon observed of Saddam Hussein and Osama bin Laden in the context of the National Security Council staff's examination of who was behind the 9/11 attacks:

> [Osama bin Laden] was deeply contemptuous of Saddam Hussein. For believers like bin Laden, Saddam was the second coming of Gamel Abdel Nasser, a secular pharaonic ruler who had destroyed the religion and oppressed the umma. There is little evidence that Saddam viewed bin Laden and his ilk any differently than Egypt's secular rulers viewed [Islamist activists] Sayyid Qutb, Shuqri Mustafa, and their successors—as religious extremists who would enjoy nothing more than to see secular rule toppled. However attractive their anti-Americanism, they could only be handled with caution. There was nothing in the record to suggest that a central precept of the state sponsors had changed: never get into bed with a group you cannot control. Both the Iranians and the Iraqis appeared to be reluctant to cooperate with an organization that might commit some enormity that could be traced back to them. The NSC analysts found it difficult to accept that al Qaeda acted alone, but no other conclusion was warranted.[42]

Indeed, for what it's worth, two high-ranking al-Qaeda leaders in U.S. custody, Abu Zubaydah and Khalid Sheikh Mohammed, al-Qaeda chief of operations until his capture on March 1, 2003, told the CIA in separate interrogations that the terrorist organization did not work with the Saddam Hussein regime. Though the idea had been discussed among al-Qaeda's leadership, Osama bin Laden rejected the idea because he did not want to be beholden to Saddam Hussein.[43] Their testimony is certainly consistent with the judgment of experts on al-Qaeda and Saddam Hussein as well as with the failure to date of U.S. intelligence authorities in Iraq to discover "smoking gun" documentation of a working relationship between al-Qaeda and the Iraqi regime.

There was always, however, one seemingly plausible scenario for Saddam's first use of WMD, including indirectly via transfer to a terrorist group, against American or Israeli targets: an American attack on Iraq that placed Saddam in a position of certain doom, thereby removing any "deterrent" obstacles to taking down as many of his enemies as possible on the way to his own extinction. Before the war, President Bush himself acknowledged that an "Iraqi regime faced with its own demise may attempt cruel and desperate measures."[44] A prewar CIA assessment concluded that Saddam, if convinced that a U.S. attack could not be deterred, might "decide that the extreme step of assisting Islamist terrorists in conducting a WMD attack against the United States would be his last chance to exact vengeance by taking large numbers of victims with him."[45] When war came, however, Saddam apparently believed that he and many of his supporters could survive it to fight another day (see chap. 7).

Though the Bush administration postulated an imminent Iraqi threat to the United States undifferentiated from the threat posed by al-Qaeda, the Iraqi threat in 2003 was in fact hypothetical, distant, and deterrable, whereas the al-Qaeda threat remains operational and undeterrable. Adding to the administration's "threat confusion" was its relative nonchalance, in the fall of 2002 and winter of 2002–3, toward North Korea's open repudiation of the 1994 Agreed Framework, its termination of the International Atomic Energy Agency (IAEA) inspection regime, its restart of its nuclear fuel production facility, its missile rattling in the Sea of Japan, and its threatened resort to nuclear war in the event of hostilities. Already a nuclear weapons–capable state with missiles greatly superior in range to any in Saddam's Iraq, North Korea remains in a position to expand its nuclear arsenal and proliferate nuclear materials to other enemies of the United States. It is also in a position, with its massive conventional forces deployed along the DMZ, to inflict unacceptable damage on the greater Seoul region.

Yet even though the United States was the target of North Korea's behavior, the Bush administration's initial reaction was to palm off the crisis to "regional diplomacy"—that is, to seek to persuade China, Russia, and Japan to persuade North Korea to reverse its course of action. Until April 2003 the administration refused to negotiate directly with Pyongyang (a course of action favored by China, Russia, Japan, and South Korea) but also made it plain that it was not prepared to go to war—indeed, how could it, given the U.S. forces gathering half a world away to attack a nuclear-weaponless regime crawling with IAEA inspectors?

What accounted for North Korea's threatened nuclear "break-out" and the lame American response relative to the sound and fury of administration policy toward Saddam's Iraq? One can only speculate about Pyongyang's motives. But having been designated, along with Iraq and Iran, an "axis of evil" state in January 2002, and having subsequently observed the Bush administration, with its new doctrine of anticipatory self-defense, moving ever more credibly toward a regime-changing invasion of Iraq, might not Pyongyang have concluded that it was next on the list? And if so, might it not have decided to launch a crash program to expand its small nuclear arsenal and to do so publicly for the purposes of strengthening deterrence of a U.S. attack as well as coercing the United States into direct negotiations? The timing of North Korea's initiation of the crisis suggests perception of an opportunity to exploit the Bush administration's strategic preoccupation with Iraq.

As for the U.S. response, the *New Republic's* Leon Wieseltier almost certainly got it right: "Pyongyang's sins of proliferation are significantly greater than Baghdad's sins of proliferation, but we will satisfy ourselves with diplomacy. We will not use force. . . . The reason that we will not use force against North Korea is simple. It's that we cannot use force. If the United States will punish North Korea militarily, North Korea will punish South Korea militarily. The prospect of such catastrophe is unacceptable. And so we are, except in the insane circumstance that Kim Jong Il prepares to launch a nuclear weapon, deterred."[46]

If anything, the spectacle of the United States undeterred by a nuclear-weaponless Iraq but deterred by a nuclear-arming North Korea could only encourage other rogue states seeking to acquire nuclear weapons to accelerate their search.[47] As Joseph S. Nye Jr. observed in January 2003, "What North Korea shows is that deterrence is working. The only problem is that we are the ones being deterred." For former national security adviser Zbigniew Brzezinski, "What the cases of North Korea and Iraq show is that if the threat is genuinely serious, the preemption doctrine is not pursued." In other words, preemption is an attractive option only against enemies that cannot strike back—a reality that does not amuse the shriller neoconservatives. According to Robin Cook, the former British foreign minister who resigned over the decision to go to war with Iraq, "[t]he truth is that the US chose to attack Iraq not because it posed a threat but because the U.S. knew that Iraq was weak and expected its military to collapse." Predictably, William Kristol and Robert Kagan denounced the Bush administration's pursuit of a diplomatic solution to the Korean nuclear crisis as "appeasement" and asked: "What will the lesson be to other would-be North Koreans? If you want an American promise against attack, build some nukes."[48]

It is imperative to differentiate not just between various terrorist organizations but even more so between al-Qaeda and rogue states such as Iraq. Effective grand strategy rests on an ability to discriminate among enemies and the threats they pose and to tailor specific plans of action accordingly. As such, it also requires recognition of the varying utility of military power relative to nonmilitary tools of statecraft in dealing with different security challenges. Rogue states are much more vulnerable than al-Qaeda and other international terrorist organizations to traditional deterrence and military destruction. Moreover, given America's unprecedented global military primacy, the United States does not need much direct military help in bringing down regimes such as the Taliban in Afghanistan and Saddam in Iraq.

Such is not the case, however, in dealing with the likes of al-Qaeda, which is neither deterrable nor subject to military extirpation. D. Robert Worley has insightfully likened the al-Qaeda threat to an international guerrilla war against the United States and its interests abroad, requiring a "counterguerrilla" strategy that orchestrates all the elements of national power while relegating the military to a supporting role. He notes that "the Romans maintained two distinct forms of warfare, *bellum* and *guerra*," the former "the form of warfare conducted against another state" and the latter "the form of warfare waged against migrating and marauding tribes." He argues that *bellum* (i.e., conventional warfare) has limited utility against irregular threats like al-Qaeda, and believes that the core of effective counter-*guerra*, like effective counterinsurgency, is an intelligence-based strategy of the hunt.[49]

> The *guerra* strategy must be relevant to the nature of the conflict. Strategies based on retaliation will fail because retaliation will not deter martyrs. Terrorist networks have nothing of value equivalent to the damage they can inflict. Strategies based on preventing rogue states from acquiring the means of attack have merit when directed at limiting the proliferation of nuclear, chemical, and biological weapons and ballistic missile delivery vehicles; they are irrelevant, however, when the means employed are commercial aircraft or other readily available instruments.[50]

It is both an intellectual and strategic error to blend together rogue states and international terrorist organizations. Though the two types of threats may have occasional common enemies and working relationships, they are fundamentally different in character, modes of operation, and vulnerability to U.S. military power.

Al-Qaeda remains a separate and distinct enemy from any rogue state, waging its own war for its own purposes. Even the loss of its Taliban ally and training bases in Afghanistan seems but a temporary setback. Whereas the doomed regime of Saddam Hussein was shattered like crystal, the organization and modus operandi of al-Qaeda have displayed extraordinary adaptability and flexibility. Al-Qaeda and al-Qaeda-inspired terrorist groups continued to attack Western targets outside the United States throughout 2002 and 2003.

Indeed, even after Saddam had been toppled from power the International Institute for Strategic Studies issued a report declaring that, notwithstanding the loss of its infrastructure in Afghanistan and the killing or capture of perhaps one-third of its leadership, al-Qaeda is "now reconstituted and doing business in a somewhat different manner, but more insidious and just as dangerous as in its pre-11 September incarnation." More insidious because the West's "counter-terrorism effort . . . perversely impelled an already highly decentralized and elusive transnational terrorist network to become even harder to identify and neutralize." The destruction of its camps in Afghanistan meant that al-Qaeda "no longer concentrated its forces in clusters discernible and targetable from the air," which meant that "the lion's share of the counter-terrorism burden rested on law enforcement and intelligence agencies."[51]

Within a year following 9/11, al-Qaeda was reconstituted along the Afghan-Pakistan border and shifting its strikes to soft Western targets in the Third World. By the summer of 2003 al-Qaeda and al-Qaeda-inspired groups had conducted deadly attacks in Saudi Arabia, Morocco, Tunisia, Pakistan, Bali, Kenya, and Yemen, and experts were openly comparing Islamic terrorism to communism and fascism, ideologies that inspired proponents regardless of occasional setbacks.[52] According to one assessment, al-Qaeda now "places priority foremost on the lands of Islam," where it gets "a double benefit. They can hit Westerners—tourists in Bali, diners in Casablanca. And they can damage the governments of Islamic states they consider to have strayed from the true path and to have allied themselves with the U.S."[53] There is also evidence of a new al-Qaeda willingness to forge alliances heretofore regarded as unlikely, including with the Shiite terrorist organization Hezbollah (al-Qaeda is Sunni), American white supremacists, the Palestinian Hamas, and even Marxist/criminal Colombian rebels.[54] Further evidence suggests that al-Qaeda was overhauling its approach to penetrating the United States by recruiting U.S. citizens or others with legitimate Western passports, who would be much harder to detect than Arab foreign nationals.[55]

For the U.S. military, Saddam Hussein was easy pickings compared to al-Qaeda, and the failure of the U.S. removal of the former to have any discernible effect on the latter is testimony to the mistake of conflating the two. The invasion of Iraq and the war on terrorism should not be confused.

5
War Aims

Controversy surrounded American war aims from the very start of the U.S.–Iraqi crisis of 2002–3. That controversy was certainly not abated by the postwar discovery that Saddam Hussein's Iraq possessed no deliverable weapons of mass destruction—perhaps no WMD at all, much less deployed systems ready to be fired at coalition forces—and that Iraq had no evident operational relationship with al-Qaeda, much less that of a supplier of WMD to Osama bin Laden. The absence of WMD served to confirm suspicions in the minds of many who opposed the war, Western and Arab critics alike, that the U.S. postulation of an imminent WMD threat was a pretext for a war waged for other purposes. Such purposes included seizure of Iraq's oil wealth; conversion of Iraq into a strategic client state; intimidation of Iran, Syria, and Saudi Arabia; protection of Israel; demonstration of America's unassailable military primacy; and domination of the Arab world and the destruction of Islam.

The first American war against Iraq was waged for the limited objective of liberating Kuwait from Iraqi occupation. It sought to reverse an act of aggression. It succeeded but left intact the aggressor regime in Baghdad. The George H. W. Bush administration hoped and believed that General H. Norman Schwarzkopf's victory, which at the time seemed more overwhelming than it actually was, would prompt a coup against Saddam Hussein. But Schwarzkopf's victory was incomplete, and Saddam survived to fight another day.

The second American war against Iraq was waged with the explicit aim of overthrowing the Iraqi regime *as a means of enabling Iraq's disarmament.* The war of 2003 sought to finish the unfinished business of 1991. But the aim of regime change imposed upon the United States a responsibility the administration of George H. W. Bush was not prepared to assume in 1991: Iraq's political and economic reconstruction. The first war was limited; the second was "total" insofar as it concerned the intended fate of the enemy.

The second war against Iraq was thus much more in keeping with American preferences for how wars should be fought. Americans have never been comfortable with limited wars—that is, wars waged for limited political objectives and by restricted employment of military power. Americans tend to separate war and politics, believing that war is a substitute for, rather than an extension of, politics. Once the shooting begins and regardless of political objective, so the thinking goes, the aim should be the enemy's complete military defeat. The "unconditional surrender" formula of Ulysses S. Grant and Franklin D. Roosevelt has been the ideal, not the compromise Korean War armistice of 1953 or the hesitant gradualism that many still believe led to America's defeat in Vietnam. Pres. George H. W. Bush himself, even as he pocketed his victory in Kuwait and ordered the troops back home, remarked on his sense of disappointment: "I haven't yet felt this wonderfully euphoric feeling that many of the American people feel. . . . I think it's that I want to see an end," he told a questioner. "You mention World War II—there was a definitive end to that conflict. And now we have Saddam Hussein still there [in power]—the man that wreaked this havoc on his neighbors."[1]

The argument for total war against actual and emerging aggressor states is a compelling one in a post–Cold War era in which the United States does not have to worry, as it did in Korea and Vietnam, that its local wars against communist states could escalate into war with the Soviet Union or China. China's surprise intervention in the Korean War was a chastening experience for American cold warriors, including Lyndon Johnson, whose fear of a Chinese surprise in Vietnam accounted in no small measure for his restrained application of U.S. military power against North Vietnam. The Truman-MacArthur controversy of late 1950 and early 1951, which was prompted by Chinese intervention, was a policy dispute over whether the United States should continue to restrict its military operations to Korea with the limited political objective of restoring South Korea's territorial integrity (the position of Truman and the Joint Chiefs of Staff), or whether the United States should instead expand its military operations to the Chinese mainland with the objective of forcing the Chinese out of Korea and reunifying the entire peninsula under American auspices (the MacArthur position, supported by a majority of the American people). For the Truman administration, an open-ended war with China was, in the famous words of JCS chairman Omar Bradley, "the wrong war, at the wrong place, at the wrong time, and with the wrong enemy," because such a war would have fixated American strategic attention and military resources on a secondary theater of operations at a time when Europe, the primary theater, lay undefended against a menacing Soviet threat.[2]

Yet as Victor Davis Hanson, a staunch proponent of the second war against Iraq, has noted, "the armistice of 1953 means that we still worry about nuclear-tipped missiles in North Korea despite a 'peace' of a half-century."

What Hanson calls "interrupted wars"—that is, wars that leave the enemy capable of political and military recovery, "simply raise the hopes of both sides that their enemies will slowly be worn down or demoralized in an extended cold war, and thus at some future date either give up or be unable to reinstate hostilities." In his view "clear victory can settle long-existing problems immediately in a way negotiated armistices cannot. . . . [I]n the long run an insistence on abject surrender saves lives when truly evil regimes capitulate rather than bargain their way out of humiliation."[3]

The Bush doctrine's explicit embrace of regime change as a principle of American security policy toward rogue states is an implicit rejection of the unpopular limited conflicts of the Cold War, Gulf War, and the Bosnian and Kosovo military interventions. It is a return to the tradition of Appomattox Court House, the Reims schoolhouse, and the deck of the *Missouri* in Tokyo Bay.

Proponents of total victory believe U.S. military power is irresistible and assume sustained public support. For them, the problem is not the enemy but rather weak, meddling politicians and overly cautious military leaders who lack the fortitude to go for the military gold. American power, however, has distinct limits against determined unconventional adversaries, and public support cannot be sustained indefinitely in wars over stakes perceived as less than compelling—especially if military performance falters or at least fails to register visible progress toward a definitive end to hostilities. The enemy has some say in how wars turn out. The United States failed in Vietnam not because the politicians would not let the military win; the Joint Chiefs of Staff were a cauldron of interservice rivalry, had no uniform, integrated strategy for victory, and were institutionally incapable of providing the White House timely and useful military advice.[4] Rather, the United States failed because its conventional military power had limited utility against a revolutionary nationalist enemy fighting for his homeland and willing to make extraordinary sacrifices; because the American public in the end did not believe that the largely abstract objectives for which the war was being fought were worth the sacrifices made in blood and treasure; and—above all—because the local client on behalf of whom we fought had no long-term political or military viability.[5] The claim that the United States denied itself victory in Vietnam is extraordinarily narcissistic; it utterly ignores the performance of the enemy and our South Vietnamese allies, to say nothing of the war's unique strategic setting.

Pursuit of regime change in Hanoi in the 1960s (Victor Davis Hanson's retrospective strategy)[6] would have necessitated an invasion and attempted occupation of North Vietnam, which almost certainly would have provoked the entry of the Chinese, who would then have been waging war alongside a Vietnamese foe fighting to defend the Communist heartland. And for what? To vanquish an impoverished Vietnamese enemy who had no imperial ambitions beyond Indochina and whose ideology remains as morally and intellectually bankrupt as it was four decades ago?

This chapter examines U.S. war aims of the second American war against Iraq. War aims can be general or specific, declared or undeclared, defensive or offensive. General war aims are broad in scope and relate to the desired political and strategic end state of conflict. Specific war aims identify particular objectives that relate military operations to desired political and strategic outcomes. Declared war aims are just that—publicly announced—whereas undeclared war aims relate to unstated larger hopes and expectations of what conflict will yield. Defensive war aims serve to preserve the status quo, whereas offensive war aims seek to change it. There can be considerable overlap between general and undeclared war aims and between specific and declared war aims.

The starting rationale for the war of 2003 was the general negative undeclared war aim of preserving American military hegemony in the Persian Gulf, which the Bush administration believed would be threatened by Saddam Hussein's acquisition of nuclear weapons. The objective was to prevent Saddam from acquiring such weapons by removing the Iraqi dictator, destroying Iraqi WMD and their associated facilities, and establishing governance in Iraq that insured benign security intentions. Preservation of U.S. hegemony in the Gulf contributed to the larger goal of perpetuating U.S. global military primacy. To permit that primacy to be effectively challenged in one region was to encourage others to challenge it elsewhere. In terms of international relations theory, the objective was to preserve the existing balance of power in the Persian Gulf.

Indeed, if "balance of power" is defined as the existing distribution of power at the global or regional levels, regardless of how out of balance they might actually be, then the goal of preserving U.S. military hegemony in the Persian Gulf was a balance-of-power goal.[7] It is a goal, moreover, that American political administrations have consistently supported or pursued since the end of World War II. During the Cold War the United States sought to contain Soviet power and influence in the Persian Gulf. During the 1980s the United States backed Iraq as a counterweight to the threatening Ayatollah Khomeini's Iran; and in the 1990s, when the primary threat was Saddam Hussein's Iraq, the United States, lacking a sufficiently powerful regional surrogate, confronted Baghdad with its own military power, going to war to eject the Iraqis from Kuwait and subsequently sanctioning Saddam militarily and economically. The second war against Iraq was the culmination of a contest that began in 1990.

Another general undeclared war aim in 2003 was the Bush administration's felt need to demonstrate America's will and capacity to use force decisively. One of the major neoconservative, and more broadly, Republican internationalist critiques of Democratic administrations going all the way back to Lyndon Johnson's presidency, but especially directed at the detested Clinton presidency, was fear of using force decisively, without constant second thoughts and searches for legitimacy via international institutional approval. Indeed, Kaplan and Kristol contend that the Vietnam War convinced "wishful liberals, and many others besides, [that] American power was now irredeemably tainted by involvement in a 'criminal' war. The suspicion of American power inherent in contemporary liberalism now became a reflexive opposition to the exercise of American power."[8]

Neoconservatives believe America's defeat in Southeast Asia produced a "Vietnam Syndrome" that traumatized subsequent Democratic administrations as well as the professional U.S. military, whose embrace of the Weinberger doctrine signaled an opposition to choosing war except in situations of threatened vital material interests and a virtual guarantee of military victory. The result was a string of half-baked military interventions, most of them nibbling at symptoms of the threat rather than the source of the threat. Regime change was attempted and accomplished in only two instances, in Grenada and Panama, against enemies that could put up little resistance; it was not attempted in the Gulf War or the Balkans.

The Vietnam War and subsequent U.S. uses of force adversely affected America's strategic reputation, encouraging enemies, including Saddam Hussein and Osama bin Laden, to believe that the United States was a "sawdust superpower," a state whose military might vastly exceeded its will to use it. The United States was defeated in Vietnam, run out of Lebanon and Somalia, and by the time of its Balkan interventions, so casualty-phobic that it placed the safety of its military forces above the missions they were assigned to accomplish.[9]

By demonstrating the credibility of American power, an invasion and occupation of Iraq, the Bush administration believed, would strengthen deterrence by putting other actual and aspiring rogue states on notice that the United States meant business. Operation Iraqi Freedom would provide a demonstration of the Bush doctrine in action as well as a demonstration of American supremacy in the realm of conventional warfare. Even China might be dissuaded from challenging American military primacy in East Asia.

This intended demonstration effect would not be confined to adversaries. To America's friends and allies, many of whom opposed the war, Operation Iraqi Freedom would demonstrate that the United States would no longer permit its freedom of military action to be constrained by a perceived need for prior international legitimization in the form of UN authorization or NATO approval—that the United States was prepared to act unilaterally even in defiance of world opinion. From the very start of its confrontation with Iraq, the Bush administration made it clear that, in the end, it would take military action against Baghdad with or without UN, NATO, or other international institutional approval. Some in the administration, including Vice Pres. Dick Cheney, opposed the very idea of soliciting a UN mandate. As for America's allies, they could follow or get out of the way. The Soviet Union's disappearance and declining U.S. dependence on major NATO allies to project U.S. power in regions outside Europe made NATO less important, especially those "old Europe" allies in sharp military decline and unable to reconcile themselves to the fact of American power and the moral imperative of American leadership. Never mind that America's strident unilateralism toward Iraq alienated key allies, brought U.S.–German and even U.S.–Canadian relations to their lowest point since 1945, and threatened to destroy the Atlantic alliance itself.

Neoconservatives believe that the exercise of American power is inherently virtuous because of the self-evident legitimacy of American political values, and that past presidents had therefore unnecessarily compromised the exercise of that power by assuming that legitimacy required international institutional approval. For the Bush administration it was "my way or the highway."

An embrace of a unilateralist foreign policy was a hallmark of the Bush administration from its very inception. It preferred "coalitions of the willing" to formal alliances, "understandings" to treaties, and military action over consultations and diplomacy. It was averse to anything that would inhibit America's freedom of military action. Unilateralism essentially repudiates the grand bargain the United States struck with its friends and allies after World War II. They accepted American power and leadership in exchange for American willingness to embed that power in international institutions for the purpose of reassuring friends and allies that American power would be used with restraint. If successful, the Bush administration's unilateralism and policy of "anticipatory self-defense" could begin the breakup of the very international system that has been the basis of America's security policy for more than half a century.

A fourth general war aim was to transform the Middle East via Iraq's democratization. This herculean goal was always high on the neoconservatives' agenda and was firmly endorsed by President Bush in his February 2003 American Enterprise Institute speech and in his March 17 speech in which he gave Saddam Hussein forty-eight hours to leave the country. "Unlike Saddam Hussein," he said, "we believe the Iraqi people are deserving and capable of human liberty. And when the dictator has departed, they can set an example to all of the Middle East of a vital and peaceful and self-governing nation."[10] For the Bush White House, regime change in Iraq meant eliminating not just Saddam but also authoritarian rule altogether in a country that had known little else in its entire history. Replacing dictatorship with democracy, even democracy initially imposed by a foreign power (in his AEI speech, Bush referred to America's success in Germany and Japan after World War II), would change Iraq from an aggressor into a peaceful state and therefore no longer a threat to global security. For the administration, the connection between tyranny and terrorism, and between freedom and the absence of terrorism, is clear. In his September 7, 2003, televised address to the nation, President Bush stated:

> In Iraq, we are helping . . . to build a decent and democratic society at the center of the Middle East. . . . The Middle East will become a place of progress and peace or it will be an exporter of violence and terror that takes more lives in America and other free nations. The triumph of democracy and tolerance in Iraq, in Afghanistan and beyond would be a grave setback for international terrorism. The terrorists thrive on the support of tyrants and the resentments of oppressed peoples. When tyrants fall, and resentment gives way to hope, men and women in every culture reject the ideologies of terror and turn to the pursuits of peace. Everywhere that freedom takes hold, terror will retreat.[11]

The very success of democracy in Iraq would thus serve as a beacon for others in the region, including U.S. allies such as Egypt and Saudi Arabia. A democratic Middle East in turn would provide the peoples of the region a powerful and ultimately irresistible alternative to the failed regimes of the so-called moderate Arab states and the Islamists' totalitarian vision of the future.

This is a truly revolutionary objective—on par with the post-1945 political transformation of Germany and Japan. But the basis on which the democratic domino theory rests has never been explicated. Is it simply hope? Ideological conviction? Even assuming that Iraq can be converted into a democracy, an ambitious assumption, how would democracy spread to the rest of the region? Joshua Micah Marshall believes that "invasion of Iraq was not merely, or even primarily, about getting rid of Saddam Hussein. Nor was it really about weapons of mass destruction. . . . Rather, the administration sees the invasion as only the first move in a wider effort to reorder the power structure of the entire Middle East." Armed with the Bush doctrine, "the administration is trying to . . . use military force, or the threat of it, to reform or topple every regime in the region . . . on the theory that it is the undemocratic nature of these regimes that ultimately breeds terrorism."[12]

The problem with this new domino theory is the same as the problem with the old one: it presumes that states and societies are essentially equal in vulnerability to the "threat" (i.e., democracy in the Middle East today, Communism in Southeast Asia in the 1960s). It ignores local circumstances, societal differences, distinct national histories, and cultural asymmetries. Then there is the problem of Islamists using democracy to win power for antidemocratic purposes, as did Hitler in Germany in 1933. "One person, one vote, one time." It was this very threat that provoked the suppression of budding democratic institutions in Algeria. Indeed, fear of an Islamist electorate accounts in no small measure for the persistence of autocratic dictatorships in Algeria, Egypt, and Pakistan. A genuinely democratic Saudi Arabia almost certainly would be much more anti-American than the present kingdom. Are U.S. strategic interests in the Muslim world really better served by hostile and unstable democracies than by friendly and stable authoritarian regimes?

U.S. destruction of Saddam Hussein's regime and creation of a democratic Iraq, to say nothing of the Middle East's democratization, would also redound to the benefit of Israel's security. Saddam's Iraq was an avowed enemy of Israel and during the Gulf War of 1991 became the only Arab state ever to launch missiles into Israeli territory. Though the Bush administration attacked Iraq on behalf of what it perceived to be threatened U.S. security interests, regime change in Baghdad served the longstanding American objective in the Middle East of enhancing Israel's security.

There is a highly speculative fifth general war aim, and it has to do with the relationship of oil and the perpetuation of U.S. global military primacy. Simply put, hostile control or massive disruption of the Persian Gulf's oil wealth would threaten U.S. capacity to maintain that primacy over the long run. Many Arabs believe that the real objective of Operation Iraqi Freedom was to gain control of Iraq's oil for America's own use. The Bush administration emphatically and convincingly denies this charge; it is committed to applying Iraq's oil wealth to Iraq's economic reconstruction, which means that it will not use Iraq's oil revenues to finance U.S. occupation costs.

The fact nonetheless remains that the United States is, and for the foreseeable future will remain, critically dependent on Persian Gulf oil. No amount of conservation, experimentation with alternative fuels, new drilling in the United States, or development of non-Gulf alternative oil sources will change this fact. This dependence means that the United States cannot afford to permit either hostile control or catastrophic disruption of the flow of Persian Gulf oil. Indeed, access to that oil at reasonable prices has been the foundational interest of U.S. security policy in the Gulf since the end of the Second World War. Cheap and plentiful energy also became critical to sustaining the American wealth creation machine that enabled the United States to gain and perpetuate its global military primacy.

But U.S. military primacy in the Persian Gulf not only guarantees U.S. access to the region's oil. Michael T. Klare observes that it also permits the United States "to maintain a stranglehold on the economies of potential rivals so that they will refrain from challenging the United States out of fear of being choked to death through denial of vital energy supplies." Klare's judgment may shock those Americans who believe their country could not be guilty of so base a motive, but the fact remains that *implicit* in our ability to stop potential enemies from closing the Strait of Hormuz to us is *our ability to close it to them.* Our potential future enemies, such as China, which is becoming increasingly dependent on Persian Gulf Oil, know this. Shibley Telhami has rightly pointed out that "to deny control of these vast resources to powerful enemies" has been "a central drive behind the American military strategy in the region . . . for more than half a century," even though "that [goal] has not been fully understood by most analysts."[13]

How does Iraq figure into this imperial calculus? Before the Iranian revolution, the United States relied upon the "twin pillars" of Iran and Saudi Arabia to secure its oil interests in the Persian Gulf. The fall of the Shah of Iran made oil-bloated but militarily weak Saudi Arabia the centerpiece of that interest, and it was the implicit threat to Saudi Arabia posed by Iraq's conquest of Kuwait that prompted Pres. George H. W. Bush's decision for war in 1991. But 9/11 fundamentally undermined the traditional U.S.–Saudi security relationship, which required, among other things, U.S. silence on the issues of the House of Saud's corruption, autocratic rule, religious and gender bigotry, and propagation of the very Islamist extremism that produced the 9/11 attacks. Security business-as-usual became impossible to sustain on the part of an administration populated by neoconservatives who believed that Saudi Arabia was part of the terrorist threat. Even were there no connection between Saudi Arabia and Islamist terrorism, there were concerns about the longevity of the Saudi regime. The combination of explosive population growth, drastic decline in per capita income, and the staggering profligacy of the thirty-thousand-member House of Saud all pointed toward inevitable collapse absent fundamental reform of the Saudi state.[14]

Uncertainty about the monarchy's strategic reliability and political future made a pro-American Iraq an irresistible alternative to neoconservative primacists. Sitting atop the Persian Gulf's second largest oil deposits, Iraq is the only state in the world that could offset the potential loss of Saudi Arabia.

Certainly, a democratic Iraq with a formal U.S. defense guarantee (modeled on the one extended to Kuwait after the 1991 war) would be a more stable and reliable security partner in the long run than the corrupt Bedouin princes of Saudi Arabia.

For neoconservatives Operation Iraqi Freedom promised the United States an opportunity to groom a new Persian Gulf heavyweight strategic partner as an insurance policy against the political uncertainties surrounding the future U.S.–Saudi relationship as well as free the United States to take a less tolerant and more demanding attitude toward the House of Saud. Together with a large, open-ended U.S. military presence, which was never sustainable in Saudi Arabia, the Bush administration's forcible regime change in Iraq strengthened its military primacy in the Gulf, which in turn strengthened its global military primacy. Thus the war of 2003 *was* about oil—as well as many other things—because U.S. military primacy cannot be perpetuated without secure access to oil and the ability, even if never exercised, to deny it to others.

With respect to specific, declared war aims, these were stated by Secretary of Defense Donald Rumsfeld on March 21, 2003, two days after U.S. military action began. At a news conference, he declared: "Our goal is to defend the American people, to eliminate Iraq's weapons of mass destruction, and to liberate the Iraqi people." He then proceeded to list eight specific objectives in apparent order of priority:

> First, to "end the regime of Saddam Hussein by striking with force on a scope and scale that makes clear to the Iraqis that he and his regime are finished."

> Second, "to identify, isolate and eventually eliminate Iraq's weapons of mass destruction, their delivery systems, production capabilities, and distribution networks."

> Third, to "search for, capture, drive out terrorists who have found safe harbor in Iraq."

> Fourth, to "collect such intelligence as we can find related to terrorist networks in Iraq and beyond."

> Fifth, to "collect such intelligence as we can find related to the global network of illicit weapons of mass destruction activity."

> Sixth, "to end sanctions and to immediately deliver humanitarian relief, food and medicine to the displaced and to the many needy Iraqi citizens."

> Seventh, to "secure Iraq's oil fields and resources, which belong to the Iraqi people, and which they will need to develop their country after decades of neglect by the Iraqi regime."

And eighth, "to help the Iraqi people create the conditions for a rapid transition to a representative self-government that is not a threat to its neighbors and is committed to the territorial integrity of that country."[15]

The first two objectives, regime change and disarmament, have been postulated by the Bush White House from the very start of the American-Iraqi crisis of 2002–3. Their accomplishment enables attempts to fulfill the remaining six objectives. In the case of disarmament, however, how far that objective extends beyond the arena of WMD remains unclear. Iraq is situated in a hostile neighborhood, and even a benign, democratic Iraq would need sizable conventional military forces to guarantee its territorial integrity from external attack and externally sponsored separatist movements. Additionally, the transition from a Stalinist state to a democracy, even if successful, is unlikely to be smooth, thus requiring a military force to maintain domestic order.

Also unanswered is the long-term role of the United States with respect to Iraq's security. Beyond a U.S. occupation force transitional to the creation of a representative, self-governing Iraq, is there going to be a declared U.S. commitment to defend Iraq against external attack? Such a commitment certainly seems inevitable if the United States exchanges Saudi Arabia for Iraq as its primary military partner in the Persian Gulf and establishes basing rights in that country. There is also the prospect of a nuclear-armed Iran, against which an Iraq stripped of its WMD would require an external guarantor.

The third, fourth, and fifth objectives relate to the larger war on terrorism. Given the nature and history of Saddam's regime, the archives of Iraq's many security services could well provide a treasure trove of information not only on international terrorist networks but also on the secret role that other states, potentially including U.S. friends and allies, played in militarily and technologically sustaining the regime before, during, and after the Gulf War of 1991. At a minimum, those archives ought to provide a clearer picture of the regime's relationship to al-Qaeda.

The objective of lifting sanctions and delivering humanitarian relief abruptly terminates a twelve-year policy that contributed to the impoverishment and collapsing health of the very Iraqi people the United States chose in 2003 to liberate and restore to their rightful place in the world. The effect of those sanctions was to punish the victims of tyranny without dislodging the tyrant. The sanctions also served as domestic cover for American politicians who wished to be tough on Saddam Hussein without incurring the risks that decisive military action against him would entail. The George W. Bush administration correctly concluded that only such military action could topple Saddam, and hopefully the American experience in sanctioning Iraq (and for that matter, Iran and North Korea) will once and for all discredit economic sanctions as a cheap and effective tool of coercing police states.

The objective of securing Iraq's oil for the Iraqi people, coupled with Saddam's removal and Iraq's disarmament, will end the diversion of enormous wealth to fuel external military ambitions. But to benefit the Iraqi people, revenues from revived oil production would have to be protected from being applied to service the massive external debt Iraq incurred under Saddam Hussein or to finance the costs of U.S. occupation. The Energy Department estimates that Iraq owes foreign creditors between $100 and $200 billion, or three to six times the anticipated annual revenues that restored oil production will likely generate.[16] The Center for Strategic and International Studies puts Iraq's total debt at $383 billion, half of which are claims against Iraq by aggrieved governments, companies, and individuals arising from the 1991 Gulf War, another third of which are debts still owed by Iraq for its heavy borrowing in the 1980s to finance its war with Iran, and the remainder consisting of pending contracts with the now-defunct regime of Saddam Hussein.[17]

If these estimates are anywhere close to correct, Iraq, even under the most generous debt rescheduling plan, cannot possibly pay off what it owes, plus service the balance while simultaneously sustaining its reconstruction expenses, prewar estimates of which ranged from $25 billion to $100 billion. (Of Iraq's estimated $15–$20 billion near-term oil earning potential, perhaps $11 billion would be required for routine government spending, leaving an estimated $4–$9 billion to finance reconstruction and debt payments.)[18] sThe only two ways out of this terrible dilemma would be for creditors to write off some or all of the debt in the name of restoring Iraq to the community of nations or for the indigenous government that eventually emerges in Iraq to repudiate Saddam's debts. The latter solution would be a drastic step but has precedent in the U.S. repudiation, after the Spanish-American War of 1898, of Cuba's foreign debt on the grounds that Spain imposed that debt upon the Cuban people without their consent. Indeed, two Harvard economists, Michael Kremer and Seema Jayachandran, contend that "odious debt" incurred by despots, as opposed to the people they rule, should be candidates for repudiation and that the precedent such repudiation would set would discourage potential lenders from bankrolling future tyrants.[19]

The implication of returning Iraq's oil to the Iraqi people is that oil revenues will not be used to finance U.S. annual occupation costs. The United States financed its occupation of Japan and Germany after World War II; neither country had oil or its functional equivalent as a means of quickly generating hard currency. Use of Iraq's oil revenues to finance some or all of U.S. occupation costs could not only cripple Iraq's economic recovery but also confirm in many Arab minds the charge that the United States, led by an administration of oilmen, invaded Iraq for the purpose of gaining control over Iraq's oil for its own purposes.

Yet even though the Bush administration is committed to reserving Iraq's oil revenues for the purpose of that country's economic recovery, congressional calls for using at least some of the money to defray occupation costs are likely. Even before Operation Iraqi Freedom, the federal government was headed for a major fiscal crisis due to the confluence of huge administration tax cuts, declining revenues as a result of recession and the impact of 9/11, and the impending retirement of the baby boomer generation. The crisis could only accelerate with the addition of war and open-ended occupation and reconstruction costs.[20]

The last objective, liberating the Iraqi people and creating the conditions for a rapid transition to representative government, was the moral cornerstone of the Bush administration's case for war against Iraq. It was not in and of itself a sufficient cause for war, even though the politically embarrassing postwar discovery of a nonexistent Iraqi WMD threat prompted the Bush administration retroactively to speak as if the liberation of the Iraqi people had been America's chief war aim all along. But this was not the case before the war. Were it so, the administration would have to explain why it was not liberating the populations of such "allies" as Saudi Arabia and Pakistan, autocracies that until 9/11 formed the two main international props of the Taliban and by extension Osama bin Laden. A Saddam Hussein who verifiably complied with all UN resolutions and was manifestly not in possession of nuclear weapons or working to acquire them would not have elicited a preventive war from the Bush administration, which until 9/11 was essentially pursuing its predecessor's policy toward Iraq. Liberation of the Iraqi people was a welcome benefit of a war initiated for other reasons. Deputy Secretary of Defense Wolfowitz told a *Vanity Fair* interviewer that freeing the Iraqi people was not a sufficient cause for war. According to the transcripts of that interview, he said that Saddam Hussein's "criminal treatment of the Iraqi people" was "not a reason to put American kids' lives at stake, certainly not on the scale we did it."[21]

Operation Iraqi Freedom was "as much about freeing Iraqis to precisely the same degree as the Anglo-American invasion of Europe was about freeing those imprisoned in Hitler's death camps," observed Andrew J. Bacevich after the fall of Baghdad. "In each instance military action resulted in liberation that was incidental, welcome and even admirable, but that was no more than a by[-]product all the same." In any case, notes Fouad Ajami, "Few Arabs believe this effort to be a Wilsonian campaign to spread the reign of liberty in the Arab world. They are to be forgiven their doubts, for American power, either be design or by default, has been built on relationships with military rulers and monarchs without popular mandates."[22]

But "the reign of liberty in the Arab world" was in fact a U.S. war aim stemming from the neoconservative vision of the region's democratization sparked by Iraq's transformation into a representative government. Critics have every reason to be skeptical of prospects for an American-imposed democracy in Iraq. One of the reasons for U.S. defeat in Indochina was the Saigon regime's dubious legitimacy in the eyes of many Vietnamese; that regime was an artificial, Cold War creation of the Americans (seen by many to be successors to the French) and, throughout its twenty-year life, utterly dependent on American money and military might for its survival. Critics have equal reason to doubt prospects for democracy in the region's other autocracies—and to fear that truly representative government in places like Saudi Arabia and Egypt would be Islamist governments hostile to the United States. The adage "be careful what you wish for because you might get it" is worth pondering when approaching the issue of democratic governance in the Middle East.

That said, the neoconservative premise that the Middle Eastern status quo is no longer acceptable to the United States is hard to refute in the wake of 9/11. There is an undeniable connection between Islamist terrorism and the failure of autocratic governments in the Middle East to provide for their populations' minimal social, economic, and political needs. The issue is not whether the Middle Eastern status quo is acceptable—it is not. The issues are how to go about changing the Middle East and whether change can be imposed by outside powers. There is also the fact that movement from autocracy to democracy has historically often been protracted and violent. The transition in Europe took centuries and was marred by bloody civil wars. Indeed, 561 years separates the Magna Carta and the founding of the American Republic, and it took another 200 years to move from the French Revolution to Europe's near complete democratization.

6

Analogies: Munich, Vietnam, and Postwar Japan

During the 2002–3 national debate over whether to go to war with Iraq, proponents and opponents of war enlisted historical analogies to bolster their arguments. Presidential use-of-force decisions have always been accompanied by reasoning by historical analogy to interpret the meaning of new events and by employing analogies to mobilize public support for a preferred policy. Presidents and other policymakers instinctively turn to what they think history teaches about what to do, or not do, in a given foreign policy crisis.[1]

This does not mean that they reason correctly. Reasoning by historical analogy is an inherently risky business. No two historical situations are identical; policymakers' knowledge of history is often poor; and it is hard to resist the lure of even faulty analogies that support existing policy bias at the expense of more informative analogies. Lyndon Johnson and his senior foreign policy advisers, when weighing the wisdom and feasibility of U.S. intervention in the Vietnam War in 1965, dismissed the unpleasant but highly informative analogy of the French-Indochinese War in favor of the more optimistic Korean War analogy.

Two analogies have dominated the foreign policy discourse over the past half century: Munich, shorthand for the consequences of the democracies' appeasement of Nazi Germany, fascist Italy, and imperial Japan in the 1930s; and Vietnam, shorthand for the dangers of intervening in a foreign civil war. The Munich analogy teaches that the only way to deal with aggressor states is through early and decisive use of force either to deter them from future aggression or to destroy them altogether. Appeasement simply whets an aggressor state's appetite for more and postpones inevitable war while raising its ultimate cost. The Vietnam analogy teaches that foreign civil wars are political quagmires lying in wait for intervening external powers.

Not surprisingly, proponents of war with Iraq repeatedly invoked the Munich analogy. In his March 17 "ultimatum" speech, President Bush counseled his audience to remember that in "the 20th century some chose to appease murderous dictators whose threats were allowed to grow into genocide and global war." Saddam Hussein was portrayed as an Arab Hitler bent on dominating the Middle East. That he was still in power in 2003 was testimony to the "interrupted war" of 1991 and subsequent spinelessness in sanctions enforcement and weapons inspections. Left unchecked, Saddam, like Hitler, was destined to commit further aggression; war was therefore the only effective policy choice. The appeal of the Munich analogy was both generational and circumstantial. As Jack Snyder observed in the *National Interest:* "The Rumsfeld generation grew to political maturity inculcated with the Munich analogy and the domino theory. It is true that an opposite metaphor, the quagmire, is readily available for skeptics to invoke as a result of the Vietnam experience. But after the September 11 attack and the easy victory over the Taliban, the American political audience is primed for Munich analogies and preventive war, not for quagmire theories."[2]

The Munich analogy permeates the entire neoconservative critique of post–Cold War U.S. foreign policy. For neoconservatives, Hitler easily translates into Saddam Hussein, and once the United States opted for war against Iraq even over UN objections, George W. Bush morphs into Winston Churchill, or at least into a president with the Churchillian virtue of a willingness to go to war to stop a tyrant bent on aggression. (Never mind that at the time of the Munich crisis Britain and France were in no military position to defend Czechoslovakia or to launch a preventive war against Germany, or that even had they been in a position to do so, they would have had to fight without their later and decisive allies, the United States and the Soviet Union.) In the years separating the two Gulf wars, neoconservatives repeatedly used the term "appeasement," that dirty word from the 1930s, to condemn the Clinton administration's policies toward Iraq, Iran, and North Korea; they also used it to characterize the stance of those within the George W. Bush administration, such as Secretary of State Colin Powell, suspected of scheming to find an alternative—for example, reinstalling the UN weapons inspection regime—to the war with Iraq the neoconservatives had wanted for so long.[3]

William Kristol, in an August 2002 *Weekly Standard* editorial directed at those he believed were backsliding on the president's declared objective of regime change in Iraq, excoriated the "axis of appeasement—stretching from Riyadh to Brussels to Foggy Bottom, from [*New York Times's* managing editor] Howell Raines to [Senator] Chuck Hagel to Brent Scowcroft— [that] has now mobilized to deflect the president from implementing his policy." In that same month, Secretary of Defense Rumsfeld, citing the appeasement of Hitler in the 1930s, defended preventive military action against Iraq as the only sure means of thwarting Saddam's inevitable aggression in the future: "Think of all the countries that said, 'Well, we don't have enough evidence.' *Mein Kampf* had been written. Hitler had indicated what he intended to do. Maybe he won't attack us. Maybe he won't do this or that. Well, there are millions dead because of [those] miscalculations." Later, he said, "it wasn't until each country got attacked that they said, 'Maybe Winston Churchill was right. Maybe that lone voice expressing concern about what was happening was right.'"[4]

If the Munich analogy argued for war against Iraq, the Vietnam analogy argued against it. The issue was not doubt regarding America's ability to overthrow Saddam Hussein; even most opponents of war against Iraq believed that a U.S. military victory was inevitable and that it could be gained in months if not weeks. There was simply no comparison between the Vietnamese Communists of the 1960s and Saddam Hussein's regime forty years later or between the strategic circumstances and operational challenges of American intervention in Vietnam and those surrounding Operation Iraqi Freedom.[5]

The "Vietnam" issue was, rather, the prospect of becoming ensnared in an open-ended postwar political quagmire inside Iraq, a country torn by deep ethnic, religious, and tribal enmities. Sandra Mackey warned against this prospect:

> Already engaged in a war against terrorism in another tribal society [Afghanistan], the United States cannot wade unaware into Iraq as it once waded into Vietnam. From one perspective, the geopolitical stakes in the Gulf are indisputable. From another perspective, there is among the Iraqis no nationalism powerful enough to inspire civilians to fight for years in the cause of their nation. Nevertheless, the ghosts of Vietnam hover around Iraq. They are there because the United States is again in danger of stumbling into the internal conflicts of another people, only to become trapped in old feuds it never comprehended. In this new era of the American experience that began on September 11, 2001, the United States can no longer afford to be seduced by its own military power or by a naïve faith that foreign worlds can be simplified and mastered.[6]

This was precisely the risk that the George H. W. Bush administration was determined to avoid in 1991. Indeed, the elder Bush invoked both Munich and Vietnam during the Gulf crisis of 1990–91: Munich to justify war to reverse Saddam Hussein's aggression against Kuwait, and Vietnam to reassure the American public that he would not permit a stalemated war by interfering with military operations the way the Johnson administration had in Vietnam. Bush sought to insulate the United States from a potential Vietnam in the Persian Gulf by abjuring any intervention not only in postwar Iraqi politics but also in the professional military's own war plan. "Nation-building" and "micromanagement" were dirty words in 1991 by virtue of the Vietnam experience.[7]

Does the Munich analogy apply to Saddam Hussein's Iraq? There are some obvious similarities. Both Saddam and Hitler were brutal dictators with agendas of conquest. Both operated in regions of indisputable importance to the United States, and both committed aggression against their neighbors. Both were high-risk gamblers who were ultimately destroyed by their recklessness. (In this respect they were quite the opposite of the cautious and patient Stalin, Saddam Hussein's role model as a dictator.)

But here the similarities begin to be overwhelmed by the differences. Hitler presided over the most powerful industrial state in Europe, and he re-created a German army that was operationally superior to that of any of his enemies, including the United States. In the end, it took the combined might of the United States, the Soviet Union, and the British Empire to bring him down, and even then only after four years of bloody military operations on a scale not witnessed before or since. Compare this challenge to that of defeating Iraq in 2003. In the space of just four weeks, a coalition ground force of less than five divisions conquered a country the size of California and did so at a cost in coalition dead of less than two hundred, a significant percentage of them from friendly fire. Iraq's military performance, if one can call it that, bears no similarity to that of the Third Reich's.

Moreover, from Hitler's accession to power in January 1933 until March 1939, six long years, no serious attempt was made to deter Hitler from violating the provisions of the Versailles Treaty, including his remilitarization of the Rhineland, incorporation of Austria, and acquisition of the German-speaking regions of Czechoslovakia and finally the rest of Czechoslovakia. By the time Britain and France mustered the backbone to extend a defense guarantee to Poland, Hitler's next intended victim, it was too late. Hitler invaded Poland in September 1939 believing that the British and the French would do nothing. "Our enemies are worms," he told his assembled generals on the eve of Germany's invasion of Poland. "I saw them at Munich."[8] And, in fact, the British and the French, other than declaring war, sat on their military hands in the west as Hitler's armies swiftly subjugated Poland. In sum, deterrence was not even attempted until it was too late, and when deterrence was finally tried, it was not credible to Hitler because of the democracies' prior record of appeasement. The historian Gerhard Weinberg also points out that at the time of the Munich Conference in September 1938, no public support for war existed in either France or Great Britain—a prerequisite for war against Germany.[9]

With respect to nuclear weapons, Hitler did not pursue their development with anything like the determination of Saddam Hussein (at least before the Gulf War). Hitler lived and died in the prenuclear world. There was a Nazi program to build an atomic bomb, but it was crippled from the start by Hitler's racial policies, which drove key Jewish nuclear physicists out of Europe, and by Hitler's confidence that he could fulfill his imperial ambitions without an atomic bomb and well before one might become available to Germany. Building an atomic bomb was never a high military research priority for Hitler, who was much more interested in jet aircraft and cruise and ballistic missiles. Wartime Germany in any event lacked the industrial organization, scientific talent, bomb materials, and financial resources that enabled the United States to detonate its first bomb in July 1945. Hitler never saw the atomic bomb as a strategic or operational necessity, and certainly not as a ticket to great power status.

The United States was aware of German interest in atomic weapons; in 1939, Albert Einstein had so warned Pres. Franklin Roosevelt, who, determined to preempt any possibility of Germany's acquiring the atomic bomb first, initiated the Manhattan Project. For the United States during World War II, the best "counterproliferation" policy was the combination of the Manhattan Project and the destruction of the Nazi regime before it could attain atomic status.

Saddam Hussein's situation in March 2003 was dismal compared to Hitler's in September 1939. Unlike Hitler, Saddam was militarily isolated and had been effectively deterred from any territorial aggression since 1991. He ruled a country in a region militarily dominated by a hostile superpower—precisely the reverse of Hitler's domination of Europe by the summer of 1940. Saddam's crippled army had not recovered from the Gulf War, and his economy was a shambles. Whatever his imperial ambitions, Saddam was, in short, in no position to act on them. By most accounts he was, however, obsessed with acquiring nuclear weapons. He apparently believed that possession of them in 1991 would have deterred the United States from forcibly overturning his aggression against Kuwait. He saw nuclear weapons as a badge of great power status and a means of challenging American military hegemony in the Persian Gulf.

The unanswered questions on the eve of Operation Iraqi Freedom—and the basis of the Bush administration's case for preventive war against Iraq—were the status of his nuclear ambitions and whether he really believed possession of nuclear weapons would permit him to act with impunity in the Gulf. The reestablishment of a UN inspection regime in Iraq in November 2002 made it virtually impossible for Saddam to proceed with whatever his nuclear program amounted to; indeed, critics of the war option argued that an expanded inspection regime was the much better alternative to war as a means of preventing Saddam from acquiring nuclear weapons. As a result of the U.S. overthrow and occupation of Iraq, we now know that Saddam's nuclear "program" had deteriorated to virtual nonexistence.

Ironically, before Operation Desert Storm, the George H. W. Bush administration significantly underestimated the scope of the Iraqi nuclear weapons program, whereas in the run-up to Operation Iraqi Freedom the George W. Bush administration had painted a terrifying Iraqi WMD threat to the United States as imminent. For example, the joint congressional resolution it sponsored authorizing the use of force against Iraq declared that "Iraq's demonstrated capability and willingness to use weapons of mass destruction" posed "the high risk that the current Iraqi regime will . . . employ those weapons to launch a surprise attack against the United States."[10] As for how Saddam might have behaved once in possession of nuclear weapons, we will never know.

The Vietnam War analogy was employed before the second war against Iraq as an argument against war, which believers in this analogy feared would not only entangle the United States in a quagmire of postwar Iraqi politics but also spark an explosion of violence against American targets throughout the Middle East. In this view, the Vietnam War was a civil war among Vietnamese, not a case of external aggression—the view of the Johnson White House, which was wedded to a Munich analogy interpretation of events in Indochina in the 1960s. Great powers enter other peoples' civil wars at great peril because of the inherent disparity of stakes between the local parties to the civil war and the intervening great power. For the former, the stakes are usually total, whereas for the latter they are usually limited; this means the local parties are prepared to fight longer and harder than the external intervening power. Michael Ignatieff invoked the Vietnam analogy with respect to Iraq:

> As the Iraqi operation looms, it is worth keeping Vietnam in mind. Vietnam was a titanic clash between two nation-building strategies, the Americans in support of the South Vietnamese versus the Communists in the north. Yet it proved impossible for foreigners to build stability in a divided country against resistance from a Communist elite fighting in the name of the Vietnamese nation. Vietnam is now one country, its civil war over and its long-term stability assured. An American operation in Iraq will not face a competing nationalist project, but across the Islamic world it will arouse the nationalist passions of people who want to rule themselves and worship as they please. As Vietnam shows, empire is no match, long-term, for nationalism.[11]

The Vietnam analogy may be informative with respect to the second war against Iraq's impact on Arab nationalism, but it runs into trouble when applied to the Iraqi state and the aftermath of Operation Iraqi Freedom. The Communists in Vietnam waged a revolutionary war on behalf of a powerful Vietnam nationalism that stretched back for two millennia. The Communists were also ethnically homogeneous, led by a charismatic leader, and they pursued a strategy of protracted war that exploited America's strategic impatience and limited war aims. There was no postwar U.S. military presence in Indochina because it was the United States, not the Vietnamese Communists, who lost the war. The war was, to be sure, a "quagmire" for the United States. It bogged down American forces in a bloody, open-ended, and ultimately futile conflict in which its South Vietnamese ally never gained sufficient political traction to survive as a viable state. But the shooting never stopped until after the United States abandoned Indochina.

In contrast the 2003 regime-destruction phase of war against Iraq was, relative to the eight-year lost war in Vietnam, a quick and decisive victory against a hated and militarily helpless dictatorship in a country of profound ethnic, religious, and tribal divisions that had been cobbled together by the British after World War II. The conventional phase of the war itself was never destined to be a quagmire, given America's crushing military superiority over Iraq and the critical differences separating the strategic and local circumstances of the Persian Gulf in 2003 and those of Indochina in the 1960s.[12]

If anyone found the Vietnam analogy attractive, it was those in Baghdad on the receiving end of American military power. Saddam Hussein clearly hoped to inflict an Arab Vietnam on the United States. He entered his first war with the United States convinced that the Vietnam War had paralyzed America's will to use force in circumstances that risked significant loss of American life—a conviction seemingly validated by the humiliating withdrawal of the United States from the Lebanese "quagmire" following a terrorist attack on the Marines in Beirut.[13]

For Saddam and his henchmen in 2003 (as in 1991), the only scenario in which Iraq's utter defeat might be avoided was a Vietnam-like protracted conflict in which the level of American casualties ultimately sapped American will to continue fighting. Saddam was known to be an admirer of Ho Chi Minh, and as the United States moved toward war with Iraq, Baghdad's military leaders were known to be spending months researching U.S. defeats in Vietnam, Lebanon, and Somalia—to the point of circulating both the book and the film *Black Hawk Down*.[14] In the fall of 2002 Iraq's deputy prime minister Tariq Aziz reportedly told a University of Warwick researcher, "People say to me, 'You are not Vietnamese. You have no jungles and swamps.' I reply, 'Let out cities be our swamps and our buildings our jungles.' "[15] Aziz and other Iraqi officials made no bones about their attraction to a protracted "casualty" strategy based on luring U.S. forces into urban warfare. Consistent with this strategy was the employment of irregular forces against the coalition's initially exposed supply lines and later against coalition occupation forces. Clearly, lessons from the 1991 war had been learned. Iraq's regular forces were prepared to abandon vast tracts of national territory and did not attempt to slug it out with the Americans in open country. Baghdad wanted a Stalingrad along the Tigris, or at least wanted the threat of such a meat-grinder battle to deter a U.S. attack.

From the start of the Bush administration's road to war with Iraq, it was not the war itself but rather the postwar situation inside that country that beckoned as a potential quagmire. Indeed, the great difference between Vietnam and Iraq is nationalism's comparative weakness in the latter country. Iraq is a relatively recent and quite artificial creation of the British foreign office, which divided up the old Ottoman Empire after World War I. Primary loyalties inside Iraq are ethnic, tribal, and religious, not national, and it is Iraqi society's very fragmentation along these lines and the long history of Sunni-Shiite and Arab-Kurdish strife that pessimists believe will engulf the U.S. occupation.

Does "quagmire" characterize the U.S. position in Iraq today? If by that term is meant an open-ended military occupation necessitated by the absence of a politically sustainable indigenous structure of governance, then the answer is: yes. In other words, if, as in Vietnam, U.S. military intervention has failed to establish a sustainable political order in place of the previous or (in the case of Vietnam) competing political order, then quagmire it is. Persistent military presence alone is not sufficient to constitute a quagmire. U.S. forces remain in Japan sixty years after Japan's defeat in World War II, but they remain there for strategic reasons external to Japan. It is military presence dictated by ongoing political failure inside the occupied territory plus persistent indigenous violence against U.S. forces that makes a quagmire. In this regard, the U.S. experience in Lebanon from 1982 to 1984 may well prove analogous to today's unfolding situation in Iraq.[16]

The Bush administration's preferred counteranalogy is, not surprisingly, MacArthur's postwar Japan, a great nation-building success story that transformed an autocratic aggressor state into a benign democratic ally. In his March 6, 2003, speech at the American Enterprise Institute, the president declared:

We will remain in Iraq as long as necessary and not a day more. America has made and kept this kind of commitment before in the peace that followed a world war. After defeating enemies, we did not leave behind occupying armies, we left behind constitutions and parliaments. We established an atmosphere of safety in which responsible, reform-minded local leaders could build lasting institutions of freedom. In societies that once bred fascism and militarism, liberty found a permanent home

There was a time when many said that the cultures of Japan and Germany were incapable of sustaining democratic values. Well, they were wrong. Some say the same of Iraq today. They are mistaken. The nation of Iraq, with its proud heritage, abundant resources and skilled and educated people is fully capable of moving toward democracy and living in freedom.[17]

The analogy is enticing, but it is also highly misleading. The United States may well succeed in creating a sustainable democracy in Iraq. It certainly did so in Japan. But the Japanese circumstances of 1945 were profoundly different from the Iraqi circumstances of today. First, the legitimacy of America's occupation of Japan and direct military governance of that country for six years was accepted by the international community, including Japan's neighbors in East Asia. Japan had been a brutal aggressor state in the 1930s and 1940s, and her victims rejoiced in America's defeat of Japan. The United States liberated East Asia from Japanese rape, pillage, and slaughter. Victims of Japanese aggression regarded the U.S. occupation of Japan as an indispensable guarantee against a resurgence of Japanese militarism.

The contrast with the U.S. occupation of Iraq could not be starker. The Bush administration's preventive war against Iraq aroused a firestorm of international political opposition—opposition underscored by U.S. failure to secure even a simple majority among UN Security Council members for use of force against Iraq: only two of the council's five permanent members, the United States and Great Britain, favored such action. This was a far cry from the solid UN mandate Pres. George H. W. Bush sought and received for war against Iraq in 1991. All major Arab states opposed America's 2003 war against Iraq, as did France, Germany, Russia, and China, and—unexpectedly—Canada, Mexico, and Turkey. Indeed, democratic Turkey's refusal to permit U.S. ground force operations from its territory was not only a political embarrassment for the Bush administration but also significantly weakened the initial force of the U.S. attack on Iraq by precluding a second, "northern front" against Iraq led by the U.S. Army's powerful 4th Infantry Division. Even among old NATO allies public opinion was profoundly averse toward the Bush administration's foreign policy. A Pew Research Center poll taken on the eve of Operation Iraqi Freedom revealed the following rates of disapproval of Bush's foreign policy: Britain—60 percent; France—87 percent; Germany—85 percent; Italy—76 percent; Spain—79 percent; and Turkey—85 percent.[18]

Second, the Japanese themselves accepted the occupation as legitimate. They understood that they had been utterly defeated; indeed, the emperor himself had legitimized Japan's unconditional surrender by breaking precedent when he directly addressed the Japanese people over the radio, calling for all Japanese to accept the war's termination. The American decision to retain the emperor, and Gen. Douglas MacArthur's shrewd use of the emperor to legitimize the American commander's revolutionary political, social, and economic reforms were indispensable keys to the spectacular success of the U.S. occupation. There is no functional Iraqi equivalent of the emperor. John Dower, author of the definitive work on Japanese society under American rule, connects the nature of Japan's defeat to susceptibility to an American-imposed revolution from above: "Because the defeat was so shattering, the surrender so unconditional, the disgrace of the militarists so complete, the misery the [war] had brought home so personal, starting over involved not merely reconstructing buildings but also what it meant to speak of a good life and good society."[19]

But it wasn't just the emperor who was critical to that success. There was MacArthur himself, a man uniquely suited to become "a stock figure in the political pageantry of Japan: the new sovereign, the blue-eyed shogun, the paternalistic military dictator, the grandiloquent but excruciatingly sincere Kabuki hero."[20] MacArthur played his role with consummate skill and with a completely free hand from Washington; by the time he departed Japan in 1951, he was revered as a godlike figure.[21]

Third, there was the nature of Japan and Japanese society. Unlike Iraq, Japan was an ancient, homogeneous, and conformist nation. The population was not only obedient to its emperor but also free of the kind of ethnic, tribal, and religious divisions that have plagued Iraq since its formation. MacArthur could take Japan's social and political cohesion for granted. And, given his use of the emperor to legitimize American rule, MacArthur never had to worry about violent Japanese resistance to U.S. occupation. (There was not a single act of politically motivated violence against U.S. occupation forces.) Here again, the contrast with Iraq could not be greater. Operation Iraqi Freedom was not an absolute victory over the Saddam Hussein regime. It failed to kill or capture Saddam Hussein or to destroy completely the Ba'athist Party infrastructure. Sufficient remnants of the regime, apparently including Saddam himself, survived to wage, in conjunction with foreign jihadists and aroused Iraqi nationalists, a mounting insurgent war against U.S. occupation forces. Continued

Ba'athist-sponsored resistance, perhaps directed by Saddam Hussein himself, served to generate fear among most Iraqis and hope among Saddam's supporters that Saddam, the ultimate survivor, might yet return to power if the Americans tired of responsibility for postwar Iraq and departed (as they had from Vietnam, Lebanon, and Somalia). Indeed, in retrospect it is possible to speculate that guerrilla warfare was a last-resort component of Saddam's strategy for dealing with the irresistible conventional military superiority of the United States (see chap. 7).

Nor did Japan possess natural resources that could spark American commercial and international political rivalry for access. Indeed, Japan's oil dependence on the United States helped set the stage for war in 1941; it was Roosevelt's imposition of an oil embargo on Japan in July that propelled the Japanese into oil-rich Southeast Asia—a move the Japanese believed they could not safely make with the Philippines under U.S. control and the Pearl Harbor–based U.S. Pacific Fleet intact.

Consider the contrast with Iraq, which not only possesses the world's second largest oil reserves but also sits between the terrorist-sponsoring states of Syria and Iran. As John Dower noted in an interview shortly after Operation Iraqi Freedom began, "In Iraq, we are going to have carpetbaggers and special interests trying to manipulate what's going on there for their own advantage. This could be disastrous. Given the incredible focus on Iraq's strategic importance, the more appropriate analogy may not be Japan proper but Okinawa, which was turned into a gross appendage of the American military empire."[22]

The novelist and former secretary of the navy James Webb summarized the dangers of faulty reasoning by historical analogy:

> The connotations of "a MacArthurian regency in Baghdad" show how inapt the comparison [with the situation in Iraq] is. Our occupation forces never set foot inside Japan until the emperor had formally surrendered and prepared Japanese citizens for our arrival. Nor did MacArthur destroy the Japanese government when he took over as proconsul after World War II. Instead, he was careful to work his changes through it, and took pains to preserve the integrity of the imperial family. Nor is Japanese culture in any way similar to Iraq's. The Japanese are a homogeneous people who place a high premium on respect, and they fully cooperated with MacArthur's forces after having been ordered to do so by the emperor. The Iraqis are a multiethnic people filled with competing factions who in many cases would view a U.S. occupation as infidels invading the cradle of Islam. Indeed, this very bitterness provided Osama bin Laden the grist for his recruitment efforts in Saudi Arabia when the United States retained bases on Saudi soil after the Gulf War.[23]

Two final points deserve mention. First, Japan's insular geography was no less significant than the Japanese nation's homogeneity. As an island state whose maritime approaches were completely dominated by U.S. naval and air power, Japan could be sealed off from externally sponsored armed infiltration by subversive groups. In contrast, Iraq is nearly land-locked by easily penetrated borders and surrounded by neighbors, particularly Iran, that are hostile both to the United States and to secular rule in Baghdad. Second, in the case of both Japan and the three western occupation zones of Germany, there was a much worse alternative to the presence of Allied forces: a Communist takeover via internal subversion or external Soviet aggression. The profound anti-Communism of the Japanese and Germans and the proximity of menacing Soviet military power contributed greatly to the stability and progress of the occupation in both countries.

7

The War

The military overthrow of Saddam Hussein's regime was never in doubt as long as America's political will to win prevailed. Iraqi's military forces were doomed to defeat by an acute inferiority in every qualitative index of military power, including morale, discipline, training, doctrine, weaponry, organization, and intelligence. U.S.–dominated coalition forces seized Baghdad just 21 days after initiating hostilities on March 19, 2003, and took just one more week to complete major combat operations in Iraq. A cautious White House waited until May 1 to declare victory. On that day, President Bush stated: "The Battle of Iraq is one victory in a war on terror that began on September 11, 2001, and still goes on."[1]

In four short weeks—ten days less than the 1991 war—the United States drove Saddam Hussein from power and seized control of Iraq. (The U.S. war plan, as written, was expected to require up to 120 days.)[2] On the eve of the conflict, the polemicist and war hawk Christopher Hitchens remarked, "[t]he best that can be said of the Iraqi army is that it has not recently lost a war against its own civilians." After the war, the British military historian John Keegan declared that "Saddam's war plan, if he had one, must be reckoned one of the most inept ever designed. . . . [It] ignored every rule of defensive warfare."[3]

Some have compared Operation Iraqi Freedom's brevity and decisiveness to the May 1940 German blitzkrieg against France and the Low Countries. The neoconservative commentator Max Boot believes that the 1940 campaign used to be "the gold standard of excellence" but is no more because the military performance of the U.S.–U.K. coalition makes "fabled generals such as Erwin Rommel and Heinz Guderian seem positively incompetent by comparison." In fact, the Germans in 1940 compelled the French to surrender in 44 days, but they permitted most of the British Expeditionary Force in France to escape to fight another day. Nor is there any useful comparison between operational balance of the two sides in 1940 and 2003; the former was far less favorable to the Germans than it was to the Americans sixty-three years later. In 1940 a total German force of 136 divisions, 2,500–2,600 tanks, 7,700 artillery pieces, and 2.5 million men faced combined French, Belgian, Dutch, and British forces of 135 divisions, 3,000 tanks, 11,200 artillery pieces, and 3.5 million men. Moreover, whereas the military outcome of 2003 was never in doubt, it was for the Germans in 1940; the German war plan was an operational and strategic gamble against numerically superior enemy forces fielding weapons commensurate in quality to those possessed by the Germans. The principal operational risk was a French intelligence discovery of the Ardennes locus of the German armored *schwerpunkt;* even absent that discovery, the German crossing of the Meuse was a very close-run affair. The main strategic risk was that the campaign would fail to achieve a quick victory and degenerate into a protracted war that the Nazi economy was not prepared to support.[4]

Allied numerical superiority was, however, quite misleading. The core of the Allied force, the French army, was politically demoralized and professionally unprepared to deal with the revolutionary technical, tactical, and organizational innovations that constituted "blitzkrieg." In these respects, Iraqi army forces of 2003 bear some comparison with the French military of 1940. Moreover, coalition ground forces in 2003 were, in comparison to German forces in 1940, quite thin in relation to the amount of enemy ground they had cover. Finally, unlike the 2003 coalition, whose forces were subjected to mounting guerrilla attacks after the cessation of major conventional military operations, the Germans achieved a strategically clean victory against the French, if not the British. The French surrender of June 1940 was formal and definitive; indigenous resistance to the German presence arose only with the disappearance of the Vichy regime in late 1942 and with Anglo-American assistance.

As short as the 2003 war was, however, it was, as wars are wont to be, full of unexpected events, both things that happened and things that did not. The purpose of this chapter is not to retrace the course of military operations or to examine the tactics and technologies employed—tasks better left to experts far more knowledgeable and experienced than I. Rather, it is to assess the relationship of the military operations as they actually unfolded, as well as the prewar expectations of those who favored and planned the war; international and domestic politics; and the war's declared and undeclared objectives.

The biggest unanswered prewar question was how hard Iraqis would—and could—fight. Optimists, including neoconservatives, believed that Saddam Hussein's Iraq was a political and military house of cards that would collapse at the first sharp U.S. military blow. Some believed the war would be effectively over within a few days; the brutalized Iraqi people were eagerly awaiting liberation and therefore would not resist invasion, and even the regime's vaunted Special Republican Guard and Republican Guard would quickly implode under the weight of U.S. ordnance and the realization that the regime was doomed. Optimists expected mass military surrenders and civilian uprisings.

Pessimism—fear that the United States could be militarily defeated or at least stalemated in Iraq (as it had been in Vietnam)—was notable for its scarcity. With some exceptions, even the strongest critics of preventive war against Iraq did not question America's ability to crush Iraq militarily; their concerns focused on the political wisdom of doing so. If, however, there were no notable pessimists, there were many who didn't buy the optimists' story line. Cautionaries (for lack of a better term), which included military professionals habituated to imagining and examining worst-case scenarios, believed that prudent planning had to anticipate the very real possibility of significant resistance. Unlike 1991, the regime would be fighting for its survival. Moreover, Iraqis might hate Saddam, but they also might not like being conquered by a foreign invader. They would be fighting a defensive war on their own territory, and the southern and western approaches to Baghdad offered many natural and man-made obstacles that could slow and bloody an advancing enemy. Baghdad itself loomed as a potential cauldron of urban warfare in which U.S. tactical and technological advantages might be significantly compromised and American casualties incurred in politically unacceptable numbers. There was, too, the likely Iraqi use of chemical and even biological weapons, which at a minimum would reduce U.S. combat effectiveness by forcing U.S. troops to button up in their protective paraphernalia and in a worst case could kill or incapacitate thousands. The optimists might be right, but planning should assume the possibility, even probability, that they were wrong.

As it turned out, neither best-case predictions nor worst-case fears materialized. Saddam's regime did not collapse in the face of initial "shock and awe" air and missile strikes, and there were no mass surrenders or mass uprisings. On the other hand, there was no Iraqi use of WMD, no strikes on Israel, minimal torching of oil wells, and little Iraqi effort to exploit the opportunities for attrition and delay in the approaches to Baghdad or for urban warfare in Baghdad itself. The vaunted Republican Guard, which in 1991 fought with determination if not skill, proved little more than bomb bait for U.S. airpower. Indeed, it is difficult to speak of Iraq's military performance; it was, if anything, a nonperformance. There were some tactical surprises, such as Iraqi irregular attacks in U.S. rear areas, but they had little ripple effect at the operational level of the conflict.

Things also did not go as planned—they rarely do in war. But in the end it really didn't make much difference. The huge disparity in fighting power between the United States and Iraq and the U.S. Central Command's exceptional operational flexibility foreclosed any prospect of U.S. defeat or even protraction of major combat operations. The Iraq that the United States attacked on March 19, 2003, was strategically isolated, militarily crippled, and politically bankrupt. The challenge was not winning the war but winning the peace.

The war the United States launched against Iraq in March 2003 was nonetheless the product of less than ideal strategic circumstances and of disputatious operational planning. There was also, on the part of some, a dubious assumption about the resilience and fighting power of the Iraqi regime. The unfortunate strategic circumstances were the war's lack of international political legitimacy and the absence of key allies among Iraq's major neighbors. The Bush administration's decision, in defiance of the United Nations and against the strong pleas of key NATO allies, for a unilateral preventive war against Iraq alienated friends and allies alike, especially in the Muslim world. Though the White House claimed that Operation Iraqi Freedom was based on a large coalition of the willing, only the United States and Britain contributed significant combat forces for the war (Australia and Poland committed token forces), making it essentially an Anglo-American attack on an Arab state. The rest of the coalition consisted mostly of nominal political supporters, some of them, such as the Marshall Islands and the Federated States of Micronesia, joke states, and others, such as former Communist states in Eastern Europe seeking NATO membership, wishing to ingratiate themselves to the United States for reasons that had nothing to do with Iraq. It was the first war in which the United States could count Albania, Eritrea, Ethiopia, Mongolia, Rwanda, and Uzbekistan as "allies." In contrast, the coalition of states contributing ground and air forces to the Gulf War of 1991 included Afghanistan, Bahrain, Bangladesh, Canada, Czechoslovakia, Egypt, France, Italy, Kuwait, Morocco, Oman, Niger, Pakistan, Qatar, Saudi Arabia, Senegal, Syria, and the United Arab Emirates. Turkey, though committing no combat forces, permitted the United States to use air bases in Turkey to launch air strikes against Iraqi targets.

An American invasion of an Arab state with which it was not at war, which posed no visible or imminent threat to U.S. security, and which was bound once again to underscore two centuries of Western humiliation of the Arab world was never going to attract the kind of coalition that Pres. George H. W. Bush assembled for the Gulf War of 1991. The limited war aims of 1991 made such a coalition possible; the unlimited aims of 2003 rendered it impossible.

The two key regional absentees in 2003 were Saudi Arabia and Turkey, whose participation in the war of 1991 permitted the United States to amass and employ overwhelming force against the Iraqis in Kuwait. The 9/11 attacks and the Bush administration's de facto abandonment of the Middle East Peace Process were turning points in U.S.–Saudi relations. Saudi Arabia's indirect complicity in the terrorist attacks undercut continued public and congressional support for the oil-for-security bargain upon which those relations were based. Certainly for the neoconservatives within the Bush administration, Saudi Arabia was part of the problem in the war on terrorism; indeed, in their view, one of the attractions of a democratic U.S. client regime in Iraq was its elimination of American dependence on Saudi Arabia. For the Saudis, the Bush administration's decision, in effect, to subcontract America's Middle East policy out to the government of Ariel Sharon (whom the president called "a man of peace") impeded a continued close security relationship with the United States. The combination of administration insistence that the PLO dump its democratically elected leader, Yasir Arafat, and apparent administration indifference to continued Israeli repression and settlement of the West Bank barred any chance that Riyadh would permit its territory to be used as a launch pad for attacks on another Arab state. The Saudi decision to invite American troops into the kingdom in 1990 for that purpose was what radicalized Osama bin Laden against both the United States and the Saudi regime. To do so again would be to play with domestic political dynamite.

In fact, in late April 2003, Secretary of Defense Rumsfeld announced the Pentagon's intention to pare down the U.S. military presence in Saudi to its small, pre-1990 training program involving 400–500 personnel; that presence had peaked at 10,000 during Operation Iraqi Freedom, double the 5,000 norm during the 1990s.[5] Though Secretary Rumsfeld said the reduction was tied to the elimination of the Iraqi threat, clearly the Bush administration viewed a continuation of anything other than a minor U.S. presence as a threat to the House of Saud's internal legitimacy.[6] Thus, ironically and inadvertently, Operation Iraqi Freedom came close to accomplishing one of Osama bin Laden's major objectives: America's military evacuation of Saudi Arabia.

In the case of Turkey, there were miscalculations on both sides. The Bush administration apparently took for granted Ankara's willingness to permit Turkish territory to be used for U.S. air and ground attacks against Iraq even though the Turkish elections of November 2002 had swept into power the Islamist Justice and Development Party (JDP). The JDP opposed Turkish support for a U.S. war on Iraq (as did more than 90 percent of the Turkish people) and mistakenly believed that the United States would not attack Iraq without active Turkish support. The JDP's blockage of Turkish participation denied the United States the opportunity to launch a powerful second front attack from the north and left the army's powerful 4th Infantry Division, slated for deployment to southeastern Turkey, off the military game board until after the fall of Baghdad. Turkey's refusal left the United States only one main axis of attack into Iraq and gave Iraqi forces in northern Iraq a free ride during the opening stages of hostilities. U.S. operational planning had to be adjusted accordingly. The decision was made to launch the southern front attack without awaiting redeployment of the 4th Infantry Division to Kuwait via the Red Sea and Arabian Gulf.[7]

The main attack, preceded by the securing of Iraqi air bases and potential Scud missile–launch areas in western Iraq by special operations forces, was conducted by three U.S. divisions—the U.S. Army's 3d Infantry and 101st Air Assault divisions and the Marine Corps 1st Marine Expeditionary Force (containing a division and associated air wing)—and a brigade combat team of the Army 82d Airborne Division. The British 1st Armored Division, assigned to secure Iraq's southern crossroads city of Basra, also participated. Attacking forces consisted of approximately 115,000 U.S. soldiers and marines and 26,000 British troops.

The road to the war plan itself was long and difficult because of civil-military disagreement on what would be required in the way of military force to bring Saddam Hussein down. Generally speaking, Secretary of Defense Rumsfeld, Deputy Secretary of Defense Wolfowitz, and other influential civilian Defense Department players, as well as the vice president and his staff, believed Saddam's regime was so hated inside Iraq and so politically brittle even inside the Iraqi armed forces that a sharp "shock and awe" stroke of intense air and missile attacks would quickly collapse the regime. Many neoconservatives believed what self-serving Iraqi opposition group leaders in exile told them—namely, that the Iraqi people were desperately awaiting liberation and would cooperate with invading American forces, that the regular Iraqi army could be persuaded not to fight, and that even key Republican Guard units would desert Saddam once they were persuaded that defeat was quick and certain. The assumption was that the Iraqi people were not only anti-Saddam but also pro-America—and by extension—pro-democracy. In a March 11, 2003, speech to the Veterans of Foreign Wars, Deputy Defense Secretary Paul Wolfowitz likened the coming U.S. invasion of Iraq to Eisenhower's liberation of France: "The Iraqi people understand what this crisis is about. Like the people of France in the 1940s, they view us as their hoped-for liberator." (Never mind that France in 1944 was occupied by a hated *foreign* enemy that had invaded France three times in the space of seventy years.) Less than a week later, Vice President Cheney told NBC's *Meet the Press:* "I think things have gotten so bad inside

Iraq, from the standpoint of the American people, my belief is we will, in fact, be greeted as liberators."[8]

"It was a fantasy," countered Judith Yaphe, the chief CIA analyst on Iraq during the 1991 Gulf War and now a professor at the National Defense University. "They had a strategic vision that we would face no opposition, that everyone would surrender, that Iraqis would throw rose petals and rice, and people would welcome us as conquering liberators."[9]

"I believe demolishing [Saddam] Hussein's military power and liberating Iraq would be a cakewalk [because] (1) it was a cakewalk last time; (2) they've become much weaker; (3) we've become much stronger; and (4) now we're playing for keeps," pronounced Ken Adelman, a prominent neoconservative and former Reagan Defense Department official, a year before the war.[10]

"I think Saddam's army will defeat Saddam," intoned Richard Perle. "There may be pockets of resistance, but very few Iraqis are going to fight to defend Saddam Hussein."[11] In early 2001—before 9/11—he predicted that Saddam would be gone in a year and told columnist Robert Novak, who asked whether major U.S. expeditionary force would be required to unseat the Iraqi dictator, "No, certainly not. I don't think that's necessary."[12]

"I don't think it would be a tough fight," declared Vice President Cheney in September 2002, a judgment echoed by Sen. John McCain: "I am very certain that this military engagement will not be very difficult," opined the outspoken neoconservative and dedicated war hawk. "[Saddam Hussein] does not have the support of his people. And I'd ask one question: What member of the Iraqi army is willing to die for Saddam Hussein when they know he's going to be taken out?"[13]

Such comments reflect an insensitivity to war's inherent fickleness. They further betray a naivete about not only the coercive power of a totalitarian regime fighting for its very survival but also how Iraqis, numbingly propagandized by Saddam and impoverished for more than a decade by economic sanctions championed most loudly by the United States and Britain, might react to an invading and occupying Anglo-American army. One is reminded of the assumption that underlay the fiasco of the U.S.–sponsored invasion of Cuba at the Bay of Pigs in 1961: that the Cuban people would rise en masse against Fidel Castro because they were eager to be liberated by the United States.[14]

That the Iraqis did not rise up was undoubtedly due in part to fear of reprisal by Saddam's security services and the especially thuggish and fanatical Saddam Fedayeen. The power of a police state to coerce should never be underestimated. Even Saddam-hating Iraqis were not about to rise as long as they remained infiltrated by regime goons and as long as there was no conclusive proof that the regime was finished. Saddam Hussein's apparent survival of Operation Iraqi Freedom and the persistence of violence by remnant Ba'athist Party militia denied definitive and reassuring "closure" to the regime.

But the absence of uprisings almost certainly was also a legacy of the 1991 experience, when the Shias and Kurds, encouraged by the United States, did rise only to be subsequently betrayed by U.S. inaction as Saddam proceeded to slaughter an estimated sixty thousand to one hundred thousand of them.[15] And there was the additional fact that most countries, however unpopular their governments might be, do not like to be invaded and conquered by foreign armies. Stalin was more of a monster than Saddam Hussein (certainly in terms of the number of regime victims), yet Hitler's invasion of the Soviet Union in 1941 excited the irresistible fury of Russian nationalism that ultimately crushed most of the German army. To be sure, this did not happen in Iraq, which has a much shorter and weaker national history than did Russia in 1941, but even weak nationalism can be strengthened by foreign invasion and occupation. "The fear factor is major," argued Richard Murphy, former assistant secretary of state for the Near East, during the middle of the war. "But I wonder whether . . . the desire to defend God and country by shooting up the invaders has more appeal than we have given it credit for."[16] Indeed, no sooner had the war ended than many Iraqis made it plain that while they welcomed America's destruction of Saddam's regime, they also wanted the United States to vacate Iraq.

The civilian war hawks were also impressed by the unexpected ease with which U.S. forces had driven the Taliban regime from power in Afghanistan. Using a combination of CIA cash (to buy off potential opponents), surrogate ground forces (the Northern Alliance), U.S. special operations forces, and precision air strikes, the United States broke the back of the Taliban's field forces, which contributed to their own destruction by attempting positional defense. Victory was facilitated by the popularity inside Afghanistan of American military action, which liberated the country from a primitive and oppressive Islamist regime that effectively imprisoned half its population (women) and denied all its people such simple pleasures as music. The cheap win in Afghanistan excited the imagination of many, especially the Pentagon civilians who were committed to what was known but never precisely defined as "defense transformation."

Afghanistan seemed to suggest that continuing trends in aerial surveillance and strike technologies would permit airpower, in conjunction with relatively small, light, high-tech ground forces, to substitute for large, firepower-heavy ground forces of the kind created to stop Soviet armor on the north German plain. Secretary Rumsfeld and his aides insisted that "the size of ground forces is no longer a key measure of capability," recounted Michael Gordon in late March 2003. "Rather, they argue, even relatively small formations can be a powerful force as a result of advanced command and control systems, improved reconnaissance, improved ground systems, and an expanded arsenal of precision-guided bombs. Small, mobile but potent [ground] forces, they say, are the wave of the future."[17]

Indeed, Secretary Rumsfeld, who was committed to defense transformation, was hostile to what he believed were doctrinally and structurally obsolete Cold War–legacy force structures, especially the army's heavy divisions, which in his view were excessively muscle-bound and not rapidly deployable overseas. He did not get along well with Gen. Eric Shinseki, the army chief of staff, even though Shinseki was attempting to develop hybrid medium-weight units that could be rapidly deployed overseas. Indeed, Rumsfeld made Shinseki a lame duck by announcing the general's replacement fourteen months in advance of Shinseki's retirement; the secretary of defense subsequently exploited the U.S. victory in Iraq to fire army secretary Thomas White, whom he viewed as hostile to his vision of transformation.[18]

Rumsfeld also believed the Clinton administration had given the professional military too much latitude in the formulation of foreign and defense policy, and he was determined to reassert the authority of the Office of the Secretary of Defense over the Joint Staff and the service chiefs. "I want to reinstate civilian control of the military!" he roared during a meeting shortly after taking office.[19] He further believed that much of the senior military leadership had not broken out of their Cold War mind-set and still suffered an excessive caution induced by the persistence of the "Vietnam syndrome." For Rumsfeld that syndrome was encapsulated in the highly restrictive Weinberger-Powell doctrine, which cautioned against using force except in the most favorable political and military circumstances, including the availability of overwhelming force. If defined as the quantity of force and the volume of firepower, overwhelming force was an example of Cold War thinking.[20]

Long before Operation Iraqi Freedom, even before 9/11, civil-military tensions inside the Pentagon were running higher than perhaps at any time since the reign of Robert McNamara, who, like Rumsfeld, was an abrasive, assertive, exceptionally self-confident man who was not afraid to impose his views on the professional military. Indeed, some military officers who opposed Rumsfeld's ideas on defense transformation and what they viewed as his unwarranted and dangerous meddling in operational planning privately compared him to McNamara, the most hated secretary of defense since the office was established in 1947. McNamara had enraged the service chiefs by concentrating in the Office of the Secretary of Defense decision-making authority on matters up to then left to the uniformed military, and had then gone on to micromanage U.S. military operations in Vietnam with disastrous results.

From the start, there was disagreement over the scope and composition of the force believed to be necessary to bring Saddam down.[21] The civilians and some "transformationist" military officers favored an aircentric strategy aimed at an early "shock and awe" attack that would shatter the regime by destroying such leadership targets as Saddam's palaces and bunkers, Ba'ath Party headquarters and gathering places, Republican Guard divisional headquarters, and police and internal security targets. It was hoped that such an attack, preceded by months of massive leaflet drops and other psychological warfare operations aimed at softening the Iraqi will to resist, would collapse the regime within a matter of days. The civilians discounted the need for significant heavy ground forces, in part because they believed that Iraq's regular army and even key Republican Guard units could be coaxed into nonresistance, even defection, by psychological warfare operations and the sheer display of irresistible American military might. In the Pentagon's jargon, Operation Iraqi Freedom was to be an "effects-based operation"—that is, an operation in which force would be applied against targets whose destruction or neutralization would alter the Iraqi leadership's psychological disposition to continue resistance. As Maj. Gen. Robert Scales, former commandant of the Army War College, put it, "[t]he old way, you would fight through an enemy. In the new way, you fight around an enemy and go for the brain. [Operation Iraqi Freedom was designed to be] a large-scale psychological take-down." "This was a strategy that favored focus over scale. It sought a TKO instead of trying to batter its foe into unconsciousness," observed the military analyst William M. Arkin. "Rather than destroy Iraq to save it, [planners] were trying to coax victory from an enemy they saw as weak . . . and uncertain about its appetite for war."[22]

Thus the source of expectations of an early regime implosion, which among other things would spare U.S. forces the prospect of protracted urban warfare in Baghdad, was twofold: the neoconservative assumption that all Iraqis but Saddam and a few of his henchmen would welcome a U.S. invasion, that this would be like Eisenhower's liberation of France; and the transformationist assumption that new technologies had rendered large heavy ground forces irrelevant to the task at hand. On March 4, 2003, the chairman of the Joint Chiefs of Staff, Gen. Richard B. Myers, said the goal was a "short conflict" that would be "much, much, much different" from the forty-three-day war in 1991 (which included only one hundred hours of ground combat). Three days before the first U.S. strikes, Vice President Cheney said that regular Iraqi forces might not put up a fight and that "significant elements of the Republican Guard . . . are likely to step aside."[23]

Consistent with this judgment was a planning assumption that Iraq would be a relatively benign environment for U.S. forces. What with almost all Iraqis expected to welcome liberation, armed resistance would be restricted, as it was in the war of 1991, to uniformed military forces. The prospect of resistance by irregular Iraqi units operating in coalition rear areas in civilian dress and using guerrilla and terrorist tactics, including suicide bombings, to harass coalition supply lines and cow potentially rebellious cities was not taken seriously. Nor was the prospect of protracted Iraqi irregular warfare after the termination of major U.S. conventional military operations. Indeed, it is not clear that planners undertook any systematic assessment of lessons that the Iraqis themselves might have drawn from their defeat in 1991.

The initial fulcrum of the war-plan dispute was what Gen. Tommy Franks, head of the U.S. Central Command, termed, in a postwar interview with Knight Ridder correspondent Joseph L. Galloway, "the off-the-shelf plan that had been put together over the course of the 10–11 years post-Desert Storm by one Cent[ral] Com[mand] commander after another."[24] That plan essentially called for a repeat of Desert Storm within post–Cold War force constraints: a massive force buildup followed by an air campaign followed by a ground invasion. Secretary Rumsfeld and his transformationist colleagues, inspired by success in Afghanistan, rejected the plan out of hand; they put enormous store in precision bombing, wanted an early war with Iraq, and initially argued for a force of 50,000 to 75,000 ground troops rich in light, special operations forces.[25] This force would launch a lightning drive from Kuwait to Baghdad, its corridors of advance paved by relentless aerial bombing of any Iraqi forces that managed to get in the way.

Within what Franks called the "bookends" of these heavy and light plans an often acrimonious argument was joined. Senior military leaders, especially army and Marine Corps commanders, favored delay and a much larger and heavier ground force, on the order of 250,000, organized around at least three—and preferably four—armored and mechanized infantry divisions. They were enthusiastic neither for war with Iraq nor for the gamble that Secretary Rumsfeld's proposed force represented. The army in particular despised the Afghan model because it suggested that airpower, more specifically, the air force, could provide a substitute for much of the army's organic fire support, including its heavy artillery and attack helicopters;

this was anathema to a service that harbored a historic distrust of air force–provided close air support.

Army and Marine Corps leaders also believed the U.S. military was already thinly stretched across residual and threatened Cold War commitments in Asia and new war-on-terrorism commitments in Afghanistan and elsewhere, and they understood that a regime-change war against Iraq would impose upon U.S. ground forces, especially the army, potentially open-ended and taxing postwar occupation responsibilities. They also took a much less casual view of the Iraqis' willingness to resist; they understood that Operation Iraqi Freedom, unlike Desert Storm, posed an existential threat to the Iraqi regime. Indeed, in August 2002, Marine Corps commandant James L. Jones used an interview with the conservative *Washington Times* to publicly attack the "cakewalk" optimists. "Afghanistan was Afghanistan. Iraq is Iraq. It would be foolish, if you were ever committed to going into Iraq, to think that the principles that were successful in Afghanistan would necessarily be successful in Iraq," Jones said. He predicted that defeating Iraq would be "hard stuff," and cautioned against primary reliance on light ground forces. "You'd better have Plan B in your hip pocket, because when you attack someone . . . on their homeland they are going to fight differently than if they engage you, say, in Kuwait. The defense of the homeland is hard stuff because they are not going anywhere."[26]

In the end, a compromise was struck. According to one authoritative account:

> As Rumsfeld and his circle argued from one bookend, Franks slowly worked his way down from the other . . . until a compromise suggested itself: the war would start with a force of a hundred thousand or less, but deployment orders would be given to a much larger force, which could be fed into the battlefield as needed, through an open "pipeline."
>
> It was an elegant solution. Rumsfeld's model would be given a chance to work, and if that failed the war would be won the Army way, with overwhelming ground force. "If the cost begins to approach a gamble," Franks says, "then you put in the pipeline forces, which guarantee success in the event you've miscalculated with the start force." As it turned out, diplomatic developments so delayed the start of the war that by the time it began Franks had more than ninety thousand [troops] and more than a hundred thousand pipeline [troops] in the area.[27]

The plan discarded not only a massive force buildup but also sequential air and ground campaigns. CENTCOM did not want to give Saddam time to destroy Iraq's oil wells, and the "rolling start" permitted an attack before waiting for all the forces to show up. This may have completely fooled the Iraqis. "The impression we have from talking to some Iraqi officers . . . is that some were expecting a Desert Storm–type campaign preceded by a long period of aerial bombardment," commented Lt. Gen. William Wallace, the Army Fifth Corps commander, after the war. "[I]nstead we actually started the ground war before we started the air war [and] I have to believe it surprised some Iraqi military officers who found themselves confronting U.S. tanks very early in the war."[28]

But the army did not get its way on heavy ground forces. When the war began, only one heavy army division—the 3d Mechanized Infantry Division—entered the fight. The 4th Mechanized Infantry Division was marooned at sea by Turkey's refusal to permit the United States to open a second front in northern Iraq. Secretary Rumsfeld had also, in November 2002, slashed CENTCOM's request for pipeline forces, specifically the heavy 1st Cavalry and 1st Armored Divisions.[29] According to a retired senior general who followed the evolution of the war plan, "The secretary of defense cut off the flow of [the 1st Cavalry and 1st Armored] divisions, saying this thing would be over in two days."[30] (The 1st Armored was later reinstated.)

These two divisions, along with the 3d Mechanized, would have given Franks three rather than the one army heavy division he had available when the war began. This left Franks with a scarcity of not just heavy forces but also ground forces in general. General Wallace, Fifth Corps commander, struck out for Baghdad via Iraq's southern oil fields (the securing of which was a preliminary objective) with only three U.S. divisions: the 3d Mechanized, the 101st Air Assault Division, and the 1st Marine Expeditionary Force. (A British division was assigned the task of securing Basra.) It was a force without an armored reserve and simply too small to perform the following tasks: (1) dash three hundred miles to and into the heavily defended capital of a country twenty-five times the size of Kuwait, which in 1991 had been liberated by coalition forces double the size of those in 2003; (2) secure its rear area from Iraqi paramilitary harassment—a mission, admittedly, not anticipated; and (3) transition quickly and effectively into a postwar stabilization force.[31] "In my judgment, there should have been a minimum of two heavy divisions and an armored cavalry regiment on the ground—that's how our doctrine reads," commented retired army general Barry McCaffrey, who commanded the 24th Mechanized Infantry during the 1991 Gulf War. Retired army major general William C. Nash agreed: "The stability of the liberated areas is clearly an issue," he said. "The postwar transition has to begin immediately in the wake of attacking forces, and they seem to be short for those important missions at this time."[32]

The military analyst William Arkin summed up the Rumsfeld war plan: "From the start, the Pentagon favored an unconventional war plan.

This plan assumed that a precision air campaign of 'shock' and 'awe,' aided by special operations and psychological warfare, would shake the regime out of power, provoking a near-bloodless unraveling of Baath rule and thus averting the need for warfare in Baghdad and for massive destruction in the nation's heartland." For McCaffrey, "Their assumptions were wrong." They believed that "the nature of warfare has fundamentally changed, that numbers don't count, that armor and artillery don't count. They went into battle with a plan that put a huge air and sea force into action with an unbalanced ground combat force."[33]

JCS chairman Myers struck back, calling the retired generals' criticisms "bogus," and "absolutely wrong, they bear no resemblance to the truth." He went on to declare that "[the critics] either weren't [in on the planning], or they don't know, or they're working another agenda. It's not helpful to have those kind of comments come out when we've got troops in combat." After the war, General Franks responded to critics who said the invasion force was too small: "I will simply say that in this particular circumstance the force that entered Iraq—had it not had the 4th ID, the 1st Armored Division, an Armored Cav Regiment en route to and beginning to download its equipment in Kuwait—this would have been a gamble. But the fact [that] the force that entered Iraq was the lead element of additional substantial combat power, the pieces of which were already beginning to unload in Kuwait, took the gamble out of the equation and placed the level at what I call prudent risk."[34]

The ratio of force to space was nonetheless daunting as coalition forces approached the outskirts of Baghdad. As former CENTCOM commander Joseph P. Hoar pointed out, CENTCOM in the 1991 war had seven-plus army divisions, two Marine Corps divisions, one British division, one French division, and sizable Arab forces "to liberate Kuwait, a country about the size of New Jersey." In contrast, Operation Iraqi Freedom set out with fewer than five divisions (three U.S., one British, and two separate U.S. brigades) "to conquer a country the size of California."[35]

Scarcity of force was also a factor in the coalition's inability to suppress the outbreak of public disorder that followed the fall of Baghdad. There were simply not enough coalition troops on the ground to halt the massive looting of countless stores and shops, presidential palaces and other public buildings, including hospitals and museums, and, ominously, small arms factories and storage sites. Some estimates concluded that the looting caused more damage and loss of wealth than that inflicted by the coalition during the war.[36] Astoundingly, coalition forces failed to secure the 120-acre Tuwaitha Nuclear Research Center before it was sacked by looters; the center was believed to have contained almost two tons of partially enriched uranium, according to prewar reports by International Atomic Energy Agency (IAEA) inspectors.[37] About the only thing coalition forces firmly secured at the outset were Iraq's oil wells and supporting oil industry infrastructure, which predictably validated, in the minds of many Iraqis and other Arabs, that the real purpose of the U.S. invasion of Iraq was to steal Iraq's oil. Subsequently, many key nodes of that infrastructure were sabotaged by regime remnants and other forces hostile to the U.S. occupation and reconstruction.

Apparently neither the Bush administration nor the U.S. Central Command anticipated the depth of the power vacuum created by its regime change in Iraq, a curious oversight given the administration's correct portrayal of Saddam's Iraq as a totalitarian state. Totalitarian states are defined by an absence of civil society and an intolerance of the slightest dissent by individuals. Like Stalin, Saddam completely atomized Iraqi society, slaughtering real and imagined enemies. The destruction of such regimes by an external invader will create a vacuum of power unless the invader moves in with overwhelming force, as the United States did in 1945 in Japan, which it swiftly secured with a twenty-three-division force of five hundred thousand troops.[38] Overwhelming force may no longer be necessary to defeat U.S. adversaries, but there is no substitute for it when it comes to filling political vacuums. "Our problem in postwar Iraq has been a paucity of force, rather than an excess," complained neoconservative war hawk Charles Krauthammer. "The way to succeed is with an occupation 'heavy.'. . . Occupation light has permitted the ad hoc seizure of power in pockets of the country by various ambitious nasties."[39]

The dispute over force size was very much an extension of the prewar argument within the Pentagon over the future size and structure of U.S. armed forces, especially the army, which, of all the services, encountered the greatest difficulties in adapting to the post–Cold War strategic environment.[40] The principal antagonists were the army, six of whose ten active duty divisions were heavy, and Secretary of Defense Rumsfeld and his transformationist supporters. The army and its backers, including retired generals free to speak in public for those inside the army who could not, saw in the apparent difficulties Operation Iraqi Freedom was encountering in its second week proof that arguments for a larger and heavier ground force had been right, and by extension, proof that the transformationist argument that the combination of smaller, lighter ground forces and precision-strike airpower could now substitute for heavy ground forces had been wrong. Yet the collapse of major Iraqi resistance just two weeks later, before the 4th Mechanized Infantry Division arrived on the scene, seemed to vindicate the transformationists. The regime had been taken down in four weeks with only one heavy army division in the field, and the regime's major military bulwark, the Republican Guard, had been wiped out or frightened into desertion largely by Special Operations Forces–directed airpower. It was not only a catastrophic defeat for Saddam Hussein but also a crushing policy defeat for those, especially senior army officers, who still clung to the quantitative interpretation of the Powell doctrine's insistence on overwhelming force.

But was the Iraqi enemy a fair test of the argument? Its military performance, or more accurately, nonperformance, and the as-yet-unknown reasons for it raise questions about Operation Iraqi Freedom's utility as a generator of meaningful lessons for future conflict. John Keegan titled an April 2003 article "Saddam's Utter Collapse Shows This Has Not Been a Real War." The only serious resistance offered was by "the Ba'ath Party militia, effectively a sort of political Mafia equipped with nothing more effective than hand-held weapons."[41] Undoubtedly, many of those who fought to overthrow Saddam Hussein's regime take issue with Keegan's characterization of the war.

But the war's extreme one-sidedness deserves examination. Aside from the coalition's qualitative supremacy, exceptional knowledge of Iraqi regime targets and force dispositions, free run of Iraqi air space, and so on, did Saddam play into American hands by convincing himself that war could be avoided, or that even if not, his regime could somehow survive it? What might have led him to reach such fantastic conclusions? The evident divisions within the Bush administration on Iraqi policy? The bitterly divisive UN debate that left the United States isolated from key allies? Turkey's surprise refusal to permit the United States to open a northern front against Iraq? Disbelief that the coalition would attempt to conquer Iraq with only four-plus divisions? Confidence that Iraqi irregular forces could disrupt coalition supply lines and inflict unacceptable casualties? Belief that the Iraqi people, however repressed, would rise against a foreign invader? The delusions of personality cultism?

Postwar testimony of former Iraqi officers and a bodyguard of Saddam Hussein's older son, Uday, portrays the Iraqi dictator as initially confident that his forces could halt the U.S. forces on the approaches to Baghdad and that the U.S. advance would in any event halt before entering Baghdad for fear of being entrapped in bloody urban combat. As in 1991 Saddam apparently believed that his forces were in a position to inflict politically unacceptable casualties upon the Americans. He appeared woefully unaware of the low state of his own forces' morale and war-fighting skills and was oblivious to the paralyzing effects of a politically balkanized Iraqi military establishment on its capacity to offer coordinated resistance to an enemy that had transformed joint military operations into an art form. Saddam was dumbstruck at the rapidity and completeness with which his forces collapsed and therefore decided to fall back on guerrilla warfare only after Baghdad fell. That option was never previously considered because Saddam was confident it would not be necessary.[42]

An alternative explanation rests on inference from Saddam's apparent survival and growing attacks on U.S. occupation forces in Baghdad and the Sunni heartland north and west of Baghdad. Perhaps Saddam at some point before the launching of Operation Iraqi Freedom concluded that a U.S. invasion was inevitable and that it would be militarily irresistible, resulting in an American occupation of Baghdad and much of the rest of Iraq. He may have hoped or even believed that regular Iraqi forces would put up more effective resistance than they did, but he had the experience of the Gulf War behind him and he could not have ignored the fact that Iraq's conventional military forces were much weaker than in 1990. The combination of probable catastrophic conventional military defeat and an iron determination to survive as a political force in postwar Iraq could have propelled Saddam into selecting a fallback guerrilla warfare strategy implemented by surviving die-hard Ba'athist cadre and militia forces and aimed at exhausting U.S. will to stay the political and military course in Iraq. The option of protracted irregular warfare against U.S. occupation forces had been presaged in paramilitary Saddam Fedayeen attacks on exposed U.S. rear areas during Operation Iraqi Freedom and had encouraging historical precedent in Lebanon and Somalia, where local irregulars imposed politically unacceptable blood costs on U.S. forces. Irregular warfare has long been the choice of the militarily weak, and Saddam Hussein is known to have admired the performance of America's enemies in Vietnam, Lebanon, and Somalia.

Growing evidence suggests that regime elements seeking to sabotage reconstruction orchestrated much of the looting and disorder that engulfed Baghdad following the entry of U.S. forces as well as subsequent attacks on U.S. forces in the capital and in the Sunni heartland north and west of Baghdad.[43] Five weeks after the termination of major operations against Iraqi conventional forces, the U.S. military commander in Iraq, army lieutenant general David McKiernan, declared that surviving Ba'athist Party remnants are "committed to a long fight that will complicate the mission of the coalition," and that until "these people are destroyed or captured, the security environment will remain problematic."[44]

None of this is to underplay the extraordinary determination, skill, and flexibility displayed by coalition forces in so quickly conquering so large a country with so little force on the ground relative to past blitzkriegs. Operation Iraqi Freedom was a dazzling military performance high-lighted by at least two very courageous decisions: to proceed with Operation Iraqi Freedom even without the expected benefit of the 4th Infantry Division opening a second front in northern Iraq, and to push on to Baghdad even in the face of irregular Iraqi attacks on exposed coalition lines of communication. A more operationally "prudent" White House and Central Command would not have left the 4th Infantry Division off the table and would have awaited reinforcements before approaching Baghdad.

But military performances are conducted for political purposes. How does Operation Iraqi Freedom rate in terms of its accomplishment of its declared and undeclared war aims?

Of Secretary of Defense Rumsfeld's declared eight specific war aims (see chap. 5), the first was to "end the regime of Saddam Hussein by striking with force on a scope and scale that makes clear to the Iraqis that he and his regime are finished." Though arguably the initial "shock and awe" strikes failed to immediately convince enough Iraqis that the game was up—major coalition military operations continued for another three weeks—this point is moot given the regime's subsequent disintegration. Though the regime fell, however, its embodiment, Saddam Hussein, appears to have survived Operation Iraqi Freedom and is reportedly orchestrating Iraqi resistance to the U.S. occupation. If so, the victory is tarnished in the same way that the U.S. victory in Afghanistan was tarnished by the apparent survival of Osama bin Laden and Taliban leader Mullah Omar. As had his father before him, Pres. George W. Bush personalized the struggle with Saddam Hussein, and once war began he authorized air and missile strikes designed to kill him. It does not suffice to say that Saddam no longer matters; he *was* the regime that occasioned America's second war against Iraq, and if he is still alive and operating against U.S. interests in Iraq, he is not only a political embarrassment for the Bush White House but also an advertisement of the limits of U.S. military power in eradicating the "man" in one-man regimes.

Saddam's apparent survival along with other regime remnants greatly complicates the U.S. role in Iraq. The mere suspicion that he and large numbers of his henchmen are still around intimidates many Iraqis from cooperating with U.S. occupation forces for fear of being targeted for revenge killing later on. Additionally, regime remnant–sponsored irregular attacks on those forces undermine the establishment of the security necessary for Iraq's reconstruction and could undermine, via a steady flow of military body bags back to the United States, U.S. public and congressional support for staying the political reconstruction course in Iraq. Continued regime resistance has also motivated others hostile to the American presence in Iraq, including al-Qaeda and al-Qaeda-inspired terrorists for whom that presence offers enticing targets for suicide bombings. By November 2003 the U.S. presence in Iraq was clearly serving as a magnet for Islamists from all over the world in much the same way that the Soviet invasion of Afghanistan had attracted into that country the likes of Osama bin Laden and other "Afghan Arab" jihadists.[45]

Rumsfeld's second declared objective was to eliminate Iraq's illegal weapons of mass destruction, which Secretary of State Powell in his February 5, 2003, presentation to the United Nations, said included up to 25,000 liters of anthrax and 400 associated bombs, 18 mobile biological weapons manufacturing facilities, 550 artillery shells with mustard gas, 30,000 empty munitions and enough precursors to stockpile as much as 500 tons of chemical agents, and several dozen Scud variant ballistic missiles.[46] The suspected presence of these weapons in Iraq and fear of a reconstituted Iraqi nuclear weapons program constituted the core public rationale for preventive war against Iraq and the centerpiece of the American argument for UN support.

Indeed, the prewar threat, especially that of a Saddam Hussein armed with nuclear weapons, was couched by the administration in urgent and near-apocalyptic terms. Consider the following statements from early August 2002 to mid-March 2003: "It is the judgment of many of us that in the not-too-distant future, [Saddam] will acquire nuclear weapons, and a nuclear-armed Saddam Hussein is not a pleasant prospect for anyone in the region or for anyone in the world for that matter" (Vice President Cheney, August 7, 2002, Commonwealth Club of California). "We know that Saddam has resumed his efforts to acquire nuclear weapons. . . . Many of us are convinced that Saddam Hussein will acquire nuclear weapons fairly soon" (Vice President Cheney, August 26, 2002, National Convention of the Veterans of Foreign Wars). "We do know that there have been shipments going . . . into Iraq . . . of aluminum tubes . . . that are only really suited for nuclear weapons programs" (National Security Adviser Condoleezza Rice, September 8, 2002, on CNN). "Iraq retains physical infrastructure needed to build a nuclear weapon. . . . Should Iraq acquire fissile material, it would be able to build a nuclear weapon within a year" (Pres. George W. Bush, September 12, 2002, speech before the United Nations). "Very likely all they need to complete a [nuclear] weapon is fissile material—and they are, at this moment, seeking that material—both from foreign sources and the capability to produce it indigenously" (Secretary of Defense Donald Rumsfeld, September 19, 2002, before the Senate Armed Services Committee). "The evidence indicates that Iraq is reconstituting its nuclear weapons program. Saddam Hussein has held numerous meetings with Iraqi nuclear scientists, a group he calls his 'nuclear mujaheddin,' his nuclear holy warriors" (President Bush, October 7, 2002, speech in Cincinnati). "We know [Saddam Hussein] has been absolutely devoted to trying to acquire nuclear weapons. And we believe he has, in fact, reconstituted nuclear weapons" (Vice President Cheney, March 16, 2003, on NBC).[47]

In his Cincinnati speech, President Bush declared:

> If the Iraqi regime is able to produce, buy, or steal an amount of highly enriched uranium a little larger than a single softball, it could have a nuclear weapon in less than a year. And if we allow that to happen, a terrible line would be crossed. Saddam Hussein would be in a position to blackmail anyone who opposes his aggression. He would be in a position to dominate the Middle East. He would be in a position to threaten America. And Saddam would be in a position to pass nuclear technology to terrorists. . . . Knowing these realities, America must not ignore the threat gathering against us. Facing clear evidence of peril, we cannot wait for the final proof—the smoking gun—that could come in the form of a mushroom cloud.[48]

It was therefore nothing short of astounding that U.S. forces and postwar WMD-hunter teams found exactly what the UN inspection teams before them had found: nothing. Contrary to the prewar expectations of U.S. planners, WMD were not employed against coalition forces or even deployed among Iraqi forces.[49] Not even traces of chemical or biological warfare agents were discovered. Nor was there any evidence of a reconstituted Iraqi nuclear weapons program. Coalition forces found what UN inspectors had found before the war: not a reconstituted nuclear program but rather a program in complete disarray. According to the report of Mohamed El Baradei, head of the International Atomic Energy Agency, to the UN Security Council, the IAEA "observed a substantial degradation in facilities, financial resources and programs throughout Iraq that might support a nuclear infrastructure. The former cadre of nuclear experts was being increasingly dispersed and many key figures were reaching retirement or had left the country." In the critical areas of uranium acquisition and concentration and centrifuge enrichment, "extensive field investigation and document analysis revealed no evidence that Iraq had resumed such activities." ElBaradei's summary of the UN inspectors' finding was hardly the threat of a mushroom cloud: "No indication of post-1991 [nuclear] weaponization activities was uncovered in Iraq."[50] No evidence of Iraqi work on nuclear weapons for *twelve years* preceding the second U.S. war against Iraq!

What happened to that reconstituted nuclear program and that terrifying chemical and biological arsenal depicted by the administration?

The evidence suggests that Saddam Hussein got rid of his WMD before—perhaps years before—the war.[51] He may have determined at some point that war was inevitable and that he was going to lose it whether he used WMD or not, so why not take action that would belie the Bush administration's most vocal rationale for war? There are even suggestions that Saddam, sometime before 1995, may have ordered all such weapons destroyed but not the plans and expertise to make them in order to ensure no discoveries by the old UNSCOM inspection regime.[52] In either case, if true, Saddam feared detection more than he valued possession of usable WMD.

Alternatively, Saddam may not have believed an American attack was inevitable and accordingly ditched his WMD years before the Bush administration took office while continuing to behave as if he had them for purposes of deterrence. Under this scenario, which is supported by the postwar testimony of Iraqi scientists to American officials, Saddam believed the United States would not go to war absent UN authorization and in the face of strong opposition within NATO.[53] Since international opposition to a U.S. preventive war on Iraq rested in the first instance on skepticism about U.S. claims of a robust Iraqi WMD threat, Saddam had every incentive to make sure that no WMD were ever uncovered by UN or other international inspectors. Physical validation of U.S. claims would undercut UN and allied opposition to war and therefore restraint on U.S. unilateral action. It was clearly in Saddam's interest to maximize the Bush administration's international political isolation. Yet it was also in his interest to behave as if he had something to hide, even when he did not because continuing U.S. suspicion of successfully secreted WMD could reinforce deterrence of an American attack via the possibility of their use. Moreover, "Saddam was too proud to concede that he no longer possessed WMD," surmises Bob Drogin. "To admit this point would have meant bowing to the West. He would have appeared weak, and weakness would have threatened his hold on power at home and his vainglorious self-image as a leader of the Arab world."[54]

Yet another explanation is offered by Rolf Ekeus, who headed the UN inspection effort in Iraq from 1991 to 1997. Ekeus believes that Iraq's acquisition and use of WMD and their associated missile delivery systems were motivated by "its structural enmity and rivalry with Iran." In his view, the Iraqi leadership had no confidence in their utility against highly mobile, well-trained, and well-equipped U.S. forces, and in any event soon discovered how rapidly chemical warfare agents, especially nerve agents, deteriorated in warheads and storage drums. Accordingly, Iraqi policy after 1991 was "to halt all production of warfare agents and to focus on design and engineering, with the purpose of activating production and shipping of warfare agents and munitions directly to the battlefield in the event of war." Thus, the real WMD threat was not stored or deployed systems, which did not exist, but rather "the combination of researchers, know-how, precursors, batch production techniques and testing."[55]

All this speculation still begs the question of why the Bush administration was not aware of the nonexistent Iraqi WMD threat. Was there, as former CIA director John M. Deutch called it, "an intelligence failure . . . of massive proportions"? If so, what does that say about the state of our intelligence community? "If the intelligence on a question so fundamental was completely wrong, the conclusion that follows is that administration policy-makers simply do not have the information they need. If true, that's a disaster waiting to happen," argues Tod Lindberg. "It was not a disaster in this instance because of the humanitarian and larger strategic case for removing Saddam" and because of "the relative ease of the military victory and its relatively low cost."[56]

Skeptics do not believe there was an intelligence failure. They suspect that the Bush administration knew how weak Iraq was—that its conventional forces were crippled and its WMD unusable, even nonexistent—and that the administration deliberately "exaggerated the Iraqi threat and hyped the sense of urgency because it wanted Saddam Hussein deposed for other reasons."[57] This conclusion would be consistent with the remarkable tardiness with which U.S. forces secured at least seven known Iraqi nuclear sites, all of which were reportedly looted or burned by the time those forces arrived.[58] An invasion of Iraq could not be sold simply on the basis of liberating an oppressed people; it had to be sold as a response to a WMD threat—Saddam's imminent acquisition of nuclear weapons capacity and the prospect of Saddam's transfer of other WMD to al-Qaeda. Pres. George H. W. Bush had the same problem with the Gulf War; public and congressional opinion was lukewarm about liberating Kuwait until the administration convinced most of the country of a possible Iraqi nuclear threat.

The evidence suggests that on the two critical issues of Iraq's postulated reconstituted nuclear weapons program and the relationship between the Saddam Hussein regime and al-Qaeda, key administration officials selectively picked intelligence reports that supported the administration's determination to go to war, treating the worst-case scenario as fact, ignoring contrary evidence, and refusing to discard suspect information.[59] The picture the administration painted of the threat was known by many experts to be at variance with the available evidence. One postwar assessment notes that even though the CIA had collected almost no new information on Iraq's WMD activities after Saddam Hussein had expelled UN inspectors in 1998, within the administration "a pattern [emerged] in which President Bush, Vice President Cheney and their subordinates—in public and behind the scenes—made allegations depicting Iraq's nuclear weapons program as more active, more certain and more imminent in its threat than the data they had would support."[60]

According to another detailed account of its handling of intelligence data, "the Bush administration culled from U.S. intelligence those assessments that supported its position and omitted those that did not. The administration ignored, and even suppressed, disagreement within the intelligence agencies and pressured the CIA to reaffirm [the administration's] preferred version of the Iraqi threat. Similarly, it stonewalled, and sought to discredit, international weapons inspectors when their findings threatened to undermine the case for war."[61] This judgment is echoed by two experts on Iraqi WMD, both of them proponents of Operation Iraqi Freedom: Kenneth Pollack, who believes that "it's pretty clear that different administration officials overstated their case," and former chief UN weapons inspector Richard Butler, who believes that "[c]learly a decision [was] made to pump up the case against Iraq." Former CIA director Stansfield Turner believes that "[t]here is no question [that policymakers] distorted the situation, either because they had bad intelligence or because they misinterpreted it." In an interview published in June 2003, Paul Wolfowitz told *Vanity Fair*'s Sam Tanenhaus that Saddam's supposed stash of WMD was not the most compelling reason for war, but that for "bureaucratic reasons we settled on one issue, weapons of mass destruction, because it was the one reason everyone could agree on." At least as important was enabling a U.S. military evacuation of Saudi Arabia—a major al-Qaeda grievance against the Saudi regime: "Just lifting that burden from the Saudis is itself going to open the door" to a more peaceful Middle East.[62]

Secretary of Defense Rumsfeld, in congressional testimony after the war, conceded that the "coalition did not act in Iraq because we had discovered dramatic new evidence of Iraq's pursuit of weapons of mass destruction. We acted because we saw the existing evidence in a new light through the prism of our experience on 9/11."[63] This is a truly startling admission. It supports the twin conclusions that the decision for preventive war was based on threat possibilities, not probabilities, and that 9/11 inevitably propelled the George W. Bush administration toward war with Iraq even though there was no connection between the two.

Military action is far easier to justify against a threat perceived to be imminent as opposed to one seen to be years away. Clearly, Iraq in March 2003 posed no imminent WMD threat to the United States or its friends and allies in the region. Its nuclear weapons program had never recovered from the 1991 war and subsequent UN inspection regimes, and it neither deployed nor transferred usable chemical or biological weapons. Its conventional forces could not even defend Iraqi territory much less invade Iraq's neighbors. Deterrence was working when the United States struck. There may have been other compelling reasons for attacking Iraq, but an imminent military threat was not one of them.

Administration hawks "understood that to get the American people on their side they had to needed to come up with something more to say than 'We've liberated Iraq and got rid of a tyrant,'" said former senator Bob Kerry, himself a hawk who served on the Senate Intelligence Committee. "So they had to find some ties to weapons of mass destruction and were willing to allow a majority of Americans to incorrectly conclude that the invasion of Iraq had something to do with the World Trade Center [attacks]."[64]

A willingness to launch a preemptive attack or preventive war presumes accurate intelligence on the enemy's capabilities and intentions. To be more specific, sound intelligence is the foundation of the Bush doctrine. The doctrine is unsustainable without it.[65] Indeed, if the U.S. intelligence community mistakenly postulated a grave WMD threat that in fact did not exist, what possible confidence could the Bush administration or any other have in its ability to accurately assess the intentions and capabilities of other potential target states of the Bush doctrine? The 9/11 attacks certainly did not enhance the prestige of the intelligence community (which had also been caught flat-footed by the Soviet Union's demise), nor did the Bush administration's opposition to any independent inquiry on the community's failure to detect the attacks. As George F. Will has observed, "the failure—so far—to find, or explain the absence of, weapons of mass destruction that were the necessary and sufficient justification for preemptive war" places the "doctrine of preemption—the core of the president's foreign policy . . . in jeopardy."[66]

This combination of poor intelligence and deliberate threat inflation best explains the scope of the gap between the postulated and actual Iraqi WMD threat. In fairness, the Bush administration is hardly the first to hype an external threat in order to mobilize public and congressional support for a war of choice—and if ever there was a war of choice it was the U.S. decision to attack Iraq in March 2003. The Johnson administration in 1965 portrayed the Communists in Vietnam as a mortal territorial threat to all of Southeast Asia and a no less deadly menace to the survival of the U.S. global alliance system. The Reagan administration postulated threatened vital U.S. interests in Lebanon and Grenada.

But deliberate threat exaggeration has penalties, not the least of which is diminished credibility at home and abroad. A discredited cry of wolf over the Iraqi WMD threat automatically undermines the credibility of postulated dire threats posed by North Korea, Iran, and other rogue states seeking WMD. Deliberate threat inflation also raises the question of motive. Was the postulation of a grave and imminent Iraqi threat simply a pretext for an invasion launched for other objectives? Former president Jimmy Carter, in a September 2002 editorial, warned of "a core group of conservatives who are trying to realize long-pent-up ambitions under the cover of the proclaimed war on terrorism." He went on to declare that "there is no current danger to the United States from Baghdad," pointing out that in the face of "intense monitoring and overwhelming American superiority, any belligerent move by Saddam Hussein against a neighbor, even the smallest nuclear test (necessary before weapons construction), a tangible threat to use a weapon of mass destruction, or sharing this technology with terrorist organizations would be suicidal."[67] Clearly, neoconservative opinion within the Bush administration saw opportunities in Iraq that stretched far beyond simply disarming the Saddam Hussein regime. A U.S. agenda limited simply to halting Iraq's acquisition of nuclear weapons could have been satisfied by an extension of the revived UN inspection regime that the threat of war compelled Saddam to accept in 2002. But President Bush in his American Enterprise Institute speech of February 2003 embraced not just disarmament and regime change in Iraq but also the political transformation of the Middle East. It was no less apparent that key administration policymakers saw a politically reconstructed Iraq as offering a substitute for Saudi Arabia and America's primary regional surrogate.

Rumsfeld's third, fourth, and fifth war objectives were to capture or drive out terrorists from Iraq, collect intelligence related to terrorist networks in Iraq and beyond, and collect intelligence on the global network of illicit WMD activity. Unquestionably the archives of Saddam Hussein's multiple security services will yield a vast amount of information on the regime's internal workings, its relationship to terrorist organizations, and its international trafficking for the purposes of acquiring chemical, biological, and—above all—nuclear munitions and their associated means of delivery. Of particular interest will be the regime's relationship to al-Qaeda and the status of its efforts, if any, to reconstitute its nuclear weapons program. The U.S. invasion and occupation of Iraq automatically achieved the goal of enabling collection of new intelligence on the regime and its activities.

The same cannot be said, however, for the goal of capturing or driving out terrorists from Iraq. On the contrary, the establishment of a large American military presence in Iraq has attracted Islamist terrorists *into* Iraq. U.S. occupation forces provide American military targets greater in numbers and vulnerability than can be found anywhere else in the Muslim world. Foreign Islamist terrorists are known to have entered Iraq during Operation Iraqi Freedom for the express purpose of killing U.S. troops (they launched several suicide attacks), and there is evidence of the postwar formation of a working alliance between surviving regime elements and Islamists dedicated to a campaign of terror against American forces.[68] Once bitter enemies, secular Saddam loyalists and antisecular Islamists may have been driven into collaboration against a common enemy. Terrorism expert Jessica Stern warned in August 2003 that the bombing of the United Nations headquarters in Baghdad was "the latest evidence that America has taken a country that was not a terrorist threat and turned it into one." Vincent Cannistraro, former CIA director of counterterrorism operations and analysis, agrees: "There was no substantive intelligence information linking Saddam to international terrorism. Now we've created the conditions that have made Iraq the place to come to attack Americans."[69]

Rumsfeld's sixth goal was to lift sanctions and deliver humanitarian relief supplies. Though UN sanctions were formally lifted within weeks of Baghdad's liberation, humanitarian relief operations were impeded from the start, initially by the collapse of civil order in much of Iraq and subsequently by persistent and growing regime remnant–sponsored attacks on U.S. occupation forces and on economic infrastructure targets essential to the restoration of basic utilities in Iraq. Ten weeks after Baghdad's liberation, Andrew Natsios, director of the U.S. Agency for International Development (USAID), commented, "we can't do our work unless there's security."[70] Security concerns compelled some nongovernmental relief organizations to abandon operations in Iraq. In late May 2003 CARE, World Vision, and the International Rescue Committee elected not to participate in a long-term initiative funded by USAID designed to foster civic participation and diminish tensions among Iraq's ethnic and religious groups; the organizations cited security concerns and excessive U.S. military oversight as reasons for their refusal.[71] Other relief organizations left Iraq as the security situation worsened in the summer, fall, and winter. Relief supplies sufficient to avert a humanitarian crisis were nonetheless delivered, and the situation steadily improved with each passing month.

Rumsfeld's seventh objective, to secure Iraq's oil fields and resources, was a major success of Operation Iraqi Freedom, notwithstanding the torching of a few oil wells. For reasons that remain unclear, the prewar fear that Saddam Hussein would incinerate Iraq's oil fields wholesale, as he had Kuwait's in 1991, never materialized. However, early hopes of quickly restoring Iraq's oil production to levels capable of contributing substantial revenues toward Iraq's reconstruction also failed to materialize. Iraq's oil infrastructure, crippled by the war of 1991 and thirteen years of international sanctions, was in an unexpectedly wretched state of disrepair, and repair efforts were severely hampered by sabotage.

Rumsfeld's last and most ambitious objective was to create in Iraq the conditions for a rapid transition to a representative self-government in Iraq that posed no threat to its neighbors and was committed to maintaining the country's territorial integrity. Such a government, at least in neoconservative opinion as reflected in neoconservative literature and in Pres. George W. Bush's February 26, 2003, American Enterprise Institute speech, would serve both as a stimulus to democratic revolution in the rest of the Arab world as well as a regional surrogate for Saudi Arabia.

What Iraq and the Middle East will look like a year, or five years, or ten years hence remains to be seen. As of November 2003, however, America's imperial enterprise in Iraq appeared decidedly inauspicious. The "victory" occasioned by completion of major U.S. combat operations against Iraq's fielded military forces was not followed by a cessation of hostilities but rather by persistent irregular warfare against U.S. forces. Moreover, it quickly became apparent that the Bush administration had paid far more attention to the planning and conduct of the war than to the planning and conduct of the "peace."

8

The "Peace"

"The primary problem at the core of American deficiencies in post-conflict capabilities, resources, and commitment is a national aversion to nation-building, which was strengthened by failure in Vietnam," concluded a widely read and insightful U.S. Army study on reconstructing Iraq published the month before Operation Iraqi Freedom was launched. "U.S. leaders need to accept this mission as an essential part of national security and better tailor and fund the military services and civilian governmental organizations to accomplish it."[1] The study went on to predict and warn:

> If the war is rapid with few civilian casualties, the occupation will probably be characterized by an initial honeymoon period during which the United States will reap the benefits of ridding the population of a brutal dictator. Nevertheless, most Iraqi and most other Arabs will probably assume that the United States intervened in Iraq for its own reasons and not to liberate the population. Long-term gratitude is unlikely and suspicion of U.S. motives will increase as the occupation continues. A force initially viewed as liberators can rapidly be relegated to the status of invaders should an unwelcome occupation continue for a prolonged time. Occupation problems may be especially acute if the United States must implement the bulk of the occupation itself rather than turn these duties over to a postwar international force. Regionally, the occupation will be viewed with great skepticism, which may be overcome by the population's rapid progress toward a secure and prosperous way of life.[2]

The study then listed 135 specific occupation and reconstruction tasks grouped into 21 categories to be conducted across 4 phases: an initial security phase, followed by a stabilization phase; then an institution-building phase, culminating in a handover to reconstituted Iraqi civil and military authority. The agenda reflected the most ambitious American nation-building attempt since the Vietnam War, which failed under relentless Communist military pressure and political subversion.

The transition to peace and nation-building in Iraq did not get off to a good start. With the cessation of major combat operations it quickly became clear that the administration had paid far more attention to planning the war than it had to planning the peace. According to one expert, "much more could have been done during and immediately after the war if the Coalition, and especially the US, had not seen conflict termination, peace-making, and nation-building as secondary missions, and if a number of senior US policymakers had not assumed the best case in terms of Iraqi reaction to the Coalition attack." One acid assessment postulated "the para-dox of American power at the start of the 21st century . . . [is] the superpower's staggering prowess at winning wars and its equally remark-able ineptitude at securing the peace. Twenty-one days of shock and awe . . . followed by 75 days in which American civilian administrators and hapless soldiers have stumbled and bumbled around like under-motivated keystone cops."[3]

As events unfolded, it quickly became clear that key Pentagon as-sumptions about postwar Iraq were wrong, as Deputy Secretary of De-fense Paul Wolfowitz conceded in July 2003.[4] Thomas L. Friedman suc-cinctly captured the difference between what the Office of the Secretary of Defense expected and what actually happened:

> The Bush Pentagon went into this war assuming that it could decapitate the Iraqi army, bureaucracy and police force, remove the Saddam loyal-ists and then basically run Iraq through the rump army, bureaucracy and police force. Wrong. What happened instead was that they all collapsed, leaving a security and administrative vacuum, which the U.S. military was utterly unprepared to fill. The U.S. forces arrived in Iraq with far too few military police and civilian affairs officers to run the country. As a result, the only way U.S. troops could stop the massive looting was by doing the only thing they knew how: shooting people. Since they didn't want to do that . . . Iraqi government infrastructure, oil equipment and even nuclear research sites were stripped bare. As a result, we are not starting at zero in Iraq. We are starting below zero.[5]

The Pentagon was counting on inheriting functioning government ministries and police forces as a precondition to a quick and smooth trans-fer of political authority to a group of Iraqi exiles clustered under the Iraqi National Congress (INC) headed by the Ahmad Chalabi. The Department of Defense airlifted Chalabi and other INC members into Iraq even before the cessation of major military operations. Wolfowitz had told journalist Trudy Rubin in November 2002 that the INC "would return to Baghdad and assume the reins of power, just as Gen. Charles DeGaulle and the Free French returned triumphantly to postwar France."[6] Subsequently, Gary Schmitt, executive director of the neoconservative Project for a New Ameri-can Century, conceded that the administration had "more of a liberation model in mind than occupation" and that there was some "wishful think-ing" about the size of the postwar force the Pentagon believed was needed in Iraq.[7] Continued Iraqi resistance certainly was not expected. As Wolfowitz subsequently admitted, "It was difficult to imagine before the war that the criminal gang of sadists and gangsters who have run Iraq for 35 years would continue fighting . . . what has been sometimes called a guerrilla war." Wolfowitz was also surprised that significant numbers of Iraqi military and police units had not quickly joined U.S. forces in rebuilding Iraq. No Iraqi units "of significant size," he said, defected to the Americans, and "the police turned out to require a massive overhaul."[8]

The Pentagon had in fact planned to withdraw most U.S. forces from Iraq by the fall of 2003. Anticipating a permissive security environment and major occupation force contributions from allies, it planned, within six months following cessation of major military operations, to cut U.S. force strength in Iraq to no more than 70,000 and possibly as little as 30,000.[9] But by mid-May 2003 the security situation in Baghdad compelled the Defense Department to suspend planned withdrawals, including the de-parture of the army's exhausted 3d Infantry Division, leaving in place a U.S. occupation force of about 150,000.[10] In July the Pentagon unveiled a plan that assumed a force presence in Iraq of 156,000 well into 2004; U.S. Army planners, to sustain that service's rotation base for Iraq, also increased most overseas deployments from six-month- to yearlong tours of duty and activated at least two National Guard brigades.[11] Clearly, unanticipated commitments in postwar Iraq had stretched the U.S. Army to the point where it had little in reserve for any other contingencies that might arise. Indeed, the U.S. Army appeared incapable of sustaining a commitment of sixteen of its thirty-three active duty combat brigades in Iraq absent a re-duction in commitments elsewhere or an expansion of its force structure. Ironically, in February 2003, when then army chief of staff general Eric K. Shinseki had warned Congress that, based on past experience in Bosnia and Kosovo, an occupation force for Iraq could number "several hundred thousand," he was hastily corrected by Wolfowitz, who declared: "It's hard to conceive that it would take more forces to provide stability in post-Saddam Iraq than it would to conduct the war itself and to secure the sur-render of Saddam's security forces and his army. Hard to imagine."[12]

The Pentagon's eagerness to leave Iraq reflected both professional military aversion to nation-building as well as concerns that a large and open-ended army force presence would stretch that service's cumulative overseas deployments to the breaking point. Yet those committed to ex-ploiting perceived political opportunities in Iraq and the Middle East af-forded by the war against Iraq seem not to have fully grasped the depth and potential policy consequences of the military's intense dislike of nation-building, a dislike that George W. Bush shared, at least until 9/11. Sen. Richard G. Lugar, the Republican chairman of the Senate Foreign Relations Committee, believes that Operation Iraqi Freedom delivered "a once-in-a-generation opportunity to change the political landscape of the Middle East" by converting Iraq into a democracy that in turn would serve as "a springboard to promote democratic reforms throughout the region and to end the pattern of autocracy and oppression that characterizes so many Arab governments." Lugar was flabbergasted at the Bush administration's lack of preparation for postwar challenges in Iraq. "Clearly, the administration's planning for the post-conflict phase in Iraq was inadequate," he wrote in May 2003. "[T]he Bush administration and Congress have not yet faced up to the true size of the task that lies ahead. . . . The administration should state clearly that we are engaged in 'nation-building.' . . . It's a complicated and uncertain business . . . not made any easier when some in the Pentagon talk about quick exit strategies or say dismissively that they don't do nation-building."[13]

A scarcity of force on the ground, fear of acting like an imperial occupier, inadequate planning, poor execution, bureaucratic infighting between the State and Defense Departments, and the prospect of occupation "fatigue" all combined to produce anarchy in Baghdad for almost two months after the collapse of Saddam's regime and to raise doubts concerning U.S. staying power in Iraq. Since order was *the* precondition for the accomplishment of all other occupation tasks, the failure to establish it in Baghdad and other parts of the country delayed implementation of such critical jobs as restoring electricity, providing potable water sources, and distributing humanitarian relief supplies. "What does it say about the situation when criminals can move freely about the city and humanitarian workers cannot?" asked a senior CARE staff member in Baghdad in May 2003.[14]

The combination of massive looting, arson, and other criminal activity was in the first instance a function of woefully insufficient numbers of "boots on the ground." A Pentagon leadership determined to prove that a relatively small ground combat force could conquer a country the size of Iraq seems not to have recognized that that same force would be inadequate to accomplish U.S. postwar objectives in Iraq. Only about 150,000 coalition troops were needed in Iraq to win the war, but more were required to secure the peace. Commented army lieutenant general David D. McKiernan, commander of U.S. ground forces in Iraq: "Imagine spreading 150,000 soldiers in the state of California and then ask yourself, 'Could you secure all of California, all the time, with 150,000 soldiers?' The answer is no."[15]

Troop shortages created not only a security vacuum but also a political vacuum into which self-proclaimed local authorities moved. This was especially the case in the Shiite-dominated southern half of Iraq, where clerics, some of them committed to theocratic rule, assumed local political and administrative authority.[16] The political vacuum also encouraged Iranian penetration of the Shiite community and permitted surviving regime loyalists in the Sunni "triangle" bounded by Baghdad, Fallujah, and Tikrit to mount a campaign of irregular warfare against U.S. occupation forces and reconstruction efforts. Not to be left out, Islamic jihadists, emboldened by visions of repeating for the United States in Iraq the humiliating defeat they had inflicted on the Soviet Union in Afghanistan, began infiltrating Iraq's porous borders and subsequently launching suicide bombing attacks on U.S. and other Western targets.

Nation-building in Iraq is an unavoidably high-risk, obstacle-laden enterprise for the United States, which is attempting to create in a fractious society not only an orderly government but also a politically revolutionary one in the form of a democracy in a country that has never known anything other than autocracy. The obstacles extend well beyond those identified in the U.S. Army study.[17]

The first obstacle is the unsuitability of U.S. combat forces now in Iraq as agents of civil pacification and nation-building. Those forces are designed for conventional warfare not for imperial policing operations and "winning the hearts and minds" of the local population. The army has always resisted such tasks, in part because of Vietnam War memories and in part because such tasks require specialized training and rules of engagement that are contrary to those necessary for the army's preferred and main mission. But the army is stuck with so-called operations other than war in Iraq because the United States has little in the way of cadre trained in civil-military operations and because the Bush administration is determined that the United States will run the show in Iraq even at the expense of excluding significant participation of countries and international institutions that are more experienced in such matters but that opposed the war on Iraq.[18] "Somewhere behind the combat forces should have been somebody in large numbers who were going to do public security," commented the peacekeeping expert William Durch of the Washington-based think tank the Stimson Center. "It's so elemental from looking at dozens of conflicts; you can't do anything without security." Lack of experience was certainly not the explanation. "Anyone familiar with NATO operations in Bosnia and Kosovo should have understood that we needed two armies for this invasion [of Iraq]," echoed Thomas L. Friedman. "The first was the fighting force that would kill Saddam's regime, and the second, following right behind it, a force of military police, civilian affairs officers, aid groups and public affairs teams to get our message across. The Pentagon prepared brilliantly for the first force, but not the second."[19]

A second obstacle is evident in the division within the administration, between the neoconservative intellectuals on the one hand and the politicians and military professionals on the other, over American purpose in Iraq. The former, who are called "democratic imperialists," have always regarded the destruction of Saddam Hussein as a means to a much more ambitious political end, whereas the latter, called "assertive nationalists," have focused primarily on removing Saddam and the postulated threat he posed to U.S. interests. The neoconservatives, who tend to take for granted public and congressional support for their ambitious global agenda, are committed to robust nation-building in Iraq and potentially elsewhere in the Middle East even at great cost in time, money, and military resources. In contrast, more pragmatic administration politicians and military professionals are more sensitive to cost and less optimistic about prospects for a U.S.–triggered democratic revolution in the Arab world. While the neoconservatives and pragmatists within the administration share a commitment to maintaining America's global military primacy, the neoconservatives believe that only democratic change in the world will provide lasting security for the United States, whereas pragmatists are more or less content with occasional military intervention as a solution to emerging security threats.

These differences are being exposed as attacks on U.S. occupation forces in Iraq continue. Neoconservative opinion assumed that Iraq's political reconstruction as a benign democracy could be accomplished in relatively short order because it assumed that virtually all segments of the Iraqi population would welcome the Americans as liberators and extend their goodwill to the Americans indefinitely, that Chalabi and the INC would have great political appeal in Iraq, and that no Saddam Hussein regime elements willing and able to resist U.S. forces would survive the war. The invalidity of all these assumptions raises doubts about the cost, duration, and even the feasibility of transforming Iraq into a stable democratic state—more specifically, doubts about America's domestic political stamina to see the establishment of democracy in Iraq through to the finish line. At some point, especially if irregular warfare expands against U.S. forces—as it did during the second half of 2003—the alternative of a stable autocracy in Baghdad that aligned itself with U.S. strategic interests in the Middle East could prove irresistible. Such a choice would constitute a profound defeat for neoconservative aims in Iraq and the region but would certainly be consistent with the traditional U.S. Middle East policy preference for stability over democracy.

A third obstacle to U.S. success in Iraq is the questionable political legitimacy of the entire enterprise in that country. The circumstances and challenges of nation-building in Iraq bear little resemblance to those that underpinned American nation-building success in post–World War II Japan and Germany. Iraq is a relatively young and highly artificial state, has no democratic experience, and suffers deep ethnic, religious, and tribal divisions. Most of the international community regards America's conquest and occupation of Iraq as illegitimate, and while many Iraqis welcomed Saddam Hussein's removal, a large and growing number of Iraqis, especially the Shiite majority, regard the continued presence of U.S. forces in their country as illegitimate. One is reminded of the Israeli invasion of southern Lebanon in 1982: the Shiite population majority at first welcomed the Israelis as liberators from the tyranny of the Palestine Liberation Organization; soon thereafter, however, they turned against their occupiers. Ultimately, southern Lebanon became a Vietnam for Israel, and after seventeen years of indecisive and costly low-intensity conflict the Israelis finally abandoned the country.

The issue of legitimacy extends to whatever indigenous political authority is ultimately established in U.S.–occupied Iraq. Any such authority, however populated and structured, will be suspect simply by virtue of American sponsorship. This will be especially the case for the minority Sunni Arab community, accustomed to dominating governance in Iraq for more than three centuries and now finding themselves out of power, as well as for those Iraqi Shiites who favor establishment of a theocratic state, which the Bush administration has declared it will not permit.

The legitimacy issue is further compounded by the postwar return from exile of expatriate political opposition leaders and organizations, most notably Ahmad Chalabi and his INC. Most politically ambitious Iraqi exiles were virtually unknown inside Iraq before the war (Chalabi fled Iraq in 1958 at the age of thirteen), and the mass of Iraqis who were forced to endure decades of fear and oppression because they could not escape are not likely to regard those who did leave—and lived in conditions of freedom and often wealth—as morally entitled to govern the country.

In the case of Chalabi and the INC, the stench of illegitimacy is especially strong. Aside from accusations that Chalabi is a crook (he has been convicted of bank fraud in Jordan) and the INC's internal disarray over Iraq's future, he and his organization remain the manifest choice of the Department of Defense for Iraq's future governance, even though the INC continues to find little political support in the country. For a decade (the INC was founded in 1992) neoconservatives and more than a few Republican members of Congress have been enamored of Chalabi and the INC, and it is testimony to the neoconservatives' influence inside the Pentagon that Chalabi and his associates were secretly airlifted into Iraq immediately after the fall of Baghdad without the knowledge of the State Department, which opposed Chalabi's installation as America's man in Iraq.

Indeed, before 9/11 provided them an opening for a direct U.S. attack on Iraq, neoconservatives argued that regime change could be accomplished in Baghdad via U.S. diplomatic recognition of the INC as Iraq's legitimate government and its establishment inside Iraq in a territorial sanctuary protected by American airpower. The very presence on Iraqi soil of a protected political alternative, they believed, would spark mass popular defection to the INC, which would in turn provide a recruiting base for an Iraqi liberation army. Astoundingly, American promoters of Chalabi continued to push this fantastic scenario after it had already been tried with dismal results in the protected Kurdish zone in northern Iraq. There, from 1992 to 1996 and with the CIA's backing, the INC failed to raise any credible military force but nonetheless participated in a disastrous Kurdish incursion into regime-controlled territory.[20] Nor was Chalabi himself fazed by his defeat in 1996 and subsequent withdrawal of CIA support. Rather, the charming expatriate continued to promote, and charmed neoconservatives continued to believe, the idea that five thousand to ten thousand INC fighters, supported by U.S. airpower, could take more than 60 percent of the country.[21]

Any Iraqi government seen as American picked or as serving U.S. interests at the expense of the Iraqi people would have great difficulty governing the country even absent the presence of Iraq's ethnic and religious fault lines. On this issue, the U.S. experience in Vietnam is quite relevant. America was defeated in Vietnam for a variety of reasons, but prominent among them was the Republic of Vietnam's failure to develop an identity independent of its Cold War creator. No Saigon regime could compete with Hanoi on the basis of nationalism; Dien Bien Phu emphatically placed the mantle of Vietnamese nationalism on the Communists' shoulders, who proceeded to portray the Americans, who had backed the French, as their neocolonial successors. This was not difficult to do. The Americans virtually handpicked Ngo Dinh Diem as the first president of the new republic, and when the Americans concluded that Diem no longer served their interests in Indochina, they helped engineer his overthrow. The Americans subsequently decided to take over the war from their South Vietnamese clients, unleashing U.S. forces and firepower in the South Vietnamese countryside. These developments essentially robbed Diem's weak successors of any hope of establishing a measure of political legitimacy strong enough to inspire South Vietnamese to fight and die in sufficient numbers for the republic to survive.

A postwar U.S. Army study of the situation in Iraq noted nationalism's short and difficult history in that country and concluded that the U.S. invasion "does not seem to have emerged as a strong test of Iraqi nationalism" because "[m]any Iraqis appeared willing to tolerate the U.S. invasion if it rid them of Saddam Hussein." The study warned, however, that the United States remained "an occupying power on probation with the Iraqi masses" because "Iraqi emotions about the continuing U.S. military presence could become quite intense should the Iraqis become offended through either U.S. conduct or the duration of the U.S. presence. Iraqi response to the U.S. troop presence or a U.S. attempt to install a pro-American government could . . . become a . . . serious flashpoint for an anti-American form of Iraqi nationalism to emerge."[22]

No less a problem than legitimacy for the U.S. nation-building enterprise in Iraq is the issue touched upon above: its dubious political sustainability back in the United States, especially if the effort turns out to be unexpectedly costly in blood and treasure. Neoconservatives seem to take for granted enduring public and congressional support for their ambitious foreign and defense policies. They appear to believe that Americans are prepared to "pay any price, bear any burden, meet any hardship, support any friend, oppose any foe" to perpetuate American primacy and transform the world into a peaceful community of democratic nations. Neoconservatives believe that the necessity and virtue of their foreign policy agenda are—or ought to be—self-evident to most Americans, and therefore that Americans are prepared to make the necessary sacrifices.

There is no question that 9/11 and the Bush administration's postulation of terrorist organizations and rogue states as an undifferentiated and undeterrable threat have produced broad public and congressional support for substantially larger defense budgets than were politically possible before 9/11. The 9/11 attacks and the Bush doctrine have buried, perhaps once and for all, the hesitation and timidity that characterized U.S. use of force in the 1990s. At the Pentagon, the Bush doctrine has replaced the once popular Vietnam-legacy Weinberger-Powell doctrine. But none of this should be taken as a public and congressional blank check for a foreign policy that encompasses preventive war and massive nation-building. Americans, as the U.S. Army study of Iraq's reconstruction noted, are averse to nation-building. In the case of Iraq, the aversion could become intolerance if U.S. occupation forces are drawn into the kind of bloody albeit low-intensity combat that eventually persuaded the Israelis to evacuate southern Lebanon.

More generally, a great majority of Americans also have no sustained interest in foreign policy issues. To the extent that average Americans focus on public policy issues, they focus on domestic public policy issues that bear on their interests and beliefs. Except in time of real war, they are not interested in costly crusades abroad. The British historian Niall Ferguson convincingly argues that Americans are not cut out to assume the burdens of empire, in part because the country's "best and brightest insist on staying home" and have little interest in the world beyond the United States, and in part because America does not have "the one crucial character trait without which the whole imperial project is doomed: stamina." In the United States "the young elites have no desire whatsoever to spend their lives running a screwed-up sun-scorched sandpit like Iraq. [They] aspire not to govern Mesopotamia, but to manage MTV; not to rule Hejaz, but to run a hedge fund; not to be a C.B.E. [Commander of the British Empire], but to be a C.E.O."[23]

Ferguson's conclusion is supported by the judgment of the *Strategic Survey 2002–2003* that the United States is likely to return to its traditional "realist" approach to the Middle East, in part because the American public is not prepared to pay the costs and run the risks necessary to realize the neoconservatives' utopian vision for the region. Joseph Nye believes that the neoconservatives "mistake the politics of primacy for those of empire" and that the chief problem in creating such an empire is "imperial understretch," or the unwillingness of the U.S. public and Congress "to invest seriously in the instruments of nation-building and governance, as opposed to military force." He points out that the combined budgets of the State Department and the U.S. Agency for International Development constitute only 1 percent of the federal budget and one-sixteenth of the Pentagon's budget. Nye also concludes that the realists will prevail in the end because the U.S. military is running the show in Iraq and because the United States has "designed a military that is better suited to kick down the door, beat up a dictator, and go home rather than stay for the harder work of building a democratic polity."[24]

Even if U.S. occupation forces are spared politically significant casualties, the financial costs of occupation, especially one that lasted many years, could generate public and congressional pressures to withdraw altogether or otherwise scale down the occupation to the point of jeopardizing Iraq's political reconstruction. The Bush administration grossly underestimated postwar U.S. military and reconstruction costs in Iraq. It also counted on substantial international troop and money contributions to postwar Iraq, and it ignored the looming federal fiscal crisis back home. It did not expect to encounter open-ended insurgent warfare against U.S. military and reconstruction targets, and it assumed that Iraq's infrastructure was in better repair than it actually was. Before the war, administration spokesmen talked of a quick military exit from Iraq once the war ended and of financing reconstruction with Iraqi oil rather than U.S. taxpayer dollars. Neither has come to pass, calling into question the political and fiscal sustainability of the administration's objectives in Iraq.

The absence of significant international participation (Great Britain excepted) in dealing with the challenges of postwar Iraq has compelled the United States to shoulder the brunt of the blood and treasure costs. (As of September 2003, about 185,000 U.S. troops were deployed in Iraq and Kuwait. Aside from the U.S. and British deployment, the coalition's other twenty-nine troop-contributing countries, none of them militarily significant, were contributing a total of 12,000 soldiers, or an average of about 430 troops per national contingent, with the United States footing the bill for most of them.)[25] The situation was likely to continue as long as the Bush administration remained unwilling to share political and military authority over Iraq's future with the United Nations or some other international consortium. U.S. troop losses in Iraq from May 1 to the end of August averaged slightly more than 1 dead per day, or an annual rate of 400, and by the end of August the number of U.S. wounded was approaching 10 per day. By mid-November, however, increasing attacks on U.S. forces—averaging 25 to 35 per day—were resulting in an average of 3 to 4 American dead each day. The dollar cost of maintaining U.S. forces in Iraq was running at $4 billion per month, or an annual rate of $48 billion. In early September President Bush announced an off-budget $87 billion request to cover mounting military and reconstruction costs in Iraq and continuing operations in Afghanistan.[26] This announcement followed an earlier off-budget appropriation of $79 billion to cover the costs of the war and its immediate aftermath.

An early September 2003 assessment provided by the *Wall Street Journal* predicted further spirals in projected postwar costs attributable to gross underestimation of near-term Iraqi oil revenues; surprise at the decrepit state of Iraq's infrastructure; extensive and continuing looting and sabotage of oil pipelines, electrical power lines, and other key reconstruction targets; downstream costs of financing expanding Iraqi government and security forces; and poor prospects for significant international donor support.[27] Within days of the *Journal* prediction, Secretary of Defense Rumsfeld informed U.S. senators that the bill for Iraq's postwar reconstruction was expected to run $55 billion higher than the $87 billion President Bush had announced less than a week earlier.[28] Thus five months after the cessation of major military operations, the total cost of the war and postwar military operations and reconstruction activities was headed beyond $200 billion with no end in sight and every dime of it borrowed money.

As of November 2003, notwithstanding rising U.S. casualties, failure to discover any Iraqi WMD, and unexpectedly high occupation and reconstruction costs, public and congressional majorities still continued to support the Bush administration's objectives in Iraq. Americans do not like to cut and run, especially when their soldiers are taking fire. Public support for the war itself remained strong, in part because the administration convinced most Americans that removing Saddam Hussein from power was integral to the war on terrorism. (A September 2003 *Washington Post* poll revealed that 69 percent of those polled believed that it was "at least likely that Saddam Hussein was involved" in the 9/11 attacks.)[29] There was also a sense that the United States simply could not afford to fail in Iraq: too much political and military capital had been invested in this very controversial enterprise, and there were too many foreign critics itching to say, "We told you so!"

There were, however, signs of growing public dissatisfaction with the way things were going in Iraq. Two polls taken in late August suggested the disappearance of any expectations of an easy or cheap endgame in that country. A *USA Today*/CNN/Gallup poll found that 63 percent of Americans still believed the war was worth fighting, but 54 percent also believed that the administration "did not have a clear plan to bring stability and democracy to the country." Respondents were almost evenly split over whether to "maintain current or increase U.S. force levels" in Iraq (51 percent) or "to cut or completely withdraw U.S. forces " (46 percent).[30] A *Newsweek* poll found that 69 percent of Americans were "very concerned" (40 percent) or "somewhat concerned" (29 percent) that the United States would be "bogged down for many years in Iraq without making much progress in achieving its goals." Nearly half—47 percent—said they were "very concerned" that the cost of maintaining U.S. forces in Iraq would lead to "a large budget deficit and seriously hurt the economy." Of those polled, 60 percent said that the estimated occupation cost of $1 billion per week was too high and believed it should be reduced. Only 15 percent said they would support the current levels of occupation costs for three years or more.[31] A subsequent *Washington Post*–ABC News poll found that 60 percent of all respondents did not support President Bush's early September request for an additional $87 billion for U.S. and military operations in Iraq and Afghanistan.[32]

The Iraq-deficit-economy connection could turn out to be a powerful influence on public and congressional attitudes. Even without Iraq costs, which so far have been financed by off-budget requests, federal deficits are expected to balloon government debt over the next decade. In August 2003 the highly respected Congressional Budget Office (CBO) projected a $480 deficit for fiscal year 2004 and a total cumulative deficit for the decade of 2002–13 of $1.40 trillion.[33] These numbers minimize the problem, however, because the CBO is legally required to base its projections only on existing laws. Thus the CBO projection assumes the scheduled expiration of the huge 2001 and 2003 tax cuts, although most observers believe they will be extended. (Both the White House and the Republican congressional leadership favor making the cuts permanent.) The CBO projection also ignores the likely passage of Medicare prescription drug and alternative minimum tax reform legislation. Altogether, these measures could, according to a *Washington Post* budget analysis, add an estimated $1.93 trillion to the total 2004–13 deficit.[34] The CBO also assumes that discretionary spending will grow only at the rate of inflation, projected to average 2.7 percent during the next decade, when in fact it has risen by an annual 7.7 percent over the past five years. Growth at the latter rate would add another estimated $1.39 trillion. According to the *Post* analysis, the sum of all these additions, plus the additional interest on the debt, could produce a total 2002–13 deficit of $4.33 trillion, or almost four times larger than the CBO projection.[35]

To be sure, these figures are estimates, and estimates are very assumption dependent. But they convey the magnitude of the federal fiscal crisis that lies ahead if the 2001 and 2003 tax cuts are not rescinded, if White House–backed prescription drug and minimum tax reform legislation is passed, and if discretionary spending runs significantly above the inflation rate. These estimates, moreover, do not include U.S. occupation and reconstruction costs in Iraq over the coming decade or the possible costs of a larger U.S. Army dictated by the impact of Iraq on that service's ability to meet its obligations worldwide. Fiscally, something has got to give in the coming years, and that something may well be a reduction of U.S. liabilities in Iraq. Such a reduction would be especially likely if more and more Americans come to see a cause-and-effect relationship between outlays for Iraq, spiraling federal deficits, and bad economic news at home.

Yet another obstacle plaguing the American effort in Iraq is the evident and continuing division within the Bush administration over U.S. policy toward Iraq and the respective roles of the State and Defense Departments in formulating and implementing that policy. Not since the Reagan administration has there been such a divide between the two departments on the role of force in U.S. foreign policy and the conditions of force employment. The dispute then was both a policy and personal quarrel between Secretary of Defense Caspar W. Weinberger and Secretary of State George

P. Shultz. Today's dispute between Secretary of Defense Rumsfeld and Secretary of State Powell seems much less personal relative to policy. The two departments have fought each other over Iraq policy ever since 9/11, and the contest has been conducted both publicly and privately.[36] It is a struggle that has pitted the neoconservatives and their allies in the Defense Department and on Capitol Hill against the "realists" in the State Department and their like-minded friends such as former national security advisers Brent Scowcroft and Zbigniew Brzezinski. From the beginning of the Iraqi crisis, Powell and his department have sought to restrain the neoconservatives within the administration. Against the ill-concealed opposition of those who pushed for war on Iraq immediately after 9/11—absent evidence of an Iraq-9/11 connection and without attempting to obtain UN authorization—and who saw in a war on Iraq an opportunity to establish a client government run by the INC, Powell argued successfully for taking down the Taliban first, for returning to the United Nations to seek an international mandate for using force against Iraq, and for not prejudicing Iraq's future governance by committing to Iraqi exiles who had no standing inside Iraq.

The departmental struggle was especially fierce on the issue of postwar Iraq. By the time Operation Iraqi Freedom was launched the State Department had, in conjunction with the Middle East Institute, conducted a year's worth of extensive interagency planning (though without the Pentagon) that anticipated many of the postwar problems the United States encountered in Iraq (including widespread power outages), but the Office of the Secretary of Defense, which did not begin serious preparation until two months before the war, was determined to run the show without any "interference" from Foggy Bottom. The Pentagon prevailed because President Bush in January 2003 signed a directive giving the Defense Department the primary lead, which the OSD used to exclude any challenge to its own assumptions about and plans for postwar Iraq. The result was an utter lack of preparation on the part of the Pentagon's chosen vehicle for running postwar Iraq, the short-lived Office of Reconstruction and Humanitarian Assistance (ORHA). Headed by Jay Garner, a retired army general, ORHA was late in establishing a presence in Iraq and subsequently overwhelmed by the tasks at hand. Only sixteen days separated Garner's arrival in Baghdad and Wolfowitz's formal dissolution of ORHA.[37] Garner was replaced by the ambassador L. Paul Bremer III, a twenty-three-year veteran of the State Department, and ORHA by the Coalition Provisional Authority (CPA), though Bremer was directed to report to the Office of the Secretary of Defense.

Powell has publicly embraced the Bush doctrine. But as a realist who may regard the neoconservative view of the world and America's role in it as naive, even dangerous, he is much friendlier to traditional diplomacy, treaties, alliances, and multilateralism than his neoconservative critics. As secretary of state and a longtime supporter of the Weinberger doctrine, Powell is predisposed to accord military power a lesser role in foreign policy than those who believe that the perpetuation of military primacy should be the chief objective of U.S. foreign policy. Whereas the primacists lean toward force and unilateralism, Powell favors persuasion and cooperation.

Though the dispute between the "idealist" and "realist" views of U.S. foreign policy aims and interests is as old as the American republic itself, it has profound implications for U.S. policy toward postwar Iraq. Neoconservatives believe Iraq can and ought to be democratized, whereas realists, who traditionally value stability over justice, question the wisdom and feasibility of doing so. Which Iraq better serves U.S. interests: a democratic but highly unstable Iraq hostile to the United States or a stable authoritarian Iraq friendly to the United States? The realist view, which governed the George H. W. Bush administration, holds that U.S. interests are best served, as Isam al Khafaji put it before the war, by "a limited change that entailed the removal of Saddam Hussein and his close associates while leaving the basic institutions of Saddam's regime intact." Absent Saddam and his cronies, "a façade of parliamentary democracy resembling the Egyptian one could be created: a 'leading' party composed of 'reformed' ex-Ba'athists would remain along with a strong authoritarian president backed by a restrained army and intelligence service."[38]

This choice is of course anathema for neoconservatives, who believe that 9/11 was in part the product of U.S.–sponsored perpetuation of such repressive regimes in the Middle East. For them, the aim of Operation Freedom was not just Saddam's removal, but Iraq's democratization—indeed, the democratization of the entire Middle East. In democratizing Iraq, they believe, the United States serves both its values and its interests. Some believe that the United States should also convert Iraq into a strategic client, even a military protectorate, complete with U.S. bases and a permanent garrison. Such a setup would provide substitutes for U.S. bases in Saudi Arabia and Turkey, which the United States is already evacuating, furnish a staging infrastructure from which to threaten and even attack Iran and Syria, and guarantee the success of Iraq's democratic experiment. The American Enterprise Institute's Tom Donnelly, in a May 2003 article for the *Weekly Standard* denounced the "idea that U.S. military forces can 'come home' from Iraq" as "spectacularly myopic" and argued that at a minimum U.S. ground and air forces should garrison western Iraq. Max Boot was disturbed that Secretary of Defense Donald Rumsfeld had denied a report that the Pentagon was planning to open permanent bases in

Iraq. "If they're not, they should be," he wrote. "That's the only way to ensure the security of a nascent democracy in such a rough neighborhood."[39]

The report Boot referred to was a front-page article in the *New York Times* on April 20, 2003, stating that the Pentagon was planning to establish up to four bases in Iraq that could be used for future military operations in the Middle East and Persian Gulf. Rumsfeld emphatically dismissed the report the next day: "I have never, that I can recall, heard the subject of permanent base[s] in Iraq discussed in any meeting. The likelihood of it seems so low that it does not surprise me that it's never been discussed."[40] Rumsfeld and the armed services seek to lighten the U.S. military "footprint" in the region by shifting reliance from combat force–garrisoned bases in Saudi Arabia and Turkey to bases of a lighter military footprint in smaller states more congenial to a U.S. military presence such as Qatar (where a newly developed command center has replaced part of the command function previously conducted from Saudi soil), Abu Dhabi, and the United Arab Emirates.[41] The United States has for more than a decade enjoyed military access to Kuwait and Oman and even longer in Bahrain.

Whether the neoconservatives will prevail on nation- and military base–building remains to be seen, and if they do, what a participatory government and U.S. basing rights in Iraq might look like. The question nonetheless remains: Is a stable democracy possible in Iraq? The fact that the circumstances we face today in Iraq are not analogous to those surrounding the U.S. successes in post–World War II Germany and Japan does not mean that any attempt to create democracy in Iraq is automatically doomed. Certainly the argument that Arabs—or Muslims—are incapable of democracy smacks of racism. On the other hand, the wave of democratization than swept much of East Asia, Latin America, and former Communist Europe during the past three decades seemingly broke on the shores of the Arab world. In the case of Iraq, moreover, an outside, Western power whose invasion and occupation of Iraq is regarded by many Arabs, Iraqis and non-Iraqis alike, as illegitimate, would be an attempt to impose democracy.

Experts are divided over prospects for democracy in Iraq. Aside from the legitimacy issue of democracy's association with a foreign occupying power, many experts on Iraq and on democracy are skeptical that a country habituated to autocracy and so ethnically, tribally, and religiously divided can be converted into a democratic polity based on the rule of law and respect for minorities.[42] A genuinely democratic Iraq would also accord the Shiite majority its proportional say on matters of governance while at the same time guaranteeing the political rights of the Kurdish and Sunni Arab minorities. But would a Shiite majority be committed to a secular state, and if not, could democracy usher in an Islamist theocracy?

"Since . . . Islamist movements enjoy considerable grassroots and local authenticity, they are the most likely to benefit from democratic openings," concluded a Carnegie Endowment assessment in 2002. "Truly free and fair elections in any country of the Middle East would likely assure Islamist parties a substantial share of the vote, or possibly even a majority, as would have happened in Algeria had the elections not been cancelled."[43]

Other experts are more optimistic. They point to impressive examples of extant democratic states that were once regarded as incorrigible autocracies—for example, Japan, South Korea, Taiwan, the Philippines, Argentina, Nicaragua. They also contend that the threat of an Islamist takeover of Iraq has been overstated, stressing Iraq's secular heritage, and believe that reconstituted Iraqi oil production will eventually revive the large and prosperous middle class that distinguished Iraq from other major Arab states before the Gulf War of 1991.[44]

But by far the most pressing postwar obstacle to American political success in Iraq remains the continuing—indeed escalating—irregular warfare against the U.S. occupation and attempted economic reconstruction of Iraq. Notwithstanding Pres. George W. Bush's declaration on May 1, 2003, that major combat operations were over, attacks on U.S. forces and subsequently on targets essential to reconstruction continued. The war, in fact, never ended, even though it is being conducted on a smaller scale. If there is a possible analogy to the emerging situation, it may be that of the Spanish-American War and its aftermath in the Philippines. In 1898 the United States easily vanquished Spanish naval and ground forces in Cuba and the Philippines, but in the latter islands quickly discovered that many Filipinos, though happy to be liberated from Spain, opposed the reimposition of colonial rule by the Americans. The result was a bloody three-year (1899–1902) insurgency that claimed far more U.S. lives—4,234 dead—than were lost against the Spanish—379.[45]

Neither the neoconservatives nor U.S. military planners expected to confront irregular warfare in postwar Iraq.[46] Attacks by regime remnants, jihadists, foreign mercenaries, criminal gangs, and aroused Iraqi nationalists on U.S. troops, on Iraqis working with Americans, and on such reconstruction targets as electrical power transmission lines and oil production infrastructure amount to a guerrilla war that can have but one aim: to force the United States to abandon its position and policy in Iraq. Such an objective seems fanciful at this time, given the enormous political capital the Bush administration has invested in Iraq. Yet most insurgencies start small, and those Iraqis who have taken up arms against the Americans and their local collaborators cannot but be encouraged by the precedents of Vietnam, Lebanon, and Somalia, where the United States abandoned its policy in the face of determined enemy resistance that it could not overcome with means consistent with the stakes at hand and necessary public support.

This is not to suggest that a debacle of Vietnam magnitude awaits the United States in Iraq. The situation in Iraq today bears little comparison to that in Indochina in the early 1960s; there is certainly not in Iraq today or for the foreseeable future an analog to the Vietnamese Communist enemy we faced four decades ago.

But we should not fool ourselves about the nature of attacks on U.S. forces. To dismiss them, as have Bush administration officials, in the context of the U.S. global war on terrorism as simply reactionary terrorist attacks having no legitimacy and requiring no response other than traditional counterterrorism is to impede our understanding of the situation we face in Iraq and to invite for the United States a West Bank in Mesopotamia. Indeed, to the extent that terrorism entails, as defined by the Bush administration's *National Security Strategy,* "premeditated, politically motivated violence perpetrated against innocents," assaults on U.S. troops, at least in Iraq, hardly qualify as terrorist attacks because those troops are combatants in an army of occupation. This does not make the sniper fire, ambushes, mine detonations, and suicide bomber attacks any less dangerous or less frightening to those subjected to them, but these attacks should be recognized for what they are: guerrilla warfare, which the Pentagon officially defines as "military and paramilitary operations conducted in enemy-held or hostile territory by irregular, predominantly indigenous forces."[47] Historically, violence against noncombatants had been a feature of guerrilla warfare, but guerrilla warfare's main object is to defeat or cause the expulsion of the larger conventional military enemy, be it a foreign or indigenous government force.

The Bush administration is understandably averse to calling the violence against U.S. forces in Iraq a guerrilla war because the term is associated with the quagmire of disastrous U.S. intervention in Vietnam and because it suggests that the violence is organized and directed by a central authority or at least an alliance of armed groups seeking to force the United States out of Iraq. In late June 2003 Secretary of Defense Rumsfeld publicly rejected the official Defense Department definition of guerrilla warfare as applicable to events in Iraq, asserting that the disparate composition of the resistance—"looters, criminals, remnants of Saddam Hussein's government, foreign terrorists and Iranian-backed Shiites . . . doesn't make it anything like a guerrilla war or an organized resistance. It makes it like four different things going on [in which the groups] are functioning more like terrorists."[48] Rumsfeld went on to declare, "We're in a global war on terrorism and there are people that don't agree with that—for the most part, terrorists."[49] The secretary of defense also rejected the term "quagmire." Less than two weeks earlier, however, Deputy Secretary of Defense Paul Wolfowitz and the vice chairman of the joint chiefs of staff, Gen. Peter Pace, testified to the House Armed Services Committee that U.S. forces might remain in Iraq for as long as ten years.[50]

None of this is meant to be alarmist. Most guerrilla wars fail, especially those isolated from external assistance. Resistance so far has been confined mainly to Baghdad and the Sunni triangle; Kurdish and Shiite Iraq remain comparatively quiescent. Moreover, the agendas of those Iraqi groups seeking to force the United States out of Iraq are sufficiently disparate as to impede formation of a single, centrally directed fighting organization. We should not be too confident on this score, however. Even before the war, Saddam Hussein was using the language of jihad and attempting to appeal to Iraqis not just as Arabs but also as Muslims. In much the same fashion that Stalin in World War II substituted Russian nationalism for Soviet Communism as the ideological basis for mobilizing the Soviet Union against the Nazi invasion, Saddam has sought to substitute Islam for secular Ba'athism as the touchstone for stimulating Iraqi resistance to the Anglo-American "crusader" enemy. Additionally, there is in Iraq an almost bottomless pit of weapons and ammunition available to those willing to kill Americans and their Iraqi collaborators; unlike most developing insurgencies, Iraqi guerrillas are well armed and independent of foreign suppliers.

A collaborative, working alliance between Saddam loyalists and Islamists, driven by a common hatred of "Christian imperial" power in Iraq, could certainly materialize, if it has not already. If so, Operation Iraqi Freedom will have succeeded in driving together secular and antisecular elements of Iraqi society heretofore mortal enemies of each other. But resistance by disparate groups need not be coordinated much less centrally directed to be effective. By September 2003 there were in fact increasing signs of emerging new Islamist and tribal-based resistance groups having no connection with the former regime and therefore committed to fight irrespective of the fate of regime remnants. Indeed, the very same week that U.S. forces cornered and killed Saddam Hussein's sons, Uday and Qusay, two new groups, including one calling itself the Army of Islamic Jihad, announced their existence and their intention to start killing Americans.[51]

The former Pakistani diplomat and prime ministerial adviser Husain Haqqani argues that the U.S. war on Iraq has weakened political moderates throughout the Arab world by increasing the number of "radical Muslims believing in the inevitability of a clash of civilizations and the need to stand up and be counted for their religious fellowship." The traditional rivalry between secular Arab nationalism and radical Islam's emphasis on pan-Islamism has given way to a "polarization between a Muslim 'us' and a Western 'them.'" The collapse of Iraq's secular Arab nationalist regime has promoted "convergence between radical Islamists and secular nationalists in the Middle East," a convergence that "could provide new sanctuaries to radical Islamists while creating operational links between ideologically opposed terrorist groups."[52]

Anatol Lieven also points out that the American project in Iraq can be derailed with much less hostile resistance than that required to force the United States out of Vietnam, where the United States enjoyed the benefit of an indigenous South Vietnamese government and substantial military and paramilitary forces capable of assuming static defense functions and constabulary duties.

> [G]uerrillas in Iraq do not have to achieve anything like the success of the Vietcong in order to thoroughly spoil US plans. In Vietnam, the US was defending a ramshackle but existing South Vietnamese state. In Iraq, the US is trying to create a new state on the ruins of Ba'ath and Sunni Arab–ruled Iraq. If it is to do so, the US urgently needs to restore the Iraqi economy.
>
> [But] Iraqi guerrillas can make this impossible. They have only to force allied soldiers to move around in large heavily armed groups, cut off from the population, to prevent them from acting as a police force. They can trap occupying forces into situations where they kill large numbers of civilians, infuriating the population. Above all, the guerrillas could kill or intimidate enough Iraqi policemen and officials to make large parts of the country ungovernable and destroy even the appearance of democratization and reconstruction.[53]

A U.S. Army expert on Iraq, W. Andrew Terrill, observes that "[t]he more disruptive an occupation is to daily life, the more likely it will generate resentment. Yet, an occupation that does not produce personal security for the population will . . . engender feelings of anger as has already been seen in Iraq. U.S. troops in the field are thus given the choice of a light footprint that limits direct friction with the population or a heavier footprint that provides more security. Whatever they are assigned to do, their actions will be criticized by multiple voices both inside and outside Iraq. There is no option which will fail to produce substantial criticism."[54]

The ultimate question, however, is not the quality and durability of Iraqi resistance to U.S. forces; it is, rather, America's political stamina. Does the United States have the stomach to stay its ambitious and potentially very costly course in Iraq?

The answer to this question is necessarily contingent on events to come. As of November 2003, however, the picture was not encouraging. Neither before nor after the war did the Bush administration advise the public or Congress of the potential costs, difficulties, and duration of the postwar phase of Operation Iraqi Freedom. Perhaps it failed to do so because it underestimated them across the board, anticipating instead the invader-friendly liberation scenario of perpetually thankful Iraqis, a clean sweep of the regime from power, intact and obedient government ministries, and a quick and smooth transfer of power to the Iraqi National Congress. In any event, the public was not warned of the possibility of persistent "postwar" guerrilla attacks on U.S. troops, on Iraqis collaborating with the Americans, and on other targets essential to Iraq's economic reconstruction.

These attacks not only undermined the "can-do" confidence of initial U.S. occupation authorities—three months after Baghdad's liberation, the city had less electricity and potable water than it did before the war.[55] The attacks also encouraged U.S. forces in Iraq to undertake protective measures that could compromise their capacity to promote the overriding goal of making Iraqis secure as a precondition to reconstruction. During the 1990s the Pentagon's obsession with force protection reached the point where it was prepared to elevate the security of the military intervention force above the intervention mission itself. This could easily be repeated in Iraq.[56] Providing security to Iraqis requires dispersed forces patrolling in an unthreatening manner among local populations and accepting the likelihood of friendly casualties; in contrast, force protection places a premium on concentrating U.S. forces and sealing them off as much as possible from contact with Iraqis.

American stamina in Iraq is also likely to be negatively affected by an absence of major allied and international help in policing and reconstructing that country. Such is the price of a foreign policy that openly disdains the United Nations, world opinion, and formal alliances and treaties that in any way limit U.S. freedom of military action. "We have undertaken very manpower-intensive operations in Afghanistan and Iraq without lining up critical support from key allies. Now the sad truth is that even though we are strained by those missions, far more troops are needed than are already in Afghanistan and Iraq," concluded the Brookings Institution defense analyst Ivo Daalder in July 2003. "Meanwhile, the nations who opposed the war in Iraq are in no mood to help us clean up that mess . . . [and] the Bush administration shows no signs of issuing [a] plea for help" from NATO. "So I think we're really in trouble in Iraq, and the likelihood that things will turn out well there is diminishing." Indeed, in mid-August

2003 the Bush administration publicly abandoned the idea of giving the United Nations a significant role in the occupation of Iraq, effectively blowing off potential participation in the occupation by France, Germany, India, and other countries that had made a greater UN role the price of their participation.[57]

Finally, there is the question of global military overstretch. With the evaporation of hopes for early major U.S. force withdrawals from Iraq, the United States, for the first time since the 1970s, faces a strategically dangerous quantitative shortfall in military power relative to extant and potential future military commitments. The service most stressed is the army, which as of the fall of 2003 still had about 185,000 troops (one-third of the army's active duty strength and more than half its combat power) deployed in and around Iraq, another 10,000 in Afghanistan, plus an additional 25,000 in South Korea and 5,000 in the Balkans. Altogether, some 370,000 army troops are deployed overseas, or some 75 percent of that service's total active duty force of 491,000.[58] The Iraqi deployment, which critics believe should be *reinforced* to provide the necessary measure of order and stability for Iraq's reconstruction, threatens the army's ability to provide a sufficient rotation base for its overseas deployments and effectively strips the army of a strategic reserve for such possible contingencies as a war on the Korean peninsula and an escalation of continuing Iraqi irregular warfare against U.S. forces in Iraq.[59] The force cupboard certainly could not support two simultaneous major regional wars.

The obvious and most immediate solution to relieve the army of its global overcommitment is to internationalize the occupation. This means bringing in substantial contingents of well-trained foreign troops, including troops from major NATO states other than Great Britain. Bringing in such contingents, however, would constitute a confession that the administration grossly miscalculated postwar U.S. force requirements in Iraq; it would also compel the administration to share occupation authority with foreign governments that opposed the U.S. war on Iraq in the first place.

Present Pentagon plans call for the formation of a Polish-led 9,000-man division consisting of Polish, Bulgarian, Romanian, Slovakian, and Hungarian troops, none of which has any combat or extensive peacekeeping experience. The Defense Department also hopes to persuade a reluctant India to contribute a division.[60] But even if the Polish and Indian divisions materialize (and the latter seems ruled out by U.S. refusal to countenance a significant UN role in Iraq), they would probably not fill the gap between order and stability requirements and available force in Iraq, especially given the approach of the 2004 U.S. presidential election, which will generate strong pressure on the White House to bring home as many U.S. troops from Iraq as possible.

The issue of U.S. force size in postwar Iraq is greatly compounded by U.S. dissolution of the 400,000-man Iraqi army and plans to replace it, within three years, with a predominantly light infantry force of only 40,000.[61] Such a replacement army would be too small to defend Iraq against its more powerful neighbors, and might prove insufficient even to police Iraq's extensive and rugged border with Iran. Indeed, such a small army, absent a major U.S. force presence or credible commitment to Iraq's defense, could invite Iranian and Turkish military intervention in Iraq. This could mean saddling U.S. forces with the mission of Iraq's external defense as well as the mission of providing internal order. Moreover, contends the regional military expert Anthony H. Cordesman, Iraqis could come to see a "token 40,000-man Iraq Army . . . as leaving Iraq defenseless, and as dependent on US and British occupiers. This problem—and the lack of any clear plan to create a meaningful self-defense capability against Iran and Turkey, the failure to deal with Iranian proliferation, and lack of any clear concept to share power equitably among Iraq's ethnic and sectarian factions—makes the new force seem like a puppet army. Even those officers who seem to support the US and British secretly [could] become increasingly nationalistic and hostile."[62]

Aside from leaving more than 100,000 career soldiers out of work, the decision, taken against the advice of Iraqi dissidents seconded to the State Department, to disband the prewar Iraqi army and to start from scratch on a new army one-tenth its size, may also encourage centrifugal political forces inside Iraq.[63] Since Iraq's creation as an independent state in 1932, the army has served as a primary vehicle for the inculcation of Iraqi nationalism, which in turn has served to subordinate, or at least weaken, loyalty to tribe, ethnic group, and religious affiliation. Does the United States wish to discourage national loyalty in Iraq? Would it not be possible and desirable to create a larger, thoroughly professional Iraqi army that posed no threat to the Iraqi people or their regional neighbors yet was capable of defending Iraq without U.S. intervention? Would not such an army also serve to check Iranian ambitions in the Persian Gulf?

Not surprisingly, the vacuum created by the Iraqi army's disbandment has encouraged militarization at the subnational level. Political party–based Kurdish militias, which thrived under the strategic protection of the United States from 1991 onward and which participated in Operation Iraqi Freedom, continue to dominate Iraqi Kurdistan, and ethnic militias have started to form in both the Sunni and Shiite Arab communities. Though communal self-defense is the primary function of these militias, their very existence not only impedes creation of an effective national army but also offers potential vehicles for armed resistance to the American presence.

Though the combination of scarce foreign troops and the deteriorating security situation in central Iraq had, by mid-November 2003, propelled the Defense Department into a pell-mell creation of new Iraqi security forces to free U.S. troops from static defense missions, "Iraqification" promised little near-term benefit. Hastily trained Iraqis were no substitute for professional foreign soldiers, nor were they a match for the increasingly sophisticated insurgents.

The postwar reconstruction struggle in Iraq has turned out to be more difficult and costly than the war itself, and the jury is still very much out on the question of whether the American people and their elected representatives can sustain the will to stay the course of counterinsurgency and democratic revolution in Iraq.

9
Dark Victory

N o one who despises tyranny can regret the destruction of the Saddam Hussein regime in Iraq. Operation Iraqi Freedom swept away more than thirty years of neo-Stalinist brutality and oppression. Whether or not Saddam Hussein posed a security threat to the United States in the spring of 2003, he had been a mortal threat to Iraqis ever since coming to power in 1968 and an open transgressor of numerous United Nations resolutions since 1990. Saddam Hussein ran one of the few totalitarian regimes to survive the collapse of Soviet Communism, which formed the last major totalitarian state threat to Western values and interests.

Nor can any student of military history ignore the extraordinary performance of U.S. forces in bringing down Saddam's regime. Allies and adversaries alike could not fail to be awed by the combination, on the one hand, of the Bush administration's unshakable determination to proceed against Iraq despite the loss of the Turkish "front" and to press on to Baghdad in the face of unexpected rear-area Iraqi resistance, and, on the other, of the remarkable operational and tactical flexibility displayed by masterfully coordinated ground, air, and naval forces. And who could not admire the courage, skill, and firmness of purpose with which U.S. soldiers, sailors, airmen, and marines went about their professional business? Operation Iraqi Freedom, coming on the heels of Operation Enduring Freedom in Afghanistan, underscored America's unchallengeable conventional military supremacy.

But the Bush administration did not attack Iraq in 2003 for the purposes of liberating its people and demonstrating America's mastery of modern warfare. It went to war to remove what it asserted was a direct and imminent threat to U.S. security and to remake Iraq as a precursor to the Middle East's political transformation. It did so, moreover, over the objections of most of its friends and allies.

This chapter assesses the wisdom of the war and its likely political consequences. Some of those consequences are already apparent; others remain speculative. Wars are not only waged for political objectives; they can also have unintended political consequences. Moreover, since the removal of the Berlin Wall the United States has encountered considerable difficulty in converting its military victories into enduring political successes. In 1991 it reversed Iraqi aggression against Kuwait but failed to remove the source of that aggression—a failure that necessitated, at least in the post-9/11 judgment of the George W. Bush White House and its neoconservative advisers, a second war against Iraq. In 1995 the United States, after much hesitation and with the assistance of Croatian ground forces, managed to halt Bosnian Serb genocide in Bosnia but only at the price of a peace enforced by a continuing NATO military presence. In 1999 the United States went to war against Serbia to stop ethnic cleansing in Kosovo, but did so in a manner that encouraged its acceleration; as in Bosnia, a residual force presence was necessary to enforce peace. In neither Bosnia nor Kosovo did the United States display a significant commitment to effective political reconstruction.

The same was true in Afghanistan. Though the Bush administration removed the Taliban regime in 2001, it was not prepared to invest the resources necessary to prevent Afghanistan's descent into that country's pre-Taliban warlordism. As of the fall of 2003, the "government" of Hamid Karzai controlled little territory outside Kabul; a brigade-sized U.S. Army force remained in Afghanistan, where it was conducting operations against a resurgent al-Qaeda presence in eastern Afghanistan and in Pakistani territory bordering Afghanistan. The central government in Kabul lacked adequate security forces, infrastructure, and foreign assistance; the absence of government forces or an outside occupation force in the countryside effectively ceded most of Afghanistan to local warlords and the continuing strategic intrigue of Iran and Pakistan; massive heroin production resumed.[1] The lack of a determined U.S. political follow-through in Afghanistan was, in the judgment of Frederick W. Kagan, "emblematic of a larger failure to recognize that the shape and nature of a military operation establishes for good or ill the preconditions for the peace to follow. It is possible, as we saw both in Afghanistan and in our earlier campaign against Iraq in 1991, to design military operations that are brilliantly successful from a strictly operational point of view but that do not achieve and may actually hamper the achievement of larger political goals."[2]

It is the central conclusion of this book that the U.S. war against Iraq in 2003 was not only unnecessary but also damaging to long-term U.S. political interests in the world. It was unnecessary because Iraq posed no measure of danger to the United States justifying war. It was damaging because the preventive, unilateralist nature of the war alienated key friends and allies and weakened international institutions that have long served

U.S. security interests and because of the evident lack of preparedness of the United States to deal with the predictable consequences of its forcible removal of Saddam Hussein. Other conclusions:

1. The Bush doctrine correctly identifies a grave and unprecedented threat to the United States—indeed, to the West as a whole: fanatical nonstate organizations seeking to acquire destructive capacity heretofore monopolized by states and not deterrable by traditional threats of punishment, denial, or destruction.

    Globalization has accelerated the role of nonstate actors in the international system, and the proliferation of WMD and their means of delivery portends a grim marriage of "radicalism and technology." The attacks of September 11 were a warning of things to come. Even if al-Qaeda did not employ WMD, there is little doubt it would have done so had the terrorist organization had access to such weapons. Moreover, against al-Qaeda or any other nondeterrable terrorist enemy that has already attacked the United States, a war of extermination, including preemptive and preventive military action, is morally justified and strategically imperative.

    The U.S. war in Afghanistan was both. The Taliban regime was an ally of al-Qaeda that provided the terrorist organization a safe haven to plan, train, and direct operations against American and other Western targets. The regime refused demands that the Taliban turn over the perpetrators of 9/11, and when the Taliban refused, the United States acted. The connection between Operation Enduring Freedom and 9/11 was clear and accounted for the legitimacy it commanded among so many countries that would later oppose the U.S. attack on Iraq.

2. Rogue states seek weapons of mass destruction for purposes that include deterrence, and so far have not employed such weapons in circumstances likely to invite unacceptable counteraction.

    This does not mean that such states pose no threat to their neighbors or to international order, simply that they can and have been deterred from using WMD. Saddam Hussein sought and used chemical weapons as a means of offsetting Iran's numerical advantage on the ground in the Iraq-Iran War; those weapons also served as a handy means of terrifying rebellious Kurds. With respect to nuclear weapons, he almost certainly would have sought to acquire them even had he not regarded the United States as an obstacle to his regional ambitions. The prestige of nuclear weapons dwarfs that of other WMD, especially chemical weapons, and of Iraq's two regional archenemies, Israel and Iran, one already had them and the other was striving to get them. Prestige and Israeli possession of nuclear weapons have been no less motivational for Iran, which also regarded Saddam's bid for nuclear weapons as a clear threat. Iranian interest in nuclear weapons began under the Shah and was undoubtedly heightened by Iraqi chemical attacks on Iranian front-line forces and missile attacks on Iranian cities during the Iraq-Iran War.

North Korea also lives in a tough neighborhood and views its actual or threatened nuclear capacity, along with its very destructive conventional military threat to Seoul, as a means of simultaneously deterring a U.S. attack and extorting food and fuel aid from the United States and Japan. Military power, especially its capacity to "go nuclear," is Pyongyang's only source of international significance, and if it has so far deterred U.S. military action against North Korea, it has also been deterred from attacking South Korea or Japan by the threat of unacceptable American retaliation.

Americans have difficulty placing themselves in another country's shoes, and when it comes to the acquisition of nuclear weapons by nondemocratic states they tend to dismiss the possibility that such states might have legitimate reasons for doing so, including a desire to deter attack by real and potential enemies, including the United States. Neoconservative opinion is, ironically, exceptional; it has long argued for "anticipatory" military action and national ballistic missile defenses precisely to prevent rogue states from deterring U.S. military action against *them*. David Hastings Dunn, in his critique of the Bush doctrine, addresses the administration's conclusion that the only purposes for which Saddam Hussein—and by implication, other rogue state dictators—sought to acquire WMD was to intimidate or attack: "The possibility that he wanted these weapons to deter or repulse an attack from the US is presumably discounted on the assumption that without such weapons he would have nothing to fear from the US. That the US sees no contradiction in applying these stringent criteria to others and yet sees no grounds for others to view its own defense policy in this way illustrates the limitations of this approach to national security policy."[3]

3.   Saddam Hussein posed no direct or imminent threat to the United
       States or U.S. interests in the Middle East because he lacked de-
       liverable WMD and offensive conventional military capacity and
       was in any event effectively deterred from any form of external
       aggression by credible American threats.

       The grim and urgent Iraqi threat depicted by the Bush ad-
ministration before the war was challenged by many at the time
and subsequently discredited by the impotent performance of Iraqi
conventional forces and U.S. failure to discover usable WMD.
The administration chose war over a continuation of a UN inspection regime that had uncovered no evidence of any WMD,
including a reconstituted nuclear weapons program, and whose
continued presence would have precluded such a program. Indeed, prewar evidence cited by the administration that Iraq had a
reconstituted nuclear weapons program and was moving from a
"smoking gun" toward a "mushroom cloud" turned out to be bogus or unreliable. As a threat to U.S. global security interests,
Saddam Hussein's Iraq paled in comparison to North Korea and
Pakistan, possessors as well as proliferators of nuclear weapons and their ballistic means of delivery, and, in the case of
autocratic Pakistan, a continuing sponsor of terrorism against
democratic India and host to rising Islamic extremism. Yet the
administration chose war against Saddam Hussein, multilateral
diplomacy for Kim Jong Il, and strategic partnership with Pervez
Musharraf.

       Saddam Hussein's behavior before and after the launching
of Operation Iraqi Freedom reflected that of a would-be aggressor who was being effectively deterred. Saddam always loved
himself more than he hated the United States. In 1990 he had no
good reason to believe the United States would go to war over
Kuwait in part because no credible American threat of retaliation
was even attempted. Once the Americans surprised him, however, he remained deterred from taking any action that risked his
regime's destruction. Though he had used WMD against helpless
Kurds and Iranians, he never used them against any enemy capable of effective retaliation, and he remained consistent on this
issue for the remainder of his time in power. His behavior in this
regard was consistent with that of Communist North Korea, which
though much better armed with WMD than post-1991 Iraq, remains deterred at both the conventional and nuclear levels of conflict. The Bush doctrine's assertion that credible deterrence is not

reliable against rogue states (as opposed to nonstate terrorist organizations) awaits validation.

4.   The primary explanation for war against Iraq is the Bush White House's post-9/11 embrace of the neoconservatives' ideology regarding U.S. military primacy, use of force, and the Middle East.

The neoconservatives who populated the upper ranks of the Bush administration had been gunning for Saddam Hussein for years before 9/11. They had an articulated, aggressive, values-based foreign policy doctrine and a specific agenda for the Middle East that reflected hostility toward Arab autocracies and support for Israeli security interests as defined by that country's Likud political party. Before 9/11, however, they served a president who was focused on domestic policies and who was a self-avowed "realist" when it came to foreign policy. Then came 9/11 and what a perceptive account in the *National Journal* called President Bush's "borrowing wholesale from neoconservative arguments about how the United States should reposition itself in the world and use its unprecedented power." As for Saddam Hussein, "[w]e were talking about Iraq a long time before 9/11, but since 9/11 it became part of the new wisdom about how to shape the Middle East," commented Meyrav Wurmser, director of the Center for Middle East Policy at the neoconservative Hudson Institute. Robert Jervis speculates that "Bush's transformation after September 11 may parallel his earlier religious conversion: Just as coming to Christ gave meaning to his previously dissolute personal life, so the war on terrorism has become the defining characteristic of his foreign policy and his sacred mission."[4]

The neoconservative foreign policy doctrine and agenda offered an intellectual explanation of the world to a decidedly nonintellectual president, and some have even argued that President Bush's embrace of it was a case of the neoconservatives duping a witless White House. "The neo-cons took advantage of Bush's ignorance and inexperience," asserts Michael Lind, adding that President Bush "seems genuinely to believe that there was an imminent threat to the US from Saddam Hussein's [WMD], something the leading neo-cons say in public but are far too intelligent to believe themselves."[5] This argument, however, does an injustice to both President Bush and the history of the office he holds. Few of America's forty-three presidents have been intellectuals, and many have been influenced by the ideas of others, as was Harry Truman by George Kennan, Dean Acheson, Paul H. Nitze, and the other intellectual and policy godfathers of Cold War containment. President Bush is certainly not the first president to believe himself embarked on a crusade against evil overseas; indeed, Bush's global democratic crusade is essentially an updated extension of Woodrow Wilson's. American foreign policy has always reflected tension between interests and values, realism and idealism.

Moreover, *any* administration that inherited the unprecedented global military primacy that the United States has enjoyed since the collapse of the Soviet Union could not fail to be tempted to use military power in circumstances where no one else could effectively challenge it. Jervis, as an established scholar of international politics, concludes that, more than 9/11 "or some shadowy neoconservative cabal" explains America's recent assertive unilateralism: "it is the logical outcome of the current unrivaled U.S. position in the international system. Put simply, power is checked by counterbalancing power, and a state that is not [counterbalanced] tends to feel few restraints at all."[6] And it is difficult to characterize as a "cabal" a group of like-minded, outspoken intellectuals whose policy views have been known for years and who do not need secretive plotting to advance their cause inside the Bush White House.

5.   Conflating Saddam Hussein and al-Qaeda was a strategic mistake of the first order because it propelled the United States into an unnecessary war and weakened potential homeland defenses against terrorist attack.

Conversion of 9/11 into a case for war against Iraq required postulation of Saddam Hussein as Osama bin Laden's friend, operational collaborator, and potential source of WMD. This postulation in turn required a willful disregard of overwhelming evidence to the contrary. To date, there is still no evidence of Iraqi complicity in the 9/11 attacks—a fact finally conceded in mid-September 2003 by Secretary of Defense Rumsfeld and National Security Adviser Rice—or in any other al-Qaeda attacks on Western targets before or since.[7] Nor has evidence emerged of an operational relationship between Saddam and Osama bin Laden. And none of this should have been a surprise, given the vastly different and inherently antagonistic identities and agendas of secular Saddam's state and antisecular Osama's stateless organization.

Postulating a monolithic enemy may have been necessary to sell the American public on war with Iraq, but it blurred key distinctions, including differing vulnerabilities to U.S. force among rogue states, terrorist organizations, and failed states that hosted such organizations. It encouraged the conclusions that war with Iraq was simply a geographical extension of the war on terrorism and that Saddam's removal would weaken the al-Qaeda threat to the United States and its interests overseas. But there was never any evidence of al-Qaeda dependency on Saddam Hussein, and there remains no evidence that Saddam's fall has adversely affected al-Qaeda's future. As if to advertise this fact, al-Qaeda launched deadly attacks in Saudi Arabia and Morocco just six weeks after the conclusion of the war against Iraq. Al-Qaeda has been damaged by U.S. and allied counterterrorist operations conducted directly against the organization, but these operations are not to be confused with the war that brought down Saddam Hussein.

If anything, post-Saddam Iraq offers al-Qaeda a marvelous new opportunity to mobilize a jihad against the United States in the middle of an unstable Arab heartland. Yet another Western military humiliation of an Arab state cannot but help al-Qaeda recruitment. U.S. occupation forces certainly provide a new target set for al-Qaeda and other terrorist suicide bombers, and armed Iraqi resistance beyond the occasional terrorist attack could emerge if the United States botches Iraq's economic and political reconstruction.

A major consequence of conflating Saddam's Iraq and al-Qaeda has been to saddle the United States with large and open-ended war and occupation costs at a time when America's homeland security remains substantially underfunded. Dollars that could be going to improve security around U.S. nuclear power plants and major seaports are instead being sent to Iraq to restore electrical power and pay demobilized Iraqi soldiers to keep them from rioting. And the costs continue to grow. By the fall of 2003 the administration had spent $80 billion and planned to spend another $80 billion on the war and postwar Iraq—with no end in sight and every dime of it borrowed money. The combined total of $160 billion exceeds by more than $60 billion the estimated $98.4 billion shortfall in federal funding of emergency response agencies in the United States over the next five years. That estimate is the product of an independent task force study sponsored by the Council on Foreign Relations and completed in the summer of 2003. The study, entitled *Emergency Responders: Drastically Underfunded, Dangerously Unprepared,* concluded that almost two years after 9/11, "the United States remains dangerously ill prepared to handle a catastrophic attack on American soil" because of, among other things, acute shortages of radios among firefighters, WMD protective gear for police departments, basic equipment and expertise in public health laboratories, and hazardous materials detection equipment in most cities.[8] And first responders represent just one of many such underfunded components of homeland security. War with Iraq has degraded homeland security.

6.   The U.S. attack on Iraq was a preventive war; as such, it was indistinguishable from aggression, alien to traditional values of American statecraft, and injurious to long-term U.S. security interests.

The U.S. war on Iraq alienated most U.S. friends and allies because it was palpably a preventive war that violated the central norm of relations among states: Thou shalt not commit aggression. That the Bush administration believed and claimed that it was acting in self-defense did not obscure the reality that Iraq posed no direct or immediate threat to the United States. Austria-Hungary, Germany, Russia, France, and Great Britain all went to war in 1914 in the name of self-defense. The Japanese attacked Pearl Harbor in 1941 in part because they were convinced, as was the Bush administration with respect to Iraq, that time was working against them, that the longer they waited the less favorable the military balance would become. This is not to argue that there was no case for attacking Iraq in 2003. As on the eve of Operation Desert Storm in 1991, Saddam was a brutal dictator who was in willful noncompliance with a host of UN resolutions. And there was never any question that he sought WMD, especially nuclear weapons.

But the United States did not go to war in 2003 on behalf of the Iraqi people and the United Nations. Nor was any potential Iraqi WMD threat realizable in the presence of an unfettered UN inspection regime and threatened U.S. preemption. The United States went to war instead on behalf of a new use-of-force doctrine whose proclamation in 2002 and implementation against Iraq in 2003 may have undermined U.S. security in the long term.

In addition to saddling the United States with a costly and open-ended political and military entanglement in Iraq, the Bush doctrine and war on Iraq work to encourage enemies to acquire WMD and to deplete resources that might otherwise be allocated to homeland defense against terrorist attack. The doctrine and its war have also weakened the United Nations, divided Europe, damaged NATO (perhaps mortally), and compromised the legitimacy of American power abroad.

To be sure, the United Nations as a collective security organization never lived up to original American expectations for it, and the Security Council's permanent membership is markedly unrepresentative of the actual distribution of state power in the world. But the Bush administration asked the United Nations to do something it was, by virtue of the unanimity rule for Security Council permanent members, incapable of doing: authorize a preventive war against a member state. On only two previous occasions had the United Nations authorized the use of force, and those were in response to flagrant territorial aggression. The administration moreover displayed contempt for the United Nations by suggesting that it was nothing but another discredited League of Nations and making clear that it would proceed against Iraq regardless of what the United Nations did. For the most powerful UN member to behave in such a fashion was to invite the diplomatic debacle that subsequently befell the Bush administration at the United Nations and to further weaken that organization as an instrument of collective security. By alienating three of the other four permanent members of the Security Council over the issue of war with Iraq, the United States forfeited any claim to international legitimacy and diminished prospects that it could ever again, as it had in 1950 and 1990, lead the United Nations into authorizing the use of force against genuine aggressors.

With respect to Europe and NATO, the United States deliberately sought to split the European Union and the Atlantic alliance over the issue of war with Iraq in order to isolate unexpectedly strong French and German opposition, and it did so by mobilizing support in former Communist Europe among states already in or seeking membership in the EU, and especially NATO, and eager to curry U.S. favor. In so doing, the United States, in the view of Henry Kissinger, "produced the gravest crisis in the Atlantic Alliance since its creation five decades ago." Charles Kupchan believes that NATO "now lies in the rubble of Baghdad," a judgment that, if true, would not be unwelcome to an administration that tends to regard formal alliances in general as encumbrances on U.S. freedom of military action and NATO in particular as a strategic pygmy that can bring little to the military table in the war on terrorism and wars against rogue states. The key criterion for judging the worth of allies is loyalty to America's cause as defined by a White House given to postulating a world divided between good and evil and intolerant of those who might have a different view. Observes Ivo H. Daalder: "The premium [primacists] place on freedom of action leads them to view international institutions, regimes and treaties with considerable skepticism. Such formal arrangements inevitably constrain the ability of the United States to make the most of its primacy. They similarly take an unsentimental view of U.S. friends and allies. The purpose of allied consultations is not so much to forge a common policy, let alone build goodwill, as to convince others of the rightness of the US cause."[9]

To be sure, NATO's future has been an open question since the end of the Cold War, and the combination of the Soviet Union's demise and Europe's continuing integration inevitably diminished the strategic importance of the trans-Atlantic relationship for both the United States and Europe. Neither side of the Atlantic is any longer militarily dependent on the other for its security. Nor is NATO, especially a continually expanded NATO, a useful engine of collective military action outside NATO territory; Operation Allied Force in Kosovo underscored the limits of the alliance's military effectiveness beyond NATO territory.

But was it necessary for the leader of the Atlantic alliance to go out of its way to divide the alliance between those who, for a variety of motives, supported the administration policy on Iraq ("new Europe") and those who, also for a variety of motives, did not ("old Europe")? Should the administration's decision for preventive war against Iraq have been employed as a loyalty test for the other eighteen members of the alliance? And should the United States continue to exclude from participation in Iraq's reconstruction those members of NATO that refused to believe that Iraq posed a credible threat to the United States and U.S. interests in the Gulf? If the existing trend in trans-Atlantic relations continues, especially "if pre-Iraq war diplomacy becomes the pattern," contends Kissinger, "[t]he international system will be fundamentally altered. Europe will be split into two groups defined by their attitude toward cooperation with America. NATO will change its character and become a vehicle for those continuing to affirm the transatlantic relationship. The United Nations, traditionally a mechanism by which the democracies vindicated their convictions against the danger of aggression, will instead turn into a forum in which allies implement theories of how to bring about a counterweight to the hyperpower United States."[10] Surely, such a divided West, Europe, and NATO cannot be in America's long-term interest, especially in a world of rising Islamist violence against Western civilization and everything it stands for.

But perhaps the most egregious legacy of the Bush doctrine and the war on Iraq is their effect on the moral legitimacy of American leadership. By embracing a doctrine of preventive war, by exhibiting ill-concealed contempt for the very institutions that for half a century have served to reassure the rest of the world that American power would be employed with restraint, and by redefining allies and enemies on the basis of whether "you are with us or against us," the United States threatens to forfeit its moral leadership. Former European Union commissioner Etienne Davignon has summed up the dismay of many in Europe and elsewhere: "After World War II, America was all-powerful and created a new world by defining its national interest broadly in a way that made it attractive for other countries to define their interests in terms of embracing America's. In particular, the United States backed the creation of global institutions, due process, and the rule of law. Now, you are again all-powerful and the world is again in need of fundamental restructuring, but without talking to anyone you appear to be turning your back on things you have championed for half a century and defining your interest narrowly and primarily in terms of military security."[11]

Former European Union ambassador to the United States Hugo Paemen is blunter: "Domestically you have a wonderful system of checks and balances, but in foreign policy you are completely unpredictable, and your pendulum can swing from one side to the other very quickly, while those of us who may be deeply affected have no opportunity even to make our voice heard, let alone to have any influence. This is really worrying because while your intentions are usually good, your actions are frequently informed by ignorance, ideology, or special interests and can have very damaging consequences for the rest of us."[12]

"Americans," wrote Francis Fukuyama on the first anniversary of 9/11, "are largely innocent of the fact that much of the rest of the rest of the world believes that it is American power, and not terrorists with weapons of mass destruction, that is destabilizing the world."[13] If so, then the Bush doctrine and the war on Iraq can only reinforce that belief.

Indeed, the doctrine and war reflect a preliminary but by no means final answer to a much larger question, perhaps the most important question of the beginning decades of the twenty-first century: How will America employ its unprecedented global military primacy? With restraint and due consideration of the interests and opinions of others? Or with arrogance and contempt? Ironically, it was presidential candidate George W. Bush who declared: "Our nation stands alone right now in the world in terms of power. And that's why we've got to be humble and project strength in a way that promotes freedom. . . . If we are an arrogant nation, they'll view us that way, but if we're a humble nation, they'll respect us."[14]

7. Perhaps the most important lesson of America's second war with Iraq is that successful military operations are not to be confused with successful political outcomes—or to put it another way, the object of war is not military victory per se but a better peace.

Though Carl von Clausewitz correctly observed that war is a continuation of politics by other means, Americans have traditionally viewed war as a substitute for politics. They like their wars unadulterated by politics. For this reason they have tended to define war's success or failure in terms of combat outcomes rather than in broader grand strategic terms, and accordingly have discounted the importance of war termination and the transition to peace. This outlook is reflected in civilian decision-makers' failure to accord war termination adequate priority and in the professional military's disdain for so-called operations other than war, especially those entailing peacemaking and nation-building responsibilities.

Regrettably, the United States was no better prepared for war termination in the Gulf in 2003 than it was in 1991, and though the George W. Bush administration is rhetorically committed to rebuilding the Iraq state, it remains to be seen whether it is really prepared to go the distance in terms of time, resources, and blood. The record in Afghanistan is not encouraging. It is moreover clear that the Defense Department's civilian leadership, which is still running the show in Iraq, despite the replacement of Jay Garner by Paul Bremer, grossly underestimated the responsibilities, costs, and dangers the United States would encounter in a post-Saddam Iraq. The situation will surely and sorely test a White House and Pentagon that are viscerally opposed to nation-building, notwithstanding the administration's commitment to the Middle East's political transformation.

Anthony H. Cordesman, in his assessment of conflict termination in Iraq, contends that the United States is paying the price for its "failure to look beyond immediate victory on the battlefield. Much more could have been done before, during and immediately after the war," he argues, "*if . . .* the US had not seen conflict termination, peacemaking, and nation building as secondary missions, and *if* a number of senior policymakers had not assumed the best case in terms of Iraqi postwar reactions to the Coalition attack." Cordesman concludes with an appeal and a warning: "This should be the last war in which there is a policy-level, military, and intelligence failure to come to grips with conflict termination and the transition to nation building. The US and its allies should address the issues involved before, during and after the conflict. They should prepare to commit the proper resources, and they should see political and psychological warfare in grand strategic terms. A war is over only when violence is ended, military forces are no longer needed to provide security, and nation building can safely take place without military protection. It does not end with the defeat of the main enemy forces on the battlefield."[15]

Unfortunately, there is no reason to believe that the second war against Iraq will be the last one marked by failure to come to grips with conflict termination and the transition to nation-building. The Defense Department is pushing a transformation of U.S. military power that would actually widen the divide between military operations and politically successful wars. In seeking to substitute the technologies of aerial precision strike at ever greater standoff distances for traditional ground forces, the Pentagon is moving toward capital-intensive force structures that are actually counterproductive to meeting the challenges of the kind we faced in Iraq once Saddam Hussein was removed from power. Frederick W. Kagan argues that the reason why "the United States [has] been so successful in recent wars [but] encountered so much difficulty in securing its political aims after the shooting stopped" lies partly in "a vision of war" that "see[s] the enemy as a target set and believe[s] that when all or most of the targets have been hit, he will inevitably surrender and American goals will be achieved." This vision ignores the importance of "how, exactly, one defeats the enemy and what the enemy's country looks like at the moment the bullets stop flying." For Kagan, the "entire thrust of the current program of military transformation of the U.S. armed forces . . . aims at the implementation and perfection of this target set mentality." But bashing targets is insufficient in circumstances where the United States is seeking regime change in a manner that secures support of the defeated populace for the new government. Such circumstances require large numbers of properly trained ground troops for the purposes of securing population centers and infrastructure, maintaining order, and providing humanitarian relief. "It is not enough to consider simply how to pound the enemy into submission with stand-off forces. . . . To effect regime change, U.S. forces must be positively in control of the enemy's territory and population as rapidly and continuously as possible. That control cannot be achieved by machines, still less by bombs. Only human beings interacting with human beings can achieve it. The only hope for success in the extension of politics that is war is to restore the human element to the transformation equation."[16]

Notes

Preface

1. "In the President's Words."
2. Quoted in M. Gordon and Trainor, *The Generals' War*, xv.
3. "Interview with Now-Vice President Richard Cheney."
4. Record, *Hollow Victory*, 156, 159.
5. T. Friedman, "Grapes of Wrath."
6. See Lemann, "How It Came to War."
7. Record, *Making War*.

Chapter 1. The Unfinished Business of 1991

1. See Mueller, *Policy and Opinion in the Gulf War*.
2. For examinations of various aspects of U.S. (and Western) strategic collaboration with Iraq during the Iraq-Iran War, see Timmerman, *The Death Lobby;* A. Friedman, *Spider's Web;* Darwish and Alexander, *Unholy Babylon;* and Chubin and Tripp, *Iran and Iraq at War,* 188–240.
3. ABC Television News, February 7, 1998, cited in Wurmser, *Tyranny's Ally,* 142; Haass quoted in Cockburn and Cockburn, *Out of the Ashes,* 37.
4. Mahnken, "A Squandered Opportunity?" 132.
5. Bush and Scowcroft, *A World Transformed,* 488, 489.
6. J. Baker with DeFrank, *The Politics of Diplomacy,* 435, 437, 432.
7. C. Powell with Persico, *My American Journey,* 526–27; emphasis in original; Schwarzkopf with Petre, *It Doesn't Take a Hero,* 497–98; emphasis in original.
8. Bush and Scowcroft, *A World Transformed,* 488; C. Powell with Persico, *My American Journey,* 526.
9. The other objectives were to destroy Iraq's military capacity to wage war; gain and maintain air supremacy; cut Iraqi supply lines; destroy Iraqi nuclear, biological, and chemical capabilities; and liberate Kuwait city with Arab forces. See *Conduct of the Persian Gulf War,* 499.
10. For the best account and assessment of the command decisions and operational errors that permitted half of the Republican Guard to survive Operation Desert Storm, see M. Gordon and Trainor, *The Generals' War,* 355–432.
11. J. Baker with DeFrank, *The Politics of Diplomacy,* 442; Bush and Scowcroft, *A World Transformed,* 488.
12. Tucker and Hendrickson, *Imperial Temptation,* 192.

13. Freedman and Karsh, *The Gulf Conflict*, 413.

14. Ibid., 411.

15. Meacham, "A Father's Words on Going to War," 43.

16. Quoted in Debusman, "Saddam Jeers at Bush."

17. Cline, "Defending the End," 370.

18. Quoted in Roger Cohen and Gatti, *In the Eye of the Storm*, 298–99.

19. Mahnken, "A Squandered Opportunity?" 123.

20. Ibid., 138–43.

21. See M. Gordon and Trainor, *The Generals' War*, 443–50; and Atkinson, *Crusade*, 1–10.

22. M. Gordon and Trainor, *The Generals' War*, 447.

23. Interview with Sandra Mackey, April 3, 2001, in Mackey, *The Reckoning*, 353.

24. Pollack, *The Threatening Storm*, 49.

25. CBS TV transcript, May 12, 1996, cited in Hiro, *Iraq in the Eye of the Storm*, 18. For a concise discussion of how many Iraqi children died after the Gulf War as a result of malnutrition and disease indirectly attributable to economic sanctions, see Pollack, *The Threatening Storm*, 137–39. Pollack's best guess is 200,000 to 225,000. "Given that the Gulf War itself probably caused no more than 10,000 to 30,000 Iraqi military casualties and another 1,000 to 5,000 civilian casualties, it raises the question of whether full-scale combat is a more humane policy than draconian sanctions."

26. Sponeck and Halliday, "Hostage Nation," 456–57.

27. Gause, "Getting It Backward on Iraq," 56.

28. See Pellett, "Sanctions," 185–203. See also Center for Economic and Social Rights, *Unsanctioned Suffering*.

29. Mueller and Mueller, "Sanctions of Mass Destruction," 43–53.

30. Mackey, *The Reckoning*, 363.

31. Rieff, "Were Sanctions Right?" 46.

32. Mackey, *The Reckoning*, 304.

33. Makiya, *Cruelty and Silence*, 148.

34. Tucker and Hendrickson, *Imperial Temptation*, 162.

35. D. Kagan and Kagan, *While America Sleeps*, 368–72.

36. Ibid., 367–68.

37. See Janice Gross Stein, "Deterrence and Compellance in the Gulf, 1990–91," 147–79.

38. Record, *Hollow Victory*, 30.

39. From the transcript of Ambassador April Glaspie's meeting with Saddam Hussein, reprinted in Sifry and Cerf, *Gulf War Reader*, 120–21.

40. Quoted in Stein, "Deterrence and Compellance in the Gulf, 1990–91," 152.

41. See Norman Cigar, "Iraq's Strategic Mindset," 1–29; and Baram, "The Iraqi Invasion of Kuwait," 277–78.

42. For a concise assessment of the wartime status of Iraqi chemical weapons programs and munitions, see Cordesman and Wagner, *Lessons of Modern War*, 4:879–83.

43. Quoted in R. Jeffrey Smith, "U.S. Warns of Retaliation."
44. Quoted in Sifry and Cerf, *Gulf War Reader,* 179.
45. See Gaffney, "Will the Next Mid East War Go Nuclear?" 532.
46. Terrill, "Chemical Warfare," 276–77.
47. Cordesman and Wagner, *Lessons of Modern War,* 4:887.
48. Pollack, *The Threatening Storm,* 266; emphasis added. See also Amatzia Baram, "An Analysis of Iraqi WMD Strategy," 35; and Ritter, *Endgame,* 102.
49. Hamza with Jeff Stein, *Saddam's Bombmaker,* 244.
50. Ibid., 237.
51. Gaffney, "Will the Next Mid East War Go Nuclear?" 532.
52. Gray, *Defining and Achieving Decisive Victory,* 11.

Chapter 2. The Neoconservative Vision and 9/11

1. The term "neoconservative" first appeared in the 1950s and referred to a group of largely Jewish and Catholic intellectuals once captivated by the ideals and promises of Communism and socialism but later disenchanted by the brutal totalitarianism of the Soviet state. These intellectuals, most of them Democrats, became hard-line cold warriors and supporters of U.S. intervention in the Vietnam War, and after the war gravitated to the conservative wing of the Democratic Party led by Sen. Henry M. "Scoop" Jackson, a hawk on the Vietnam War and a steadfast friend of Israel. Many subsequently became followers of Pres. Ronald Reagan, who discarded détente with the Soviet Union in favor of uncompromising hostility to Communism around the world. For accounts of the origins of neoconservatism and the neoconservatives' rise to influence within the George W. Bush administration, see Kosterlitz, "The Neoconservative Moment"; Drew, "The Neocons in Power," 20–22; Lind, "The Weird Men Behind George W. Bush's War," 10–13; Frachon and Vernet, "The Strategist and the Philosopher"; Fidler and Baker, "America's Democratic Imperialists"; L. Kaplan, "Regime Change," 21–23; Rhodes, "Imperial Logic of Bush's Liberal Agenda," 131–54; Greenberger and Leggett, "Bush Dreams of Changing Not Just Regime"; Judt, "The Way We Live Now," 6–10; Harding, "The Figure in the White House Shadows"; Elliott and Carney, "First Stop, Iraq"; "The Shadow Men," 21–23; and FitzGerald, "George Bush and the World."
2. Lieven, "The Push for War."
3. Ibid.
4. Rhodes, "Imperial Logic of Bush's Liberal Agenda," 133, 137; "Text of the President's Speech at West Point."
5. *National Security Strategy,* iii.
6. For two key examples of primacist literature of the 1990s, see Khalilzad, *From Containment to Global Leadership;* and Muravchik, *The Imperative*

of American Leadership. Later works include R. Kagan, "The Benevolent Empire," 24–35; and "American Power—For What?" 21–47.
7. Stephens, "Present at the Destruction of the World's Partnership."
8. "Statement of Principles."
9. R. Kagan and Kristol, "National Interest and Global Responsibility," 4.
10. Ibid., 6–7.
11. Ibid., 9, 13–14, 16–17.
12. Ibid., 17–18.
13. Ibid., 23–24.
14. Wolfowitz, "Statesmanship in the New Century," 325, 319, 320.
15. T. Barry, "A Strategy Foretold," 1–3; and Cramp, "The Bush Doctrine."
16. L. Kaplan and Kristol, *The War over Iraq,* 37.
17. Ibid., 38, 64.
18. Ibid., 81–83, 99.
19. Keller, "Sunshine Warrior," 51.
20. See, for example, Ledeen, *The War against the Terror Masters.*
21. P. Gordon, "Bush's Middle East Vision," 156.
22. James, "An Interview with Richard Perle."
23. Perle, "Why the West Must Strike First"; Rice, "Transforming the Middle East."
24. Packer, "Dreaming of Democracy," 49.
25. Mead, *Special Providence,* xvii.
26. Bush quoted in Lemann, "The Next World Order," 44.
27. L. Kaplan and Kristol, *The War over Iraq,* 71.
28. Ibid., 72.
29. *Strategic Survey 2002–2003,* 177.
30. Frum, *The Right Man,* esp. 195–202, 224–45; quote on 231.
31. Pollack, *The Threatening Storm,* 105.
32. Woodward, *Bush at War,* 49.
33. Ibid.
34. Ibid., 83–85.
35. Elliott and Carney, "First Stop, Iraq"; Peel, Graham, Harding, and Dempsey, "War in Iraq."

Chapter 3. The Bush Doctrine

1. Frum, *The Right Man,* 196.
2. LaFeber, "The Bush Doctrine," 549; *National Security Strategy,* 13.
3. *National Security Strategy,* 1, iii.
4. Gaddis, "A Grand Strategy"; "Text of the President's Speech at West Point"; *National Security Strategy,* 30, 27.
5. Restated in *National Security Strategy,* 13.
6. Rumsfeld, "The Price of Inaction."
7. *National Security Strategy,* 14.
8. See Easterbrook, "Term Limits," 22–25.

9. Quoted in Whitelaw and Mazzetti, "Why War?"; emphasis added.
10. Quoted in Dunn, "Myths, Motivations and 'Misunderstandings,'" 295.
11. *National Security Strategy,* 15; "Text of the President's Speech at West Point."
12. Quoted in Kristol, "Taking the War beyond Terrorism."
13. "President's State of the Union Address"; "Text of the President's Speech at West Point"; *National Security Strategy,* 15.
14. Quoted in Peterson, "Can Hussein Be Deterred?"
15. Quoted in Heisbourg, "A Work in Progress," 76.
16. *National Security Strategy,* 14.
17. Rumsfeld, "We Must Act to Prevent a Greater Evil"; Rumsfeld, "The Price of Inaction."
18. "Text of the President's Speech at West Point"; *National Security Strategy,* 15.
19. *Department of Defense Dictionary of Military and Associated Terms,* 333, 336.
20. Quoted in Sanger, "Beating Them to the Prewar."
21. Freedman, "Prevention, Not Preemption," 107.
22. Levy, "Declining Power," 91.
23. On the incidence of preemptive strikes and preventive wars in the twentieth century, see Reiter, "Exploding the Powder Keg Myth," 5–34.
24. Webster quoted in Elliot, "Strike First, Explain Yourself Later." Webster was referring to an incident in 1837 in which Canadian forces attacked a U.S. ship, the *Caroline,* above Niagara Falls; the ship was believed to be conveying supporters of a rebellion against British rule in Canada. The British claimed to have acted in self-defense, a claim Webster rejected with his dictum on preemption. Brown, "Self-Defense in an Imperfect World," 2; Hendrickson, "Toward Universal Empire," 7, 1.
25. "President Bush's Speech on the Use of Force."
26. Waltzer, "No Strikes," 20; Haass, *Intervention,* 51.
27. See, for example, Gaddis, "A Grand Strategy"; Daalder, Lindsay, and Steinberg, "Bush National Security Strategy"; Lemann, "The Next World Order"; Falk, "The New Bush Doctrine"; "The Bush Doctrine," editorial; Duffy, "Does Might Make Right?" 39; Thompson, "The Bush Doctrine"; Webb, "A New Doctrine for New Wars"; Elliott, "Strike First, Explain Yourself Later"; Mazzetti, "Ready. Aim. Fire First"; and Record, "The Bush Doctrine," 1–18.
28. Mayer, "A Doctrine Passes."
29. *Report of the Quadrennial Defense Review,* 12–13.
30. Ikenberry, *After Victory.*
31. Interview with Colin Powell in Dao, "Powell Defends First-Strike Option."
32. Sagan, *Moving Targets,* 20–22.
33. Quoted in May and Zeilkow, *The Kennedy Tapes,* 122, 207.
34. Quoted in Thomas, *Robert Kennedy,* 215.
35. Quoted in May and Zeilkow, *The Kennedy Tapes,* 244.

36. Quoted in Purdum, "The Missiles of 1962."
37. Hendrickson, "Toward Universal Empire," 5.
38. "Second Presidential Debate"; Brown, "Self-Defense in an Imperfect World," 5.
39. Falk, "The New Bush Doctrine."
40. See Sagan, "The Perils of Proliferation," 77–81.
41. Truman, *Memoirs,* 2:383.
42. Quoted in Sagan, "The Perils of Proliferation," 78.
43. Ikenberry, "America's Imperial Ambition," 45. See also Nye, *The Paradox of American Power.*
44. Kissinger, "Custodians of the World?"
45. Quoted in Kitfield, "Fractured Alliances," 721.
46. Howard, "Smoke on the Horizon."
47. McIntyre, *Understanding the New National Security Strategy,* 4.
48. Daalder, Lindsay, and Steinberg, "Bush National Security Strategy," 8; Jowitt, "Rage, Hubris, and Regime Change," 37.
49. Falk, *The Great Terror War,* 112.
50. Heisbourg, "A Work in Progress," 86.
51. Maj. Gen. Orville A. Anderson, quoted in Rankin, "U.S. Could Wipe Out Red A-Nests."

Chapter 4. Enemies: Osama's Al-Qaeda and Saddam's Iraq

1. Clausewitz, *On War,* 88.
2. *National Security Strategy,* i.
3. Hoffman, "Defining Terrorism," 19–20.
4. Schmid, Jongman, et al., *Political Terrorism,* 5–6.
5. Laqueur, *The New Terrorism,* 6. For an insightful discussion of terrorism as a strategic challenge, see Kiras, "Terrorism and Irregular Warfare," 208–32.
6. Laqueur, *The New Terrorism,* 5.
7. *Department of Defense Dictionary of Military and Associated Terms,* 428.
8. Gearty, "Terrorism and Morality," 36–37.
9. Falk, *The Great Terror War,* xviii–xiv.
10. Gilbert, *Israel,* 135–46.
11. Laqueur, *The New Terrorism,* 8.
12. Judt, "America and the War," 21; Atwood, "What Is Terrorism?" 27.
13. *National Strategy for Combating Terrorism,* 6–10.
14. Quoted in Lemann, "The War on What?" 41. See also Margalit, "The Wrong War," 5.
15. Worley, *Waging Ancient War,* 8.
16. President Bush's Speech at the National Cathedral, Washington, D.C., September 14, 2001, excerpt reprinted in *National Security Strategy,* 5.
17. Hart, "A Detour from the War on Terrorism."
18. See Gunaratna, *Inside Al Qaeda;* Bergen, *Holy War, Inc;* Bodansky, *Bin Laden.*

19. Benjamin and Simon, *The Age of Sacred Terror*, 385.

20. Benjamin, "In the Fog of War."

21. Huband, "Bin Laden Breaks Silence."

22. Harvey, *Global Disorder*, 67.

23. Quoted in Allen, "Bush: Hussein, Al Qaeda Linked."

24. Quoted in Milbank and Deane, "Hussein Link to 9/11 Lingers in Many Minds."

25. Pollack, *The Threatening Storm*, 153.

26. Judt, "The Wrong War at the Wrong Time"; Frank Rich, "The Waco Road to Baghdad," *New York Times*, August 17, 2002.

27. *Report of the Quadrennial Defense Review*, 12–13.

28. Hart, "A Detour from the War on Terrorism."

29. All excerpts from President Bush's news conference of March 6, 2003, are extracted from transcript reprinted in "'We're Calling for a Vote' at the U.N."

30. Scowcroft, "Don't Attack Iraq"; Seib, "Saddam Hussein and Terror"; Albright, "Where Iraq Fits."

31. Quoted in Stone, "Can We Fight Iraq *and* Hunt Al Qaeda?"

32. Rice, "Promoting the National Interest," 61.

33. Quoted in Whitelaw and Mazzetti, "Why War?" 5.

34. Bobbitt, *The Shield of Achilles*, 685.

35. L. Kaplan and Kristol, *The War over Iraq*, 124.

36. For an excellent and concise presentation of this argument, see Pollack, "Why Iraq Can't Be Deterred."

37. Pollack, "Why Iraq Can't Be Deterred." For a rejoinder, see Chapman, "Is Hussein Too Crazy for Us to Control?" See also Matlock, "Deterring the Undeterrable," 47.

38. Interviewed by and quoted in Mayer, "A Doctrine Passes." For a comparison of Saddam, Stalin, and Hitler as risk-takers, see Pollack, *The Threatening Storm*, 252–56.

39. Betts, "Suicide from Fear of Death?" 39.

40. Mearsheimer and Walt, "An Unnecessary War," 52–53.

41. Krauthammer, "The Obsolescence of Deterrence," 24. See also Lindberg, "Deterrence and Prevention," 24–28.

42. Benjamin and Simon, *The Age of Sacred Terror*, 264.

43. Risen, "Captives Deny Qaeda Worked with Baghdad."

44. "President Bush's Speech on the Use of Force."

45. Cited in Mitchell and Hulse, "C.I.A. Warns that a U.S. Attack May Ignite Terror."

46. Wieseltier, "Against Innocence," 27.

47. See Fuerth, "Outfoxed by North Korea."

48. Nye and Brzezinski quoted in Dobbs, "N. Korea Tests Bush's Policy of Preemption"; Cook, "Iraq's Phantom Weapons and Iran," 29; Kristol and Kagan, "North Korea Goes South."

49. Worley, *Waging Ancient War*, viii.

50. Ibid., x.
51. *Strategic Survey 2002–2003,* 9, 10.
52. See Meyer, "Al Qaeda May be Back"; Elliott, "How Al-Qaeda Got Back on the Attack."
53. Elliot, "Why the War on Terror Will Never End."
54. Stern, "The Protean Enemy," 27–40.
55. Thomas, "Al Qaeda in America," 40–46.

Chapter 5. War Aims

1. See *Public Papers of the Presidents: George Bush,* 201.
2. Quoted in Foot, *The Wrong War,* 23.
3. Hanson, "The Utility of War," 13.
4. See MacMaster, *Dereliction of Duty.*
5. See Record, *The Wrong War.*
6. Hanson, "The Utility of War," 15.
7. See Sheehan, *The Balance of Power,* 1–23.
8. L. Kaplan and Kristol, *The War over Iraq,* 57.
9. See Record, "Force Protection Fetishism," 4–11; and Record, *Failed States and Casualty Phobia.*
10. "Bush Speech on Iraq."
11. "Bush: 'We Will Do What Is Necessary.'"
12. Marshall, "Practice to Deceive," 29.
13. Klare, "For Oil and Empire?" 134; Telhami, *The Stakes,* 140.
14. See, for example, Baer, "Fall of the House of Saud," 53–62.
15. Quoted in Shanker and Schmitt, "Rumsfeld Says Iraq Is Collapsing."
16. Solomon, Bravin, and Whalen, "Iraq's Creditors Get in Line."
17. Figures cited in Murray, "U.S. Faces Messy Negotiations"; Bruce Bartlett, "'Odious Debt' Relief."
18. Vieth, "Iraq Debts Add Up to Trouble."
19. Bartlett, "'Odious Debt' Relief."
20. See Madrick, "The Iraqi Time Bomb," 48–51.
21. Quoted in Kristol, "What Wolfowitz Really Said."
22. Bacevich, "Freedom Is Just a Bonus"; Ajami, "Iraq and the Arabs' Future," 5.

Chapter 6. Analogies: Munich, Vietnam, and Postwar Japan

1. See May, *"Lessons" of the Past;* Neustadt and May, *Thinking in History;* Khong, *Analogies at War;* Hemmer, *Which Lessons Matter?* and Record, *Making War, Thinking History.*
2. "Bush Speech on Iraq"; Snyder, "Imperial Temptations," 39.
3. See Dyer, "Laying on that Old Munich Smear."
4. Kristol, "The Axis of Appeasement"; both Rumsfeld quotations in Dyer, "Laying on the Old Munich Smear."

5. See Karnow, "Do Not Compare Iraq with Vietnam"; Wilson, "Iraq Is Not Vietnam"; Boot, "Forget Vietnam."

6. Mackey, *The Reckoning,* 396.

7. For an analysis of Bush's use of the Munich and Vietnam analogies during the Gulf War, see Record, *Making War, Thinking History,* 101–4.

8. Quoted in Doughty, *The Seeds of Disaster,* 36, 38.

9. Weinberg, "No Road from Munich to Iraq."

10. Senate Joint Resolution, 45.

11. Ignatieff, "The American Empire."

12. See Wilson, "Iraq Is Not Vietnam"; Karnow, "Do Not Compare Iraq with Vietnam."

13. See Cigar, "Iraq's Strategic Mindset," 1–29; and Record, "Defeating Desert Storm," 125–40.

14. See Beeston, "Lessons of Vietnam"; Anderson, "Saddam's Greater Game."

15. Quoted in Schell, "From Sands to Quagmire."

16. See Ajami, "Beirut, Baghdad"; Baer, "Where Do They Go From Here?"; and Nordland, "The Lebanon Scenario."

17. "In the President's Words."

18. "Sinking Views of the United States."

19. Dower, *Embracing Defeat,* 25.

20. Ibid., 204.

21. See Manchester, *American Caesar,* 459–544; and Bix, *Hirohito and the Making of Modern Japan,* 533–44.

22. "Occupation Preoccupation," 9.

23. Webb, "Heading for Trouble."

Chapter 7. The War

1. Quoted in DeYoung, "Bush Proclaims Victory in Iraq."

2. Thomas and Brant, "The Education of Tommy Franks."

3. Hitchens, *A Long Short War,* 68; Keegan, "Saddam's Utter Collapse."

4. Boot, "The New American Way of War," 44. For the lineup of opposing forces in 1940, see Record, "France 1940."

5. See Schmitt, "Rumsfeld Says U.S. Will Cut Forces in Gulf," and Schmitt, "U.S. to Withdraw All Combat Units from Saudi Arabia."

6. MacLeod, "Why U.S. Is Pulling Out of Saudi Arabia."

7. For a summary of events leading up to the Turkish refusal, see *Strategic Survey 2002–2003,* 127–38.

8. Wolfowitz and Cheney quoted in Page, "Prewar Predictions Coming Back to Bite."

9. Quoted in Drogin and Miller, "Plan's Defect: No Defectors."

10. Adelman, "Cakewalk in Iraq."

11. Quoted in Scarborough, "War in Iraq Seen as Quick Win"; and Jim Rutenberg, "Conservatives Tailor Their Tone to Fit Setbacks in War."

12. Quoted in Novak, "Iraqis Eating Into Coalition 'Cakewalk.'"
13. Cheney and McCain quoted in Scarborough, "War in Iraq Seen as Quick Win."
14. See Higgins, *The Perfect Failure;* and Peter Wyden, *Bay of Pigs.*
15. Trofomiv, Pope, and Waldman, "History of Betrayal Makes Shiites Wary of Liberators."
16. Quoted in Ford, "Why U.S. Is Getting Wary Welcome."
17. M. Gordon, "New Reality, Hard Choices."
18. Novak, "Rumsfeld's Army"; and Galloway, "An Army Transformed."
19. Quoted in Priest, *The Mission,* 24.
20. For assessments of the Weinberger-Powell doctrine, see Record, "Weinberger-Powell Doesn't Cut It," 35–36; and Record, *Making War, Thinking History,* 130–41.
21. See McGrory, "Hesitant Hawks"; Jaffe, "Problems with Iraq-Invasion Plan"; Ricks, "Some Top Military Brass Favor Status Quo in Iraq"; Norton-Taylor and Borger, "Iraq Attack Plans Alarm Top Military"; Ricks, "Timing, Tactics on Iraq War Disputed"; Capaccio, "U.S. Generals' Cautions on Iraq Unheeded"; Keegan, "'Heavy' Invasion Is Best Option"; Jaffe and Hiatt, "Bush Views Iraq Invasion Plan"; Bowman, "Debate Builds over War Plans for Iraq"; Keegan, "Heavy Risk of the 'Light' Solution"; C. Gordon, "Military Concern over 2-Front Conflict"; Klare, "War Plans and Pitfalls"; Kelly, "Rummy and the Brass"; C. Cooper, "Iraqi Forces Aren't Expected to Put Up Much of a Fight"; Schmitt and Shanker, "War Plan Calls for Precision Bombing"; Michaels, "Lessons from 1991"; R. Cooper and Hendren, "Strategy Boiled Down to Light v. Heavy"; Clark, "Battle Lines Drawn at Pentagon"; M. Gordon, "A Swift, and Risky, Attack"; Boot, "Sting Like a Bee"; and Ricks, "Calibrated War Makes a Comeback."
22. Scales quoted in Diamond, Moniz, and Kelly, "Urgency to Take Out Saddam"; Arkin, "A War of Subtle Strategy."
23. Myers quoted in Schmitt, "Top General Concedes Aerial Bombardment Did Not Fully Meet Goal"; Cheney quoted in Balz, "Conduct of War Defended."
24. Galloway, "General Tommy Franks Discusses Conducting the War in Iraq."
25. Ibid.; and Boyer, "The New War Machine."
26. Quoted in Rennie and La Guardia, "Top U.S. General Attacks Hawks' Strategy on Iraq."
27. Boyer, "The New War Machine."
28. Quoted in Kitfield, "Attack Always."
29. See Galloway, "Risks of Iraqi War Emerging"; Peters, "Shock, Awe, and Overconfidence"; and Kitfield, "The Army's Gamble."
30. Quoted in Galloway, "General Tommy Franks Discusses Conducting the War in Iraq."
31. See Loeb, "Rumsfeld Faulted for Troop Dilution"; and Hersh, "Offense and Defense."
32. McCaffrey and Nash quoted in Loeb and Ricks, "Questions Raised about Invasion Force."

33. Arkin, "Too Little Shock, Not Enough Awe"; McCaffrey quoted in M. Gordon, "The Test for Rumsfeld."
34. Myers quoted in Shanker and Tiernay, "Head of Military Denounces Critics"; Franks quoted in Galloway, "General Tommy Franks Discusses Conducting the War in Iraq."
35. Hoar, "Why Aren't There Enough Troops in Iraq?"
36. See Drogin and Vieth, "Looting Thwarts Plans for Quick Iraq Recovery"; Gellman, "Looting Is a Double Loss for U.S. Forces"; Chandrasekaran, "'Our Heritage Is Finished'"; and Bowman, "U.S. Misjudged Power Vacuum."
37. Gellman, "U.S. Has Not Inspected Iraqi Nuclear Facility."
38. Crane and Terrill, *Reconstructing Iraq,* 15.
39. Krauthammer, "The Shiite 'Menace.'"
40. See Record, "Operation Allied Force," 15–23.
41. Keegan, "Saddam's Utter Collapse."
42. See Moore, "A Foe That Collapsed from Within"; McAllester, "Ex-Bodyguard for Uday"; and Zucchino, "Iraq's Swift Defeat Blamed on Leaders."
43. See Slevin, "Hussein Loyalists Blamed for Chaos"; Martin, "Iraqi 'Secret Plan' Orders Mayhem"; Martin, "Saddam Faithful Refuse to Surrender"; and Trofomiv, "U.S. Faces Two Baghdads."
44. Quoted in Slevin, "Hussein Loyalists Blamed for Chaos."
45. MacFarquhar, "Rising Tide of Islamic Militants."
46. "U.S. Secretary of State Colin Powell Addresses the U.N. Security Council."
47. All statements quoted in "Sounding the Drums for War."
48. "Remarks by President Bush on Iraq."
49. Lindberg, "Did Saddam Have WMD?"
50. Quoted in Jahn, "Weapons Inspectors."
51. See Delpech, "The Weapons Hunt"; Broad, "Some Skeptics Say Arms Hunt Is Fruitless"; Fialka and Dreazen, "Are Hints of 'Smoking Gun' in Iraq Enough?"; J. Miller, "Illicit Arms Kept Till Eve of War"; and Curl, "Bush Believes Saddam Destroyed Arms."
52. D. Kelley, "Regime's Priority Was Blueprints."
53. See Drogin. "The Vanishing"; J. Barry and Isikoff, "Saddam's Secrets"; Pincus and Sullivan, "Scientists Still Deny Iraqi Arms Programs"; and M. Gordon, "Weapons of Mass Confusion."
54. Drogin, "The Vanishing."
55. Ekeus, "Iraq's Real Weapons Threat."
56. Deutch quoted in Pincus, "Deutch Sees Consequences in Failed Search for Arms"; Lindberg, "Did Saddam Have WMD?"
57. Richard Cohen, "Never Mind the Weapons." See also Fireman, "Iraq's Weapons of Mass Distraction?"; and Hersh, "Selective Intelligence."
58. Gellman, "Seven Nuclear Sites Looted." See also Gellman, "Frustrated, U.S. Arms Team to Leave Iraq."

59. See Stone, "Were Qaeda-Iraq links Exaggerated?"; Duffy, "Weapons of Mass Disappearance"; Thomas, Wolffe, and Isikoff, "Where Are Iraq's WMDs?"; Auster, Mazzetti, and Pound, "Truth and Consequences"; G. Miller, "Pentagon Defends Role of Intelligence Unit"; Pincus and Priest, "Analysts Cite Pressure on Iraq Judgments"; Huband and Fidler, "Did Intelligence Agencies Rely Too Much on Unreliable Data?"; Meyerson, "Enron-Like Unreality"; S. Weisman, "Truth Is the First Casualty"; Zakaria, "Exaggerating the Threats"; Hersh, "Who Lied to Whom?"; and Gellman and Pincus, "Depiction of Threat Outgrew Supporting Evidence."

60. Gellman and Pincus, "Depiction of Threat Outgrew Supporting Evidence."

61. Judis and Ackerman, "The First Casualty."

62. Pollack quoted in S. Weisman, "Truth Is the First Casualty"; Butler quoted in Zakaria, "Exaggerating the Threats"; Turner quoted in Diamond, "Ex-CIA Director Says Administration Stretched Facts on Iraq"; Tanenhaus, "Bush's Brain Trust."

63. Quoted in Schrader, "Rumsfeld Defends the Decision for War."

64. Quoted in Hersh, "Selective Intelligence."

65. See Treverton, "Intelligence," 9–11.

66. Will, "The Bush Doctrine at Risk."

67. Carter, "The Troubling New Face of America."

68. See Johnson, "Unholy Allies"; Martin, "Saddam Loyalists Ally with Islamists"; and M. Gordon with Jehl, "Foreign Fighters Add to Resistance in Iraq."

69. Stern, "How America Created a Terrorist Haven"; Cannistraro quoted in Walcott, "Some in Administration Uneasy."

70. Quoted in O'Brien, "Crime and Poor Security."

71. Bank, "Three U.S. Humanitarian Groups."

Chapter 8. The "Peace"

1. Crane and Terrill, *Reconstructing Iraq*, 17.

2. Ibid., 18–19.

3. Cordesman, "What Went Wrong"; G. Baker, "With Troops under Fire."

4. Slevin and Priest, "Wolfowitz Concedes Errors on Iraq."

5. T. Friedman, "Bad Planning."

6. Rubin, "Bush Never Made Serious Postwar Plans."

7. Quoted in Dinmore, "Political Fallout."

8. M. Kelley, "Pentagon's Wolfowitz Admits U.S. Erred in Iraq."

9. M. Gordon with Schmitt, "U.S. Plans to Reduce Forces in Iraq"; and M. Gordon, "How Much Is Enough?"

10. M. Gordon, "Fear of Baghdad Unrest Prompts a Halt in Sending Troops Home"; and M. Gordon, "Allies to Retain Larger Force."

11. Loeb, "Plan to Bolster Forces in Iraq in Unveiled."

12. Quoted in Slevin and Priest, "Wolfowitz Concedes Errors in Iraq."

13. Lugar, "A Victory at Risk."

14. Slevin, "Baghdad Anarchy Spurs Call for Help."
15. Quoted in Chandrasekaran and Slevin, "Iraq's Ragged Reconstruction."
16. See Kessler and Priest, "U.S. Planners Surprised"; Wright, "Rise of Shiite Leaders in Iraq"; Shadid, "Unfulfilled Promises"; and Browne, "Radical Islam."
17. See Kosterlitz, "Occupational Hazards," 910–17; Fallows, "The Fifty-First State?" 53–64; and R. Kaplan, "A Post-Saddam Scenario," 88–90.
18. See Loeb and Lynch, "U.S. Cool to New U.N. Vote."
19. Durch quoted in Slevin and Loeb, "Plan to Secure Postwar Iraq Faulted"; T. Friedman, "Bad Planning."
20. See Cockburn and Cockburn, *Out of the Ashes,* 164–90.
21. Pollack, *The Threatening Storm,* 97.
22. Terrill, *Nationalism,* 13.
23. Ferguson, "The Empire Slinks Back," 57, 54.
24. *Strategic Survey 2002–2003,* 176–79; Nye, "U.S. Power and Strategy after Iraq," 70, 71.
25. Rubin, "More Than Soldiers Needed in Iraq."
26. Loeb, "Number of Wounded in Action on the Rise"; address to the nation by Pres. George W. Bush, September 7, 2003, reprinted in "Bush: 'We Will Do What Is Necessary,'" *Washington Post,* September 8, 2003.
27. King and Cummins, "The Postwar Bill for Iraq."
28. Efron, Wright, and Hook, "Quick Help with Iraq Unlikely."
29. Milbank and Deane, "Hussein Link to 9/11 Lingers in Many Minds."
30. Data contained in Benedetto, "Most Say Iraq War Was Worth Fighting."
31. Data contained in Barett, "When Is Enough Enough?"
32. Morin and Balz, "Public Says $87 Billion Too Much."
33. *The Budget and Economic Outlook.*
34. "Deficit Delusions." See also Andrews, "Congressional Deficit Estimate"; Shapiro, "Fiscal Recklessness"; J. Weisman, "2004 Deficit to Reach $480 Billion"; and Firestone, "Dizzying Drive."
35. "Deficit Delusions."
36. See Kessler, "Powell Cites 'Real' Divide"; Thomas, "Rumsfeld's War"; Michael Hirsh, "Powell's Battle"; Dao and Schmitt, "Rift over Plan to Impose Rule on Iraq"; O'Hanlon, "How the Hard-Liners Lost"; J. Donnelly, "Tension Seen on Iraq Building"; Morgan, "Deciding Who Rebuilds Iraq"; Lake, "Split Decision," 116–18; Daniszewski and Marshall, "Disarray in Iraq"; DeYoung and Slevin, "Pentagon, State Spar on Team to Run Iraq"; Wright, "White House Divided over Reconstruction"; Ignatius, "The Battle over Postwar Iraq"; Reynolds, "Pentagon's Free Rein"; Fred Barnes, "Bum Advice"; Kessler, "State-Defense Policy Rivalry Intensifying"; Blankley, "Winning the War"; Slavin, "Gingrich Takes Swipe at State Department"; Ignatius, "Bush's Confusion"; Gingrich, "The Next Challenge for Bush"; Hunt, "Loose Cannon"; S. Weisman, "Under Fire"; Seib, "Powell-Rumsfeld Feud"; B. Powell, "The War over the Peace"; Hammer and Soloway, "Who's In Charge Here?"

37. For three detailed and well-informed accounts of the "war" between the state and defense departments over postwar Iraq, see Fineman, Wright, and McManus, "Preparing for War"; G. Baker and Fidler, "The Best Laid Plans?"; and Slavin and Moniz, "How Peace in Iraq Became So Elusive."
38. Khafaji, "A Few Days After," 87.
39. T. Donnelly, "There's No Place Like Iraq"; Boot, "American Imperialism?"
40. Shanker and Schmitt, "Pentagon Expects Long-Term Access to Key Iraq Bases"; Rumsfeld quoted in Graham, "U.S. Won't Seek Bases in Iraq."
41. See Grier, "A Shrinking Global Footprint"; Knowlton, "U.S. Weighs Shift of Forces in Gulf"; and M. Gordon with Schmitt, "U.S. Will Move Air Operations to Qatar Base."
42. See, for example, Mackey, *The Reckoning;* Marr, "Iraq 'The Day After,'" 13–29; Yaphe, "Iraq before and after Saddam," 7–12; Ottoway, Carothers, Hawthorne, and Brumberg, "Democratic Mirage"; Freedberg and Hegland, "Reinventing Iraq"; and Khalaf, "A Divided Country."
43. Ottoway, Carothers, Hawthorne, and Brumberg, "Democratic Mirage," 4.
44. See, for example, Karsh, "Making Iraq Safe for Democracy," 22–28; Dawisha and Dawisha, "How to Build a Democratic Iraq," 36–50; Hanson, "Democracy in the Middle East," 23–26; and Byman and Pollack, "Democracy in Iraq?" 119–36.
45. Boot, *The Savage Wars of Peace,* 125.
46. Ricks, "Experts Question Depth of Victory."
47. *Department of Defense Dictionary of Military and Associated Terms,* 181.
48. Quoted in Loeb, "No Iraq 'Quagmire.'"
49. Quoted in G. Miller, "U.S. Defends Its Role in Iraq."
50. Squitieri, "U.S. Troops May Be in Iraq for Ten Years."
51. Fattah, "Random Death."
52. Haqqani, "Islam's Weakened Moderates," 61.
53. Lieven, "Help for America Must Have Strings Attached."
54. Terrill, *Nationalism,* 31.
55. Schmitt and Shanker, "Water and Electricity in Baghdad."
56. See Byman, "Building the New Iraq," 57–71.
57. Daalder quoted in Kitfield, "NATO Could Help in Iraq"; S. Weisman with Barringer, "U.S. Abandons Idea of Bigger U.N. Role."
58. Shanker, "Officials Debate Whether to Seek a Bigger Military."
59. See O'Hanlon, "Breaking the Army"; O'Hanlon, "Do the Math"; Zakaria, "Iraq Policy Is Broken"; Kramer, "W and Rummy in Denial"; F. Kaplan, "Blow-Back in Baghdad"; and Hutcheson, "Bush Says Troop Size in Iraq Just Fine."
60. Zakaria, "Iraq Policy Is Broken"; and O'Hanlon, "Breaking the Army."
61. See Chandrasekaran, "U.S. to Form New Iraqi Army"; and Tyler, "U.S.-British Project."
62. Cordesman, *Iraq and Conflict Termination,* 7.
63. Grossman, "Powell's Advisory Panel."

Chapter 9. Dark Victory

1. See F. Kagan, "Did We Fail in Afghanistan?" 39–45; *Unfinished Business;* Bearak, "Unreconstructed," 40–47, 62, 64, 96, 101; Kitfield, "Wounded, Not Crippled," 574–78; Matthews, "Out of Limelight"; McGirk and Ware, "Losing Control?"; and Baldauf and Tohid, "Taliban Appears to Be Regrouped and Well-Funded."
2. F. Kagan, "Did We Fail in Afghanistan?" 44–45.
3. Dunn, "Myths, Motivations and 'Misunderstandings,'" 295.
4. Kosterlitz, "The Neoconservative Moment"; Wurmser quoted in Kosterlitz, "The Neoconservative Moment"; Jervis, "The Compulsive Empire," 83.
5. Lind, "The Weird Men behind George W. Bush's War," 13.
6. Jervis, "The Compulsive Empire," 84.
7. "No Proof Linking 9/11 to Hussein."
8. *Emergency Responders,* 1.
9. Kissinger, "Role Reversal and Alliance Realities"; Kupchan, "The Atlantic Alliance"; Daalder, "The End of Atlanticism," 152.
10. Kissinger, "America Must Rebuild."
11. Quoted in Prestowitz, *Rogue Nation,* 8.
12. Ibid.
13. Fukuyama, "Us vs. Them."
14. "Second Presidential Debate."
15. Cordesman, *Iraq and Conflict Termination,* 22, 23.
16. F. Kagan, "War and Aftermath," 4–5, 27.

Bibliography

Adelman, Ken. "Cakewalk in Iraq." *Washington Post,* February 13, 2002.

Ajami, Fouad. "Beirut, Baghdad." *Wall Street Journal,* August 25, 2003.

————. "Iraq and the Arabs' Future." *Foreign Affairs* 82, no. 1 (January–February 2003): 2–18.

Albright, Madeleine K. "Where Iraq Fits in the War on Terror." *New York Times,* September 13, 2002.

Allen, Mike. "Bush: Hussein, Al Qaeda Linked." *Washington Post,* September 26, 2002.

"American Power—For What? A Symposium." *Commentary* 109, no. 1 (January 2000): 21–47.

An Analysis of the U.S. Military's Ability to Sustain an Occupation of Iraq. Washington, D.C.: Congressional Budget Office, September 3, 2003.

Anderson, Gary. "Saddam's Greater Game." *Washington Post,* April 2, 2003.

Andrews, Edmund. "Congressional Deficit May Exceed a Half-Trillion." *New York Times,* August 26, 2003.

Arkin, William M. "Too Little Shock, Not Enough Awe." *Los Angeles Times,* March 30, 2003.

————. "A War of Subtle Strategy." *Los Angeles Times,* March 23, 2003.

Atkinson, Rick. *Crusade: The Untold Story of the Persian Gulf War.* Boston: Houghton Mifflin, 1993.

Atwood, Paul L. "What Is Terrorism?" *Joiner Center Newsletter* 5, no. 1 (March 2003): 26–27.

Auster, Bruce B., Mark Mazzetti, and Edward T. Pound. "Truth and Consequences." *U.S. News and World Report,* June 9, 2003.

Bacevich, Andrew J. "Freedom Is Just a Bonus." *Los Angeles Times,* April 13, 2003.

Baer, Robert. "The Fall of the House of Saud." *Atlantic Monthly,* May 2003, 53–62.

————. "Where Do They Go From Here? We Pulled Out of Beirut. We Can't Abandon Iraq." *Washington Post,* August 24, 2003.

Baker, Gerard. "With Troops under Fire and the Costs Mounting, Does the U.S. Have the Will for the Long Haul in Iraq?" *Financial Times,* June 30, 2003.

Baker, Gerard, and Stephen Fidler. "The Best Laid Plans? How Turf Battles and Mistakes in Washington Dragged Down the Reconstruction of Iraq." *Financial Times,* August 4, 2003.

Baker, James A., III, with Thomas M. DeFrank. *The Politics of Diplomacy: Revolution, War, and Peace, 1989–1992.* New York: G.P. Putnam's Sons, 1995.

Baldauf, Scott, and Oqais Tohid. "Taliban Appears To be Regrouped and Well-Funded." *Christian Science Monitor,* May 8, 2003.

Balz, Dan. "Conduct of War Defended." *Washington Post,* March 26, 2003.

Bank, David. "Three U.S. Humanitarian Groups Spurn Reconstruction Effort in Iraq." *Wall Street Journal,* May 29, 2003.

Baram, Amatzia. "An Analysis of Iraqi WMD Strategy." *Nonproliferation Review* 8, no. 2 (summer 2001): 25–39.

———. "The Iraqi Invasion of Kuwait." In *The Saddam Hussein Reader,* ed. Turi Munthe, 277–78.

Barett, Jennifer. "When Is Enough Enough?" MSNBC, September 5, 2002.

Barnes, Fred. "Bum Advice." *Weekly Standard,* April 14, 2003.

Barry, John, and Michael Isikoff. "Saddam's Secrets." *Newsweek,* June 30, 2003.

Barry, Tom. "A Strategy Foretold." *Foreign Policy in Focus* (October 2002): 1–3.

Bartlett, Bruce. "'Odious Debt' Relief." *Washington Times,* April 9, 2003.

Bearak, Barry. "Unreconstructed." *New York Times Magazine,* June 1, 2003.

Beeston, Richard. "Lessons of Vietnam Absorbed by Another U.S. Foe." *London Times,* March 26, 2003.

Benedetto, Richard. "Most Say Iraq War Was Worth Fighting." *USA Today,* August 28, 2003.

Benjamin, Daniel. "In the Fog of War, a Greater Threat." *Washington Post,* October 31, 2002.

Benjamin, Daniel, and Steven Simon. *The Age of Sacred Terror.* New York: Random House, 2002.

Bergen, Peter L. *Holy War, Inc.: Inside the Secret World of Osama bin Laden.* New York: Free Press, 2001.

Betts, Richard K. "Suicide from Fear of Death?" *Foreign Affairs* 82, no. 1 (January–February 2003): 34–43.

Bix, Herbert. *Hirohito and the Making of Modern Japan.* New York: HarperCollins, 2000.

Blankley, Tony. "Winning the War, Losing the Peace." *Washington Times,* April 23, 2003.

Bobbitt, Philip. *The Shield of Achilles: War, Peace, and the Course of History.* New York: Alfred A. Knopf, 2002.

Bodansky, Yossef. *Bin Laden: The Man Who Declared War on America.* New York: Prima, 1999.

Boot, Max. "American Imperialism? No Need to Run Away from Label." *USA Today,* May 6, 2003.

———. "Forget Vietnam—History Deflates Guerrilla Mystique." *Los Angeles Times,* April 6, 2003.

———. "The New American Way of War." *Foreign Affairs* 82, no. 4 (July–August 2003): 41–58.

———. "Rumsfeld's War." *Foreign Affairs* 82, no. 4 (July–August 2003): 41–58.

———. *The Savage Wars of Peace: Small Wars and the Rise of American Power.* New York: Basic Books, 2002.

————. "Sting Like a Bee." *Wall Street Journal,* March 21, 2003.

Bowman, Tom. "Debate Builds over War Plans for Iraq." *Baltimore Sun,* August 12, 2002.

————. "U.S. Misjudged Power Vacuum, Critics Claim." *Baltimore Sun,* April 25, 2003.

Boyer, Peter. "The New War Machine." *New Yorker,* June 30, 2003.

Broad, William J. "Some Skeptics Say Arms Hunt Is Fruitless." *New York Times,* April 18, 2003.

Brown, Chris. "Self-Defense in an Imperfect World." *Ethics and International Affairs* 17, no. 1 (2003): 2–8.

Browne, Anthony. "Radical Islam Starts to Fill Iraq's Power Vacuum." *London Times,* June 3, 2003.

The Budget and Economic Outlook: An Update, August 2003. Washington, D.C.: Congressional Budget Office, August 2003.

Bush, George, and Brent Scowcroft. *A World Transformed.* New York: Alfred A. Knopf, 1998.

"The Bush Doctrine." Editorial. *New York Times,* September 22, 2002.

"Bush Speech on Iraq: 'Saddam Hussein and His Sons Must Leave.'" *New York Times,* March 18, 2003.

"Bush: 'We Will Do What Is Necessary.'" Transcript of President George W. Bush's address to the nation, September 7, 2003, *Washington Post,* September 8, 2003.

Byman, Daniel L. "Building the New Iraq: The Role of Intervening Forces." *Survival* 45, no. 2 (summer 2003): 57–71.

Byman, Daniel L., and Kenneth M. Pollack. "Democracy in Iraq?" *Washington Quarterly* 26, no. 3 (summer 2003): 119–36.

Capaccio, Tony. "U.S. Generals' Caution on Iraq Unheeded, Levin Says." Bloomberg.com, August 6, 2002.

Carter, Jimmy. "The Troubling New Face of America." *Washington Post,* September 5, 2002.

Center for Economic and Social Rights. *Unsanctioned Suffering: A Human Rights Assessment of United Nations Sanctions on Iraq.* New York: CESR, 1996.

Chandrasekaran, Rajiv. "'Our Heritage Is Finished.'" *Washington Post,* April 13, 2003.

————. "U.S. to Form New Iraqi Army." *Washington Post,* June 24, 2003.

Chandrasekaran, Rajiv, and Peter Slevin. "Iraq's Ragged Reconstruction." *Washington Post,* May 9, 2003.

Chapman, Steve. "Is Hussein Too Crazy for Us to Control?" *Chicago Tribune,* October 3, 2002.

Chubin, Shahram, and Charles Tripp. *Iran and Iraq at War.* Boulder, CO: Westview Press, 1988.

Cigar, Norman. "Iraq's Strategic Mindset and the Gulf War: Blueprint for Defeat." *Journal of Strategic Studies* 15, no. 1 (March 1992): 1–29.

Clark, Wesley. "Battle Lines Drawn at Pentagon over New Kind of War." *London Times,* March 20, 2003.

Clausewitz, Carl von. *On War.* Ed. and trans. Michael Howard and Peter Paret. Princeton, NJ: Princeton University Press, 1976.

Cline, Lawrence E. "Defending the End: Decision Making in Terminating the Gulf War." *Comparative Strategy* 17, no. 4 (1998): 345–62.

Cockburn, Andrew, and Patrick Cockburn. *Out of the Ashes: The Resurrection of Saddam Hussein.* New York: HarperCollins, 1999.

Cohen, Richard. "Never Mind the Weapons." *Washington Post,* May 7, 2003.

Cohen, Roger, and Claudio Gatti. *In the Eye of the Storm: The Life of General H. Norman Schwarzkopf.* New York: Farrar, Straus, and Giroux, 1991.

Conduct of the Persian Gulf War: Final Report to Congress. Washington, D.C.: U.S. Government Printing Office, 1992.

Cook, Robin. "Iraq's Phantom Weapons and Iran." *New Perspectives Quarterly* 20, no. 3 (summer 2003): 28–30.

Cooper, Christopher. "Iraqi Forces Aren't Expected to Put Up Much of a Fight." *Wall Street Journal,* November 13, 2002.

Cooper, Richard T., and John Hendren. "Strategy Boiled Down to Light v. Heavy." *Los Angeles Times,* March 19, 2003.

Cordesman, Anthony H. *Iraq and Conflict Termination: The Road to Guerrilla War?* Washington, D.C.: Center for Strategic and International Studies, July 20, 2003.

———. "What Went Wrong: The Iraq War and the Lessons of Conflict Termination, Peacemaking, and Nation Building." Unpublished assessment provided the author via e-mail.

Cordesman, Anthony H., and Abraham R. Wagner. *The Lessons of Modern War.* Vol. 4, *The Gulf War.* Boulder, CO: Westview Press, 1996.

Cramp, James G. "The Bush Doctrine: From Theory to Practice." Air War College paper submitted to the author in 2003 in partial fulfillment of graduation requirements.

Crane, Conrad C., and W. Andrew Terrill. *Reconstructing Iraq: Insights, Challenges, and Missions for Military Forces in a Post-Conflict Scenario.* Carlisle Barracks, PA: Strategic Studies Institute, U.S. Army War College, February 2003.

Curl, Joseph. "Bush Believes Saddam Destroyed Arms." *Washington Times,* April 26, 2003.

Daalder, Ivo H. "The End of Atlanticism." *Survival* 45, no. 2 (summer 2003): 147–66.

Daalder, Ivo H., James Lindsay, and James B. Steinberg. "The Bush National Security Strategy: An Evaluation." Brookings Institution Policy Brief. Washington, D.C.; Brookings Institution, October 4, 2002.

Daniszewski, John, and Tyler Marshall. "Disarray in Iraq Threatens U.S. Goals." *Los Angeles Times,* May 25, 2003.

Dao, James. "Powell Defends First-Strike Option." *New York Times,* September 8, 2002.

Dao, James, and Eric Schmitt. "Rift over Plan to Impose Rule on Iraq." *New York Times,* October 10, 2002.

Darwish, Adel, and Gregory Alexander. *Unholy Babylon: The Secret History of Saddam's War.* New York: St. Martin's Press, 1991.

Dawisha, Adeed, and Karen Dawisha. "How to Build a Democratic Iraq." *Foreign Affairs* 82, no. 3 (May–June 2003): 36–50.

Debusman, Bernd. "Saddam Jeers at Bush, Claims Iraq Won the War." *Washington Times,* January 17, 1992.

Defense Reorganization: The Need for Change. Staff Report to the Committee on Armed Services. S. Prt. 99–86. 99th Congress: 1st sess. Washington, D.C.: U.S. Government Printing Office, 1985.

"Deficit Delusions." *Washington Post,* August 29, 2003.

Delpech, Therese. "The Weapons Hunt." *Wall Street Journal,* April 16, 2003.

Department of Defense Dictionary of Military and Associated Terms. Joint Publication 1-02. Washington, D.C.: Department of Defense, April 12, 2002.

DeYoung, Karen. "Bush Proclaims Victory in Iraq." *Washington Post,* May 2, 2003.

DeYoung, Karen, and Peter Slevin. "Pentagon, State Spar on Team to Run Iraq." *Washington Post,* April 1, 2003.

Diamond, John. "Ex-CIA Director Says Administration Stretched Facts on Iraq." *USA Today,* June 19, 2003.

Diamond, John, Dave Moniz, and Jack Kelly. "Urgency to Take Out Saddam Leads to Shift in U.S. Strategy." *USA Today,* March 21, 2003.

Dinmore, Guy. "Political Fallout over Iraq Rattling Washington." *Financial Times,* June 25, 2003.

Dobbs, Michael. "N. Korea Tests Bush's Policy of Preemption." *Washington Post,* January 6, 2003.

Dodge, Toby, and Steven Simon, eds. *Iraq at the Crossroads: State and Society in the Shadow of Regime Change.* Adelphi Paper 354. London: International Institute for Strategic Studies, 2003.

Donnelly, John. "Tension Seen on Iraq Rebuilding." *Boston Globe,* May 3, 2003.

Donnelly, Tom. "There's No Place Like Iraq . . . for U.S. Military Bases." *Weekly Standard,* May 5, 2003.

Doughty, Robert Allan. *The Seeds of Disaster: The Development of French Army Doctrine, 1919–1939.* Hamden, CT: Archon Books, 1985.

Dower, John W. *Embracing Defeat: Japan in the Wake of World War II.* New York: W. W. Norton, 1999.

Drew, Elizabeth. "The Neocons in Power." *New York Review of Books,* June 12, 2003, 20–22.

Drogin, Bob. "The Vanishing." *New Republic,* July 21, 2003.

Drogin, Bob, and Greg Miller. "Plan's Defect: No Defectors." *Los Angeles Times,* March 28, 2003.

Drogin, Bob, and Warren Vieth. "Looting Thwarts Plans for Quick Iraq Recovery." *Los Angeles Times,* April 18, 2003.

Duffy, Michael. "Does Might Make Right?" *Time,* September 30, 2002, 39.

———. "Weapons of Mass Disappearance." *Time,* June 9, 2003.

Dunn, David Hastings. "Myths, Motivations and 'Misunderstandings': The Bush Administration and Iraq." *International Affairs* 79, no. 2 (2003): 279–97.

Dyer, Gwynne. "Laying on That Old Munich Smear." *Toronto Star,* September 2, 2002.

Easterbrook, Gregg. "Term Limits, the Meaninglessness of WMD." *New Republic,* October 7, 2002, 22–25.

Efron, Sonni, Robin Wright, and Janet Hook. "Quick Help with Iraq Unlikely, U.S. Says." *Los Angeles Times,* September 12, 2003.

Ekeus, Rolf. "Iraq's Real Weapons Threat." *Washington Post,* June 29, 2003.

Elliott, Michael. "How Al-Qaeda Got Back on the Attack." *Time,* October 28, 2002.

———. "Strike First, Explain Yourself Later." *Time,* June 24, 2002.

———. "Why the War on Terror Will Never End." *Time,* May 26, 2003.

Elliott, Michael, and James Carney. "First Stop, Iraq." *Time,* March 23, 2003.

Emergency Responders: Drastically Underfunded, Dangerously Unprepared. Report of an Independent Task Force Sponsored by the Council on Foreign Relations. New York: Council on Foreign Relations, 2003.

Falk, Richard. *The Great Terror War.* New York: Olive Branch Press, 2003.

———. "The New Bush Doctrine." *Nation,* July 25, 2002.

Fallows, James. "The Fifty-First State?" *Atlantic Monthly,* November 2002, 53–64.

Fattah, Hassan. "Random Death." *New Republic,* August 11, 2003.

Ferguson, Niall. "The Empire Slinks Back." *New York Times Magazine,* April 27, 2003, 52–57.

Fialka, John J., and Yochi J. Dreazen. "Are Hints of 'Smoking Gun' in Iraq Enough for the U.S.?" *Wall Street Journal,* April 18, 2003.

Fidler, Stephen, and Gerard Baker. "America's Democratic Imperialists: How the Neo-Conservatives Rose from Humility to Empire in Two Years." *Financial Times,* March 6, 2003.

Fineman, Mark, Robin Wright, and Doyle McManus. "Preparing for War, Stumbling to Peace." *Los Angeles Times,* July 18, 2003.

Fireman, Ken. "Iraq's Weapons of Mass Distraction?" *Long Island Newsday,* May 4, 2003.

Firestone, David. "Dizzying Drive to Red Ink Poses Stark Choices for Washington." *New York Times,* September 14, 2003.

FitzGerald, Frances. "George Bush and the World." *New York Review of Books,* September 26, 2002.

Foot, Rosemary. *The Wrong War: American Policy and the Dimensions of the Korean Conflict, 1951–1953.* Ithaca, NY: Cornell University Press, 1985.

Ford, Peter. "Why U.S. Is Getting Wary Welcome." *Christian Science Monitor,* March 27, 2003.

Frachon, Alain, and Daniel Vernet. "The Strategist and the Philosopher." *Le Monde,* April 15, 2003, trans. Mark K. Jensen.

Freedberg, Sydney J., Jr., and Corine Hegland. "Reinventing Iraq." *National Journal,* March 22, 2003.

Freedman, Lawrence. "Prevention, Not Preemption." *Washington Quarterly* 26, no. 2 (spring 2003): 105–14.

Freedman, Lawrence, and Efraim Karsh. *The Gulf Conflict, 1990–1991: Diplomacy and War in the New World Order.* Princeton, NJ: Princeton University Press, 1993.

Friedman, Alan. *Spider's Web: The Secret History of How the White House Illegally Armed Iraq.* New York: Bantam Books, 1993.

Friedman, Thomas L. "Bad Planning." *New York Times,* June 25, 2003.

———. "Grapes of Wrath." *New York Times,* March 12, 2003.

Frum, David. *The Right Man: The Surprise Presidency of George W. Bush.* New York: Random House, 2003.

Fuerth, Leon. "Outfoxed by North Korea." *New York Times,* January 1, 2003.

Fukuyama, Francis. "Us vs. Them." *Washington Post,* September 11, 2002.

Gabriel, Richard A. *Military Incompetence: Why the American Military Doesn't Win.* New York: Hill and Wang, 1985.

Gaddis, John Lewis. "A Grand Strategy." *Foreign Policy* (November–December 2002).

Gaffney, Mark. "Will the Next Mid East War Go Nuclear?" In *The Saddam Hussein Reader,* ed. Turi Munthe, 532.

Galloway, Joseph L. "An Army Transformed, Thanks to a Retiring General." *Philadelphia Inquirer,* June 5, 2003.

———. "General Tommy Franks Discusses Conducting the War in Iraq." Knight Ridder Washington Bureau, June 19, 2003.

———. "Risks of Iraq War Emerging." *Philadelphia Inquirer,* March 25, 2003.

Gause, F. Gregory, III. "Getting It Backward on Iraq." *Foreign Affairs* 78, no. 3 (May–June 1999): 54–65.

Gearty, Conor. "Terrorism and Morality." *RUSI Journal* 147, no. 5 (October 2002): 34–39.

Gellman, Barton. "Frustrated U.S. Arms Team to Leave Iraq." *Washington Post,* May 11, 2003.

———. "Looting Is a Double Loss for U.S. Forces." *Washington Post,* April 18, 2003.

———. "Seven Nuclear Sites Looted." *Washington Post,* May 10, 2003.

———. "U.S. Has Not Inspected Iraqi Nuclear Facility." *Washington Post,* April 25, 2003.

Gellman, Barton, and Walter Pincus. "Depiction of Threat Outgrew Supporting Evidence." *Washington Post,* August 10, 2003.

Gilbert, Martin. *Israel, A History.* New York: William Morrow, 1998.

Gingrich, Newt. "The Next Challenge for Bush." *Washington Times,* April 24, 2003.

Gordon, Craig. "Military Concern over 2-Front Conflict." *Long Island Newsday,* October 30, 2002.

Gordon, Michael R. "Allies to Retain Larger Iraq Force as Strife Persists." *New York Times,* May 29, 2003.

———. "Fear of Baghdad Unrest Prompts a Halt in Sending Troops Home." *New York Times,* May 15, 2003.

————. "How Much Is Enough?" *New York Times,* May 30, 2003.

————. "New Reality, Hard Choices." *New York Times,* March 28, 2003.

————. "A Swift, and Risky, Attack by Land, with Surprise in Mind." *New York Times,* March 21, 2003.

————. "The Test for Rumsfeld: Will Strategy Work?" *New York Times,* April 1, 2003.

————. "Weapons of Mass Confusion." *New York Times*, August 1, 2003.

Gordon, Michael R., with Douglas Jehl. "Foreign Fighters Add to Resistance in Iraq, U.S. Says." *New York Times,* June 22, 2003.

Gordon, Michael R., with Eric Schmitt. "U.S. Plans to Reduce Forces in Iraq, with Help of Allies." *New York Times,* May 3, 2003.

————. "U.S. Will Move Air Operations to Qatar Base." *New York Times,* April 28, 2003.

Gordon, Michael R., and Bernard E. Trainor. *The Generals' War: The Inside Story of the Conflict in the Gulf.* New York: Little, Brown, 1995.

Gordon, Philip H. "Bush's Middle East Vision." *Survival* 45, no. 1 (spring 2003): 131–53.

Graham, Bradley. "U.S. Won't Seek Bases in Iraq, Rumsfeld Says." *Washington Post,* April 22, 2003.

Gray, Colin S. *Defining and Achieving Decisive Victory.* Carlisle, PA: Strategic Studies Institute, U.S. Army War College, April 2002.

Greenberger, Robert S., and Karby Leggett. "Bush Dreams of Changing Not Just Regime, but Region." *London Telegraph,* March 18, 2003.

Grier, Peter. "A Shrinking Global Footprint of U.S. Forces." *Christian Science Monitor,* April 22, 2003.

Grossman, Elaine. "Powell's Advisory Panel in Iraqi Military Remains Idle after War." *Inside the Pentagon,* July 10, 2003.

Gunaratna, Rohan. *Inside Al Qaeda: Global Network of Terror.* New York: Columbia University Press, 2002.

Haass, Richard N. *Intervention: The Use of American Military Force in the Post–Cold War Era*. Washington, D.C.: Carnegie Endowment for World Peace, 1994.

Halloran, Richard. *To Arm a Nation, Rebuilding America's Endangered Defenses.* New York: Macmillan, 1986.

Hammer, Joshua, and Colin Soloway, "Who's in Charge Here?" *Newsweek,* May 26, 2003.

Hamza, Khidir, with Jeff Stein. *Saddam's Bombmaker: The Daring Escape of the Man Who Built Iraq's Secret Weapon.* New York: Simon and Schuster, 2000.

Hanson, Victor Davis. "Democracy in the Middle East." *Weekly Standard,* October 21, 2002, 23–26.

————. "The Utility of War." *Quarterly Journal of Military History* 15, no. 2 (winter 2003): 1–15.

Haqqani, Husain. "Islam's Weakened Moderates." *Foreign Policy* (July–August 2003): 61–63.

Harding, James. "The Figure in the White House Shadows Who Urged the President toward War in Iraq." *Financial Times,* March 22–23, 2003.

Hart, Gary. "A Detour from the War on Terrorism." *Washington Post,* March 9, 2003.

Hart, Gary, with William S. Lind. *America Can Win, The Case for Military Reform.* Bethesda, MD: Adler and Adler, 1986.

Harvey, Robert. *Global Disorder, America, and the Threat of World Conflict.* New York: Carroll and Graf, 2003.

Heisbourg, Francois. "A Work in Progress: The Bush Doctrine and Its Consequences." *Washington Quarterly* 26, no. 2 (spring 2003): 75–88.

Hemmer, Christopher. *Which Lessons Matter? American Foreign Policy Decision Making in the Middle East, 1979–1987.* Albany, NY: State University of New York, 2000.

Hendrickson, David C. "Toward Universal Empire: The Dangerous Quest for Absolute Security." *World Policy Journal* 19, no. 3 (fall 2002): 1–10.

Hersh, Seymour M. "Offense and Defense." *New Yorker,* April 7, 2003.

———. "Selective Intelligence." *New Yorker,* May 12, 2003.

———. "Who Lied to Whom?" *New Yorker,* March 31, 2003.

Higgins, Trumbull. *The Perfect Failure: Kennedy, Eisenhower, and the C.I.A. at the Bay of Pigs.* New York: W. W. Norton, 1987.

Hiro, Dilip. *Iraq in the Eye of the Storm.* New York: Thunder's Mouth Press, 2002.

Hirsh, Michael. "Powell's Battle." *Newsweek,* September 16, 2002.

Hitchens, Christopher. *A Long Short War: The Postponed Liberation of Iraq.* New York: Plume, 2003.

Hoar, Joseph P. "Why Aren't There Enough Troops in Iraq?" *New York Times,* April 2, 2003.

Hoffman, Bruce. "Defining Terrorism." In *Terrorism and Counterterrorism: Understanding the New Security Environment,* ed. Russell D. Howard and Reid L. Sawyer. Guilford, CT: McGraw-Hill/Dushkin, 2003.

Hosmer, Stephen T. *The Conflict over Kosovo: Why Milosevic Decided to Settle When He Did.* Santa Monica, CA: Rand, 2001.

Howard, Michael. "Smoke on the Horizon." *Financial Times,* September 8, 2002.

Huband, Mark. "Bin Laden Breaks Silence with Suicide Attack Call." *Financial Times,* April 9, 2003.

Huband, Mark, and Stephen Fidler. "Did Intelligence Agencies Rely Too Much on Unreliable Data from Iraqi Exiles, or Did Politicians Exaggerate the Evidence Presented to Them?" *Financial Times,* June 4, 2003.

Hunt, Al. "Loose Cannon." *Wall Street Journal,* April 24, 2003.

Hutcheson, Ron. "Bush Says Troop Size in Iraq Just Fine." *Philadelphia Inquirer,* July 3, 2003.

Ignatieff, Michael. "The American Empire (Get Used to It)." *New York Times Magazine,* January 5, 2003.

Ignatius, David. "The Battle over Postwar Iraq." *Washington Post,* April 4, 2003.

———. "Bush's Confusion, Baghdad's Mess." *Washington Post,* April 23, 2003.

Ikenberry, G. John. *After Victory: Institutions, Strategic Restraint, and the Rebuilding of Order after Major Wars.* Princeton, NJ: Princeton University Press, 2001.

———. "America's Imperial Ambition." *Foreign Affairs* 85, no. 5 (September–October 2002): 44–60.

"In the President's Words: 'Free People Will Keep the Peace of the World.'" Transcript of President Bush's speech to the American Enterprise Institute (AEI), Washington, D.C., February 26, 2003, *New York Times,* February 27, 2002.

"Interview with Now-Vice President Richard Cheney." *New York Times,* April 13, 1991. Reprinted in the *Nation,* November 11, 2002.

Jaffe, Greg. "Problems with Iraq Invasion Plan Push U.S. to Weight a New Strategy." *Wall Street Journal,* July 25, 2002.

Jaffe, Greg, and Greg Hiatt. "Bush Views Iraq Invasion Plan Requiring Fewer U.S. Troops." *Wall Street Journal,* August 6, 2002.

Jahn, George. "Weapons Inspectors: Iraq Nuke Program Was in Disarray." *USA Today,* September 9, 2003.

James, Barry. "An Interview with Richard Perle." *International Herald Tribune,* April 12–13.

Jervis, Robert. "The Compulsive Empire." *Foreign Policy* (July–August 2003): 83–87.

Johnson, Scott. "Unholy Allies." *Newsweek,* June 16, 2003.

Jowitt, Ken. "Rage, Hubris, and Regime Change." *Policy Review* 118 (April–May 2003): 33–43.

Judis, John B., and Spencer Ackerman. "The First Casualty." *New Republic,* June 30, 2003.

Judt, Tony. "America and the War." In *Striking Terror: America's War,* ed. Robert B. Slivers and Barbara Epstein, 15–30. New York: New York Review of Books, 2002.

———. "The Way We Live Now." *New York Review of Books,* March 27, 2003, 6–10.

———. "The Wrong War at the Wrong Time." *New York Times,* October 20, 2002.

Kagan, Donald, and Frederick W. Kagan. *While America Sleeps: Self-Delusion, Military Weakness, and the Threat to Peace Today.* New York: St. Martin's Press, 2000.

Kagan, Frederick W. "Did We Fail in Afghanistan?" *Commentary* 115, no. 3 (March 2003): 39–45.

———. "War and Aftermath." *Policy Review* 120 (August and September 2003): 3–27.

Kagan, Robert. "The Benevolent Empire." *Foreign Policy* (summer 1998): 24–35.

Kagan, Robert, and William Kristol. "National Interest and Global Responsibility." In *Present Dangers: Crisis and Opportunity in American Foreign and Defense Policy,* ed. Kagan and Kristol. San Francisco, CA: Encounter Books, 2000.

Kaplan, Fred. "Blow-Back in Baghdad." Slate.msn.com.

Kaplan, Lawrence F. "Regime Change." *New Republic,* March 3, 2003, 21–23.

Kaplan, Lawrence F., and William Kristol. *The War over Iraq: Saddam's Tyranny and America's Mission.* San Francisco, CA: Encounter Books, 2003.

Kaplan, Robert D. "A Post-Saddam Scenario." *Atlantic Monthly,* November 2002, 88–90.

Karnow, Stanley. "Do Not Compare Iraq with Vietnam." *Boston Globe,* April 20, 2003.

Karsh, Efraim. "Making Iraq Safe for Democracy." *Commentary* 115, no. 4 (April 2003): 22–28.

Kaysen, Carl, Steven E. Miller, Martin B. Main, William D. Nordhaus, and John Steinbrunner. *War with Iraq: Costs, Consequences, and Alternatives.* Cambridge, MA: Committee on International Security Studies, American Academy of Arts Sciences, 2002.

Keegan, John. "'Heavy' Invasion Is Best Option." *London Daily Telegraph,* August 6, 2002.

———. "Heavy Risk of 'Light' Solution to Desert Storm II." *London Daily Telegraph,* September 26, 2002.

———. "Saddam's Utter Collapse Shows This Has Not Been a Real War." *London Daily Telegraph,* April 8, 2003.

Keller, Bill. "The Sunshine Warrior." *New York Times Magazine,* March 2, 2003, 48–55, 84, 88, 96–97.

Kelley, David. "Regime's Priority Was Blueprints, Not Arsenal, Defector Told." *Los Angeles Times,* April 26, 2003.

Kelley, Matt. "Pentagon's Wolfowitz Admits U.S. Erred in Iraq." Associated Press, July 24, 2003.

Kelly, Jack. "Rummy and the Brass." *New York Post,* November 3, 2002.

Kessler, Glenn. "Powell Cites 'Real' Divide Internally on Iraq Policy." *Washington Post,* September 4, 2002.

———. "State-Defense Policy Rivalry Intensifying." Washingtonpost.com, April 22, 2003.

Kessler, Glenn, and Dana Priest. "U.K. Planners Surprised by Strength of Iraq Shiites." *Washington Post,* April 23, 2003.

Khafaji, Isam al. "A Few Days After: State and Society in Post-Saddam Iraq." In *Iraq at the Crossroads: State and Society in the Shadow of Regime Change,* ed. Toby Dodge and Steven Simon. Adelphi Paper 354. London: International Institute for Strategic Studies, 2003.

Khalaf, Roula. "A Divided Country: Will Iraq Descend into Chaos and Ethnic Hatred after Saddam's Demise?" *Financial Times,* March 18, 2003.

Khalilzad, Zalmay. *From Containment to Global Leadership: America and the World after the Cold War.* Santa Monica, CA; Rand, 1995.

Khong, Yuen Foong. *Analogies at War: Korea, Munich, Dien Bien Phu, and the American Decisions of 1965.* New York: Simon and Schuster, 1992.

King, Neil, Jr., and Chip Cummins. "The Postwar Bill for Iraq Surges Past Projections." *Wall Street Journal,* September 5, 2003.

Kinnard, Douglas. *The War Managers: American Generals Reflect on Vietnam.* New York: Da Capo Press, 1979.

Kiras, James D. "Terrorism and Irregular Warfare." In *Strategy in the Contemporary World: An Introduction to Strategic Studies,* ed. John Baylis, James Wirtz, Eliot Cohen, and Colin S. Gray. New York: Oxford University Press, 2002.

Kissinger, Henry A. "America Must Rebuild Its Transatlantic Relationships." *San Diego Union-Tribune,* April 13, 2003.

———. "The Custodians of the World?" *San Diego Union-Tribune,* September 8, 2002.

———. "Role Reversal and Alliance Realities." *Washington Post,* February 10, 2003.

Kitfield, James. "The Army's Gamble." *National Journal,* March 29, 2003.

———. "Attack Always." *National Journal,* April 26, 2003.

———. "Fractured Alliances." *National Journal,* March 8, 2003, 720–24.

———. "NATO Could Help in Iraq, but Will It?" *National Journal,* July 26, 2003.

———. *Prodigal Soldiers, How the Generation of Officers Born of Vietnam Revolutionized the American Style of War.* New York: Simon and Schuster, 1995.

———. "Wounded, Not Crippled." *National Journal,* February 22, 2003, 574–78.

Klare, Michael T. "For Oil and Empire? Rethinking War with Iraq." *Current History* 102, no. 662 (March 2003): 129–35.

———. "War Plans and Pitfalls." *Nation* 275, no. 13 (October 21, 2002): 14–18.

Knowlton, Brian. "U.S. Weighs Shift of Forces in Gulf." *International Herald Tribune,* April 28, 2003.

Kosterlitz, Julie. "The Neoconservative Moment." *National Journal,* May 17, 2003, 1,540–46.

———. "Occupational Hazards." *National Journal,* March 22, 2003, 910–17.

Kramer, Michael. "W and Rummy in Denial." *New York Daily News,* July 7, 2003.

Krauthammer, Charles. "The Obsolescence of Deterrence." *Weekly Standard,* December 9, 2002, 22–24.

———. "The Shiite 'Menace.'" *Washington Post,* May 2, 2003.

Krepinevich, Andrew F. *The Army and Vietnam.* Baltimore, MD: Johns Hopkins University Press, 1986.

Kristol, William. "Axis of Appeasement." *Weekly Standard,* August 26/September 2, 2002.

———. "Taking the War beyond Terrorism." *Washington Post,* January 31, 2002.

———. "What Wolfowitz Really Said." *Weekly Standard,* June 9, 2003.

Kristol, William, and Robert Kagan. "North Korea Goes South." *Weekly Standard,* January 20, 2003.

Kupchan, Charles. "The Atlantic Alliance Lies in the Rubble." *Financial Times,* April 10, 2003.

LaFeber, Walter. "The Bush Doctrine." *Diplomatic History* 26, no. 4 (fall 2002): 543–58.

Lake, Eli J. "Split Decision." *New Republic,* May 5, 2003, 16–18.

Laqueur, Walter. *The New Terrorism: Fanaticism and the Arms of Mass Destruction.* New York: Oxford University Press, 1999.

Ledeen, Michael. *The War against the Terror Masters: Why It Happened. Where We Are Now. How We'll Win.* New York: St. Martin's Press, 2002.

Lemann, Nicholas. "How It Came to War." *New Yorker,* March 21, 2003.

———. "The Next World Order." *New Yorker*, April 1, 2002.

———. "The War on What?" *New Yorker,* September 16, 2002, 36–44.

Levy, Jack. "Declining Power and Preventive Motivation for War." *World Politics* (October 1997).

Lieven, Anatol. "Help for America Must Have Strings Attached." *Financial Times,* July 2, 2003.

———. "The Push for War." *London Review of Books,* October 3, 2002.

Lind, Michael. "The Weird Men behind George W. Bush's War." *New Statesman,* April 7, 2003, 10–13.

Lindberg. Tod. "Deterrence and Prevention." *Weekly Standard,* February 3, 2003, 24–28.

———. "Did Saddam Have WMD?" *Washington Times,* May 6, 2003.

Locher, James R., III. *Victory on the Potomac: The Goldwater-Nichols Act Unifies the Pentagon.* College Station, TX: Texas A&M Press, 2003.

Loeb, Vernon. "No Iraq 'Quagmire,' Rumsfeld Asserts." *Washington Post,* July 1, 2003.

———. "Number of Wounded in Action on the Rise." *Washington Post,* September 2, 2003.

———. "Plan to Bolster Forces in Iraq in Unveiled." *Washington Post,* July 24, 2003.

———. "Rumsfeld Faulted for Troop Dilution." *Washington Post,* March 30, 2002.

Loeb, Vernon, and Colum Lynch. "U.S. Cool to New U.N. Vote." *Washington Post,* August 2, 2003.

Loeb, Vernon, and Thomas E. Ricks. "Questions Raised about Invasion Force." *Washington Post,* March 25, 2003.

Lugar, Richard G. "A Victory at Risk." *Washington Post,* May 22, 2003.

MacFarquhar, Neil. "Rising Tide of Islamic Militants See Iraq as Ultimate Battlefield." *New York Times,* August 13, 2003.

Mackey, Sandra. *The Reckoning: Iraq and the Legacy of Saddam Hussein.* New York: W. W. Norton, 2002.

MacLeod, Scott. "Why U.S. Is Pulling Out of Saudi Arabia." Time.com, April 29, 2003.

MacMaster, H. R. *Dereliction of Duty: Lyndon Johnson, Robert McNamara, the Joint Chiefs of Staff, and the Lies That Led to Vietnam.* New York: Harper Collins, 1997.

Madrick, Jeff. "The Iraqi Time Bomb." *New York Times Magazine,* April 6, 2003, 48–51.

Mahnken, Thomas G. "A Squandered Opportunity? The Decision to End the Gulf War." In *The Gulf War of 1991 Reconsidered,* ed. Andrew J. Bacevich and Efraim Inbar, 121–48. London: Frank Cass, 2003.

Makiya, Kanan. *Cruelty and Silence: War, Tyranny, Uprising, and the Arab World.* New York: W. W. Norton, 1993.

Manchester, William. *American Caesar: Douglas MacArthur, 1880–1964.* Boston: Little, Brown, 1978.

Margalit, Avishai. "The Wrong War." *New York Review of Books,* March 13, 2003, 5.

Marr, Phebe. "Iraq 'The Day After.'" *Naval War College Review* 56, no. 1 (winter 2003): 13–29.

Marshall, John Micah. "Practice to Deceive." *Washington Monthly* 35, no. 4 (April 2003): 28–34.

Martin, Paul. "Iraqi 'Secret Plan' Orders Mayhem." *Washington Times,* June 9, 2003.

———. "Saddam Faithful Refuse to Surrender." *Washington Times,* June 17, 2003.

———. "Saddam Loyalists Ally with Islamists." *Washington Times,* May 27, 2003.

Matlock, Jack F., Jr., "Deterring the Undeterrable." *New York Times Book Review,* October 20, 2002, 11.

Matthews, Mark. "Out of Limelight, Afghanistan Slides Back toward Chaos." *Baltimore Sun,* May 26, 2003.

May, Ernest R. *"Lessons" of the Past: The Use and Misuse of History in American Foreign Policy.* New York: Oxford University Press,1973.

May, Ernest R., and Philip D. Zeilkow, eds. *The Kennedy Tapes: Inside the White House during the Cuban Missile Crisis.* Cambridge, MA: Belknap Press of the Harvard University Press, 1997.

Mayer, Jane. "A Doctrine Passes." *New Yorker,* October 14, October 21, 2002.

Mazzetti, Mark. "Ready. Aim. Fire First." *U.S. News and World Report,* October 7, 2002.

McAllester, Matthew. "Ex-Bodyguard for Uday Tells of Near Misses, Defiance, Defeat." Newsday.com, July 25, 2003.

McCaffrey, Barry. "We Need More Troops." *Wall Street Journal,* July 29, 2003.

McGirk, Tim, and Michael Ware. "Losing Control?" *Time,* November 8, 2002.

McGrory, Mary. "Hesitant Hawks." *Washington Post,* May 30, 2002.

McIntyre, Dave. *Understanding the New National Security Strategy of the United States.* Institute Analysis 009. Washington, D.C.: ANSER Institute for Homeland Security, September 2002.

Meacham, Jon. "A Father's Words on Going to War." *Newsweek,* March 31, 2003, 43.

Mead, Walter Russell. *Special Providence: American Foreign Policy and How It Changed the World.* New York: Alfred A. Knopf, 2002.

Mearsheimer, John J., and Stephen M. Walt. "An Unnecessary War." *Foreign Policy* (January–February 2003): 50–59.

Meyer, Josh. "Al-Qaeda May Be Back, and Stronger." *Los Angeles Times,* | May 14, 2003.

Meyerson, Harold. "Enron-Like Unreality." *Washington Post,* May 13, 2003.

Michaels, Jim. "Lessons from 1991 Shape Iraqi Strategy." *USA Today,* March 12, 2003.

Milbank, Dana, and Claudia Deane. "Hussein Link to 9/11 Lingers in Many Minds." *Washington Post,* September 6, 2003.

Miller, Greg. "Pentagon Defends Role of Intelligence Unit on Iraq." *Los Angeles Times,* June 5, 2003.

———. "U.S. Defends Its Role in Iraq." *Los Angeles Times,* July 1, 2003.

Miller, Judith. "Illicit Arms Kept Till Eve of War, An Iraqi Scientist Said to Assert." *New York Times,* April 23, 2003.

Mitchell, Alison, and Carl Hulse. "C.I.A. Warns That a U.S. Attack May Ignite Terror." *New York Times,* October 9, 2002.

Moore, Molly. "A Foe That Collapsed from Within." *Washington Post,* July 20, 2003.

Morgan, Dan. "Deciding Who Rebuilds Iraq Is Fraught with Infighting." *Washington Post,* May 4, 2003.

Morin, Rick, and Dan Balz. "Public Says $87 Billion Too Much." *Washington Post,* September 14, 2003.

Mueller, John. *Policy and Opinion in the Gulf War.* Chicago: University of Chicago Press, 1994.

Mueller, John, and Karl Mueller. "Sanctions of Mass Destruction." *Foreign Affairs* 78, no. 3 (May–June 1999): 43–53.

Munthe, Turi, ed. *The Saddam Hussein Reader: Selections of Leading Writers on Iraq.* New York: Thunder's Mouth Press, 2002.

Muravchik, Joshua. *The Imperative of American Leadership: A Challenge to Neo-Isolationism.* Washington, D.C.: AEI Press, 1996.

Murray, Alan. "U.S. Faces Messy Negotiations over Iraq's Outstanding Debt." *Wall Street Journal,* April 15, 2003.

National Security Strategy of the United States of America. The White House, September 17, 2002.

National Strategy for Combating Terrorism. Washington, D.C.: White House, February 2003.

Neustadt, Richard E., and Ernest R. May. *Thinking in History: The Uses of History for Decision-Makers.* New York: Free Press, 1986.

"No Proof Linking 9/11 to Hussein, Officials Say." *Los Angeles Times,* September 17, 2003.

Nordland, Rod. "The Lebanon Scenario." *Newsweek,* September 22, 2003.

Norton-Taylor, Richard, and Julian Borger. "Iraq Attack Plans Alarm Top Military." *London Guardian,* July 30, 2002.

Novak, Robert. "Iraqis Eating into Coalition 'Cakewalk.'" *Chicago Sun Times,* March 27, 2003.

———. "Rumsfeld's Army." *Washington Post,* May 1, 2003.

Nye, Joseph S., Jr. *The Paradox of American Power: Why the World's Only Superpower Can't Go It Alone.* New York: Oxford University Press, 2002.

———. "U.S. Power and Strategy after Iraq" *Foreign Affairs* 82, no. 4 (July–August 2003).

O'Brien, Timothy L. "Crime and Poor Security Hurt the Aid Effort in Iraq, U.N. and American Officials Say." *New York Times,* June 25, 2003.

"Occupation Preoccupation: Questions for John W. Dower." *New York Times Magazine,* March 30, 2003, 9.

O'Hanlon, Michael. "Breaking the Army." *Washington Post,* July 3, 2003.

———. "Do the Math: We Need More Boots on the Ground." *Los Angeles Times,* August 12, 2003.

———. "How the Hard-Liners Lost." *Washington Post,* November 10, 2002.

Ottoway, Marina, Thomas Carothers, Amy Hawthorne, and Daniel Brumberg. "Democratic Mirage in the Middle East." *Policy Brief 20.* Washington, D.C.: Carnegie Endowment for International Peace, October 2002.

Packer, George. "Dreaming of Democracy." *New York Times Magazine,* March 2, 2003, 44–49, 60, 90, and 104.

Page, Susan. "Prewar Predictions Coming Back to Bite." *USA Today,* April 1, 2003.

Palmer, Bruce, Jr. *The Twenty-five-Year War: America's Military Role in Vietnam.* Lexington, KY: University Press of Kentucky, 1984.

Peel, Quentin, Robert Graham, James Harding, and Judy Dempsey. "War in Iraq: How the Die Was Cast before Transatlantic Diplomacy Failed." *Financial Times,* May 27, 2003.

Pellett, Peter L. "Sanctions, Food, Nutrition, and Health in Iraq." In *Iraq under Siege: The Deadly Impact of Sanctions and War,* ed. Anthony Argrove, 185–203. Cambridge, MA: South End Press, 2000.

Perle, Richard. "Why the West Must Strike First against Saddam Hussein." *London Daily Telegraph,* August 9, 2002.

Peters, Ralph. "Shock, Awe, and Overconfidence." *Washington Post,* March 23, 2003.

Peterson, Scott. "Can Hussein Be Deterred?" *Christian Science Monitor,* September 10, 2002.

Pincus, Walter. "Deutch Sees Consequences in Failed Search for Arms." *Washington Post,* July 25, 2003.

Pincus, Walter, and Dana Priest. "Analysts Cite Pressure on Iraq Judgments." *Washington Post,* June 5, 2003.

Pincus, Walter, and Kevin Sullivan. "Scientists Still Deny Iraqi Arms Programs." *Washington Post,* July 31, 2003.

Pollack, Kenneth M. "Securing the Gulf." *Foreign Affairs* 82, no. 4 (July–August 2003): 2–16.

———. *The Threatening Storm: The Case for Invading Iraq.* New York: Random House, 2002.

———. "Why Iraq Can't Be Deterred." *New York Times,* September 26, 2002.

Powell, Bill. "The War over the Peace." *Fortune,* April 28, 2003.

Powell, Colin, with Joseph E. Persico. *My American Journey.* New York: Random House, 1995.

"President Bush's Speech on the Use of Force." *New York Times,* October 8, 2002.

"The President's State of the Union Address." Washington, January 29, 2002.

Prestowitz, Clyde. *Rogue Nation: American Unilateralism and the Failure of Good Intentions.* New York: Basic Books, 2003.

Priest, Dana. *The Mission: Waging War and Keeping Peace with America's Military.* New York: W. W. Norton, 2003.

Public Papers of the Presidents of the United States: George Bush. Book 1, January 1 to June 30, 1991. Washington, D.C. : U.S. Government Printing Office, 1992.

Purdum, Todd S. "The Missiles of 1962 Haunt the Iraq Debate." *New York Times,* October 13, 2003.

Rankin, Allen. "U.S. Could Wipe Out Red A-Nests in a Week, Gen. Anderson Asserts." *Montgomery Advertiser,* September 1, 1950.

Record, Jeffrey. "The Bush Doctrine and War with Iraq." *Parameters* 33, no. 1 (spring 2003): 1–18.

———. "Collapsed Countries, Casualty Dread, and the New American Way of War." *Parameters* 32, no. 2 (summer 2002): 4–23.

———. "Defeating Desert Storm (and Why Saddam Didn't)." *Comparative Strategy* 12, no. 2 (April–June 1993): 125–40.

———. *Failed States and Casualty Phobia: Implications for Force Structure and Policy Choices.* Occasional Paper No. 18. Maxwell Air Force Base, AL: Center for Strategy and Technology, Air War College, October 2000.

———. "Force Protection Fetishism: Sources, Consequences, and (?) Solutions." *Aerospace Power Journal* (summer 2000): 4–11.

———. "France 1940 and NATO Center 1980: A Disquieting Comparison." *Strategic Review* 8, no. 3 (summer 1980): 67–74.

———. *Hollow Victory: A Contrary View of the Gulf War.* Washington, D.C.: Brassey's (U.S.), 1993.

———. "How America's Own Military Performance Aided and Abetted the 'North's' Victory." In *Why the North Won the Vietnam War,* ed. Marc Jason Gilbert, 117–36. New York: Palgrave, 2002.

———. *Making War, Thinking History: Munich, Vietnam, and Presidential Uses of Force from Korea to Kosovo.* Annapolis, MD: Naval Institute Press, 2002.

———. "Operation Allied Force: Yet Another Wake-Up Call for the Army?" *Parameters* 30, no. 4 (winter 1999–2000): 15–23.

———. *Serbia and Vietnam: A Preliminary Comparison of U.S. Decisions to Use Force.* Occasional Paper No. 8. Maxwell Air Force Base, AL: Center for Strategy and Technology, Air War College, May 1999.

———. "Weinberger-Powell Doesn't Cut It." *Proceedings* 126, no. 10 (October 2000): 35-36.

———. *The Wrong War: Why We Lost in Vietnam.* Annapolis, MD: Naval Institute Press, 1998.

Reiter, Dan. "Exploding the Powder Keg Myth." *International Security* 20, no. 2 (fall 1995): 5–34.

"Remarks by President Bush on Iraq." Cincinnati Museum Center–Cincinnati Union Terminal, Cincinnati, Ohio, October 7, 2002.

Rennie, David, and Anton La Guardia. "Top General Attacks Hawks' Strategy on Iraq." *London Daily Telegraph,* August 28, 2002.

Report of the Quadrennial Defense Review. Washington, D.C.: Department of Defense, September 2001.

Reynolds, Maura. "Pentagon's Free Rein Raises Tensions in Administration." *Los Angeles Times,* April 13, 2003.

Rhodes, Edward. "The Imperial Logic of Bush's Liberal Agenda." *Survival* 45, no. 1 (spring 2003): 131–54.

Rice, Condoleezza. "Promoting the National Interest." *Foreign Affairs* 79, no. 1 (January–February 2000): 45–62.

———. "Transforming the Middle East." *Washington Post,* August 7, 2003.

Rich, Frank. "The Waco Road to Baghdad." *New York Times,* August 17, 2002.

Ricks, Thomas E. "Calibrated War Makes a Comeback." Washingtonpost.com, March 21, 2003.

———. "Experts Question Depth of Victory." *Washington Post,* June 27, 2003.

———. "Some Top Military Brass Favor Status Quo in Iraq." *Washington Post,* July 28, 2002.

———. "Timing, Tactics on Iraq War Disputed." *Washington Post,* August 1, 2002.

Rieff, David. "Were Sanctions Right?" *New York Times Magazine,* July 27, 2003, 40–46.

Risen, James. "Captives Deny Qaeda Worked with Baghdad." *New York Times,* June 9, 2003.

Ritter, Scott. *Endgame: Solving the Iraq Problem—Once and for All.* New York: Simon and Schuster, 1999.

Rubin, Trudy. "Bush Never Made Serious Postwar Plans." *Philadelphia Inquirer,* June 26, 2003.

———. "More Than Soldiers Needed in Iraq." *Philadelphia Inquirer,* August 29, 2003.

Rumsfeld, Donald. "The Price of Inaction Can Be Truly Catastrophic." *Asahi Shimbun* (Japan), September 10, 2002.

———. "We Must Act to Prevent a Greater Evil, Even If That Act Means War." *London Independent,* September 8, 2002.

Rutenberg, Jim. "Conservatives Tailor Their Tone to Fit Setbacks in War." *New York Times,* March 28, 2003.

Sagan, Scott. *Moving Targets: Nuclear Strategy and National Security.* Princeton, NJ: Princeton University Press, 1989.

———. "The Perils of Proliferation: Organization Theory, Deterrence Theory, and the Spread of Nuclear Weapons." *International Security* 8 (spring 1994): 66–107.

Sanger, David. "Beating Them to the Prewar." *New York Times,* September 28, 2002.

Scarborough, Rowan. "War in Iraq Seen as Quick Win." *Washington Times,* September 8, 2002.

Schell, Orville. "From Sands to Quagmire." *San Francisco Chronicle,* March 31, 2003.

Schmid, Alex P., Albert J. Jongman, et al. *Political Terrorism: A New Guide to Actors, Authors, Concepts, Data Bases, Theories, and Literature.* New Brunswick, NJ: Transaction Books, 1988.

Schmitt, Eric. "Rumsfeld Says U.S. Will Cut Forces in Gulf." *New York Times,* April 29, 2003.

———. "Top General Concedes Bombardment Did Not Fully Meet Goal." *New York Times,* March 26, 2003.

———. "U.S. to Withdraw All Combat Units from Saudi Arabia." *New York Times,* April 30, 2003.

Schmitt, Eric, and Thom Shanker. "War Plan Calls for Precision Bombing Wave to Break Iraqi Army Early in Attack." *New York Times,* February 2, 2003.

———. "Water and Electricity in Baghdad Are Still below Prewar Levels, Officials Say." *New York Times,* July 8, 2003.

Schrader, Esther. "Rumsfeld Defends the Decision for War." *Los Angeles Times,* July 10, 2003.

Schwarzkopf, H. Norman, with Peter Petre. *It Doesn't Take a Hero.* New York: Bantam Books, 1992.

Scowcroft, Brent. "Don't Attack Iraq." *Wall Street Journal,* August 15, 2002.

"Second Presidential Debate between Gov. Bush and Vice President Al Gore." *New York Times,* October 12, 2000.

Seib, Gerald F. "Powell-Rumsfeld Feud Is Now Hard to Ignore." *Wall Street Journal,* April 25, 2003.

———. "Saddam Hussein and Terror: Two Very Different Threats." *Wall Street Journal,* September 25, 2002.

Senate Joint Resolution 45, To Authorize the Use of United States Armed Forces Against Iraq. 107th Congress, 2d Session, September 26, 2002.

Shadid, Anthony. "Unfulfilled Promises Leave Iraqis Bewildered." *Washington Post,* May 27, 2003.

"The Shadow Men." *Economist,* April 26–May 2, 2003, 21–23.

Shanker, Thom. "New Top General Tells Legislators U.S. Will Probably Need a Larger Army." *New York Times,* July 30, 2003.

———. "Officials Debate Whether to Seek a Bigger Military." *New York Times,* July 21, 2003.

———. "Rumsfeld Doubles Estimate for Cost of Troops in Iraq." *New York Times,* July 10, 2003.

Shanker, Thom, and Eric Schmitt. "Pentagon Expects Long-Term Access to Key Iraq Bases." *New York Times,* April 20, 2003.

———. "Rumsfeld Says Iraq Is Collapsing, Lists 8 Objectives of War." *New York Times,* March 23, 2003.

Shanker, Thom, and John Tiernay. "Head of Military Denounces Critics of Iraq Campaign." *New York Times,* April 2, 2003.

Shapiro, Walter. "Fiscal Recklessness Means More Danger Ahead." *USA Today,* August 27, 2003.

Sheehan, Michael. *The Balance of Power: History and Theory.* New York: Routledge, 1996.

Sifry, Micah L., and Christopher Cerf, eds. *The Gulf War Reader: History, Documents, Opinions.* New York: Random House, 1991.

————. *The Iraq War Reader: History, Documents, Opinions.* New York: Simon and Schuster, 2003.

"Sinking Views of the United States." *New York Times,* March 23, 2003.

Slavin, Barbara. "Gingrich Takes Swipe at State Department." *USA Today,* April 23, 2003.

Slavin, Barbara, and Dave Moniz. "How Peace in Iraq Became So Elusive." *USA Today,* July 22, 2003.

Slevin, Peter. "Baghdad Anarchy Spurs Call for Help." *Washington Post,* May 9, 2003.

————. "Hussein Loyalists Blamed for Chaos." *Washington Post,* May 15, 2003.

Slevin, Peter, and Vernon Loeb. "Plan to Secure Postwar Iraq Faulted." *Washington Post,* May 19, 2003.

Slevin, Peter, and Dana Priest. "Wolfowitz Concedes Errors on Iraq." *Washington Post,* July 24, 2003.

Smith, R. Jeffrey. "U.S. Warns of Retaliation If Iraq Uses Poison Gas." *Washington Post,* August 9, 1990.

Snyder, Jack. "Imperial Temptations." *National Interest* 71 (spring 2003): 29–40.

Solomon, Jay, Jess Bravin, and Jeane Whalen. "Iraq's Creditors Get in Line to Collect on Hussein's Debts." *Wall Street Journal,* March 26, 2003.

Sorrells, Niels C., and Colin Clark. "Undermanned and Overdeployed? Congress Debates Expanded Army." *Congressional Quarterly Weekly,* August 2, 2003.

"Sounding the Drums of War." *Washington Post,* August 10, 2003.

Sponeck, Hans von, and Denis Halliday. "The Hostage Nation." In *The Saddam Hussein Reader,* ed. Turi Munthe, 456–57.

Squitieri, Tom. "U.S. May Be in Iraq for Ten Years." *USA Today,* June 19, 2003.

"Statement of Principles." Project for a New American Century, June 3, 1997. http://www.newamericancentury.org/statementofprinciples.htm.

Stein, Janice Gross. "Deterrence and Compellance in the Gulf, 1990–91." *International Security* 17, no. 2 (fall 1992): 147–79.

Stephens, Philip. "Present at the Destruction of the World's Partnership." *Financial Times,* March 7, 2003.

Stern, Jessica. "How American Created a Terrorist Haven." *New York Times,* August 20, 2003.

————. "The Protean Enemy." *Foreign Affairs* 82, no. 4 (July–August 2003): 27–40.

Stevenson, Richard W. "78% of Bush's Postwar Spending Plan Is for Military." *New York Times,* September 9, 2003.

Stone, Peter H. "Can We Fight Iraq *and* Hunt Al Qaeda?" *National Journal,* February 22, 2003, 579.

———. "Were Qaeda-Iraq Links Exaggerated?" *National Journal,* August 9, 2003.

Strategic Survey 2002–2003, An Evaluation and Forecast of World Affairs. London: International Institute for Strategic Studies, 2003.

Tanenhaus, Sam. "Bush's Brain Trust." *Vanity Fair,* July 2003.

Telhami, Shibley. *The Stakes: America and the Middle East.* Boulder, CO: Westview Press, 2002.

Terrill, W. Andrew. "Chemical Warfare and 'Desert Storm': The Disaster That Never Came." *Small Wars and Insurgencies* 4, no. 2 (autumn 1993): 263–79.

———. *Nationalism, Sectarianism, and the Future of the U.S. Presence in Post-Saddam Iraq.* Carlisle Barracks, PA: Strategic Studies Institute, July 2003.

"Text of the President's Speech at West Point." http://www.nytimes.com/2002/ 06/01international/02PTEX-WEB.html.

Thomas, Evan. "Al Qaeda in America: The Enemy Within." *Newsweek,* June 23, 2003, 40–46.

———. *Robert Kennedy: His Life.* New York: Simon and Schuster, 2000.

———. "Rumsfeld's War." *Newsweek,* September 16, 2002.

Thomas, Evan, and Martha Brant. "The Education of Tommy Franks." *Newsweek,* May 19, 2003.

Thomas, Evan, Richard Wolffe, and Michael Isikoff. "(Over)selling the World on War." *Newsweek,* June 9, 2003, 25–30.

———. "Where Are Iraq's WMDs?" *Newsweek,* June 9, 2003.

Thompson, Loren B. "The Bush Doctrine." *Wall Street Journal,* June 13, 2002.

Timmerman, Kenneth R. *The Death Lobby: How the West Armed Iraq.* New York: Houghton Mifflin, 1991.

Treverton, Gregory F. "Intelligence: The Achilles Heel of the Bush Doctrine." *Arms Control Today* 33, no. 6 (July–August 2003): 9–11.

Trofomiv, Yaroslav. "U.S. Faces Two Baghdads: One a Friend, One a Foe." *Wall Street Journal,* June 5, 2003.

Trofomiv, Yaroslav, Hugh Pope, and Peter Waldman. "History of Betrayal Makes Shiites Wary of Liberators." *Wall Street Journal,* April 1, 2003.

Truman, Harry S. *Memoirs.* Vol. 2, *Years of Trial and Hope.* Garden City, NY: Doubleday, 1956.

Tucker, Robert W., and David C. Hendrickson. *The Imperial Temptation: The New World Order and America's Purpose.* New York: Council on Foreign Relations, 1992.

Tyler, Patrick E. "U.S.-British Project: To Build a Postwar Iraqi Armed Force of 40,000 Soldiers in Three Years." *New York Times,* June 24, 2003.

Unfinished Business in Afghanistan: Warlordism, Reconstruction, and Ethnic Harmony. Washington, D.C.: U.S. Institute for Peace, April 2003.

"U.S. Secretary of State Colin Powell Addresses the U.N. Security Council." http://www.whitehouse.gov.

Vieth, Warren. "Iraq Debts Add Up to Trouble." *Los Angeles Times,* April 4, 2003.

———. "Iraq Estimates Were Too Low, U.S. Admits." *Los Angeles Times,* September 9, 2003.

Walcott, John. "Some in Administration Uneasy over Bush Speech." *Philadelphia Inquirer,* September 9, 2003.

Waltzer, Michael. "No Strikes." *New Republic,* September 30, 2002, 19–22.

Webb, James. "Heading for Trouble." *Washington Post,* September 4, 2002.

———. "A New Doctrine for New Wars." *Wall Street Journal,* November 30, 2002.

Weinberg, Gerhard L. "No Road from Munich to Iraq." *Washington Post,* November 3, 2002.

Weisman, Jonathan. "2004 Deficit to Reach $480 Billion, Report Forecasts." *Washington Post,* August 27, 2003.

Weisman, Steven R. "Truth Is the First Casualty: Is Credibility the Second?" *New York Times,* June 8, 2003.

———. "Under Fire, Powell Receives Support from White House." *New York Times,* April 24, 2003.

Weisman, Steven R., with Felicity Barringer, "U.S. Abandons Idea of Bigger U.N. Role in Iraq Occupation." *New York Times,* August 14, 2003.

"'We're Calling for a Vote' at the U.N., Says Bush." *Washington Post,* March 7, 2003.

Whitelaw, Kevin, and Mark Mazzetti. "Why War?" *U.S. News and World Report,* October 14, 2002.

Wieseltier, Leon. "Against Innocence." *New Republic,* March 3, 2003.

Will, George F. "The Bush Doctrine at Risk." *Washington Post,* June 22, 2003.

Wilson, George C. "Iraq Is Not Vietnam." *National Journal,* April 12, 2003.

Wolfowitz, Paul. "Statesmanship in the New Century." In *Present Dangers: Crisis and Opportunity in American Foreign and Defense Policy,* ed. Robert Kagan and William Kristol. San Francisco, CA: Encounter Books, 2000.

Woodward, Bob. *Bush at War.* New York: Simon and Schuster, 2002.

Worley, D. Robert. *Waging Ancient War: Limits on Preemptive Force.* Carlisle, PA: Strategic Studies Institute, U.S. Army War College, February 2003.

Wright, Robin. "Rise of Shiite Leaders in Iraq Gives U.S. Pause." *Los Angeles Times,* April 25, 2003.

———. "White House Divided over Reconstruction." *Los Angeles Times,* April 2, 2003.

Wurmser, David. *Tyranny's Ally: America's Failure to Defeat Saddam Hussein.* Washington, D.C.: AEI Press, 1999.

Wyden, Peter. *Bay of Pigs: The Untold Story.* New York: Simon and Schuster, 1979.

Yaphe, Judith S. "Iraq before and after Saddam." *Current History* 102, no. 660 (January 2003): 7–12.

Zakaria, Fareed. "Exaggerating the Threats." *Newsweek,* June 16, 2003, 33.

———. "Iraq Policy Is Broken. Fix It." *Newsweek,* July 14, 2003.

Zucchino, David. "Iraq's Swift Defeat Blamed on Leaders." *Los Angeles Times,* August 11, 2003.

Index

Abrams, Eliot, 22
Abu Dhabi, 132
Acheson, Dean, 146
Adelman, Ken, 96
Afghanistan, 28, 93, 97–98, 142
Agency for International Development, U.S. (USAID), 115, 126
Ajami, Fouad, 77
Albania, 93
Albright, Madeleine, 9–10, 54
allies, 93–94, 149
Allison, Graham, 34
al-Qaeda: focus on after 9/11, 27–28; guerrilla war against United States, 62–63; Iraq as magnet for, 108; presence in Afghanistan, 142; suspected link to Iraq, 51–52, 59, 61–62, 147–49; threat of, 49–52
American Enterprise Institute, 19
analogies: Japan, 85–89; Munich, 78–83; Vietnam, 78, 80–81, 83–85
anticipatory self-defense. *See* preemption strategy
appeasement, 78, 79
Arafat, Yasir, 46, 94
Arkin, William M., 99, 102–3
Armitage, Richard, 32
Army, U.S.: force size in Iraq, 101, 104–5, 120–21; on nation-building, 117; overcommitment of, 138; study of nationalism in Iraq, 125; unanticipated postwar commitments and, 119
Army of Islamic Jihad, 135
assassination, 47
assertive nationalists, 122
Atwood, Paul L., 47
Aziz, Tariq, 14, 84–85

Ba'athist Party, 87–88, 96–97, 105, 106, 131, 135
Bacevich, Andrew J., 76–77
Baer, Robert, 54
Bahrain, 93
Baker, James A., III, 3–4
Bali, 63
Ball, George, 39
ballistic missile defense, 56–57
Bangladesh, 93
bellum warfare, 62
Benjamin, Daniel, 49–50
Bennet, William J., 20
Betts, Richard K., 57
bin Laden, Osama: common ground with neoconservatives, 23–24; major objective of, 94; suspected link to Iraq, 147–49; view of Saddam Hussein, 49–50, 59
biological weapons. *See* weapons of mass destruction
Black Hawk Down, 84
Bobbitt, Philip, 56–57
Bolton, John, 22
Boot, Max, 90, 131–32
Bosnia, 66, 142
Bradley, Omar, 65
Bremer, L. Paul, III, 130, 153
Brookings Institution, 43, 137
Brown, Chris, 35, 40
Brzezinski, Zbigniew, 53–54, 61, 130
Bush, George H. W., and administration: disappointment over limited victory in Iraq, 65; foreign policy of, 1–4; green light to Saddam, 57; nuclear weapons and, 83; on Saddam's hold on power, 5, 7; use of force, 37; Vietnam issue and, 80–81. *See also* Gulf War (1991)

Bush, George W.: arguments for war, 2; changes to foreign policy after 9/11, 26–29; David Rieff on, 10–11; on democratization of the Middle East, 70; on freedom, 18–19; global reach and, 47–48; Hussein and, 107; on Iraq obtaining nuclear weapons, 109; Munich analogy and, 78–83; neoconservatives view of, 19; on preventive war, 40; reservations about attacking Iraq, 28–29; on terrorism, 46–47; on use of WMD upon Iraq's demise, 60

Bush, George W., administration of: Afghanistan and, 142; conclusions about Iraq War, 2003, 142–55; foreign policy divisions within, 129–32; global reach of war on terror, 47–48; Japan analogy and, 85–89; North Korea and, 60–61; on nuclear weapons in Iraq, 82–83; postwar situation as quagmire and, 85; realistic regime change and, 131; reasons for war with Iraq, 52–60; rhetoric of terrorism, 46–47; suspected ties between Iraq and al-Qaeda, 51–52; underestimation of reconstruction costs, 126–27; undifferentiated terrorist threats, 49–51. See also Iraq War, 2003

Bush doctrine: adoption of neoconservative view, 30–31; Cold War concepts and, 32–33; conclusions about, 143; identification of threat agents, 31–32; influence of Pentagon, 125; preemption strategy and, 33–37; world view of, 40–44. See also preventive war; regime change

Butler, Richard, 112

Canada, 86, 93
Cannistraro, Vincent, 115
CARE, 115, 120
Carter, Jimmy, 114

CENTCOM, 101–2, 103
Center for Security Policy, 19
Central Command, U.S., 93, 104
Chalabi, Ahmad, 118, 122, 123–24
chemical weapons, 15, 56. See also weapons of mass destruction
Cheney, Dick: on Iraq obtaining nuclear weapons, 108; mentioned by Lieven, 17; opposition to soliciting UN mandate, 69; PNAC and, 19–20, 22; view of Iraqis as pro-American, 95–96, 100
China: appeasement of, 20–21; neoconservatives obsession with, 26; opposition to Iraq War, 86; Persian Gulf oil and, 72; preventive war and, 40, 65; regional diplomacy and, 60
CIA, 60, 111–12, 124
Clausewitz, Carl von, 45, 153
Cline, Lawrence E., 7–8
Clinton, William: appeasement and, 79; criticism of, 19, 98; rejection of Clinton policy, 26; sanctions and, 10; use of force, 37
Coalition Provisional Authority (CPA), 130
Cohen, Eliot, 22
Cold War, 54–55, 66, 67
Commentary, 19
Congressional Budget Office (CBO), 129
containment, 32–33, 39
Contras, 47
Cook, Robin, 61
Cordesman, Anthony H., 15, 139, 154
Council on Foreign Relations, 148–49
Cuban Missile Crisis, 39
Czechoslovakia, 12, 93

Daalder, Ivo, 137, 151
Davignon, Etienne, 152
declaratory doctrine, 39–40. See also preventive war
Defense Planning Guidance (1992), 19
deficit, United States, 128–29
democracy, 69–70, 131–33

democratic imperialists, 122
Department of Defense, 37, 129–31, 154.
    See also Pentagon
deterrence, 13, 16, 23, 32–33
Deutch, John M., 111
Dien Bien Phu, 124–25
disarmament, 74
Dobriansky, Paula, 22
Donnelly, Tom, 131
Dower, John, 87, 88
Drogin, Bob, 110
Duelfer, Charles, 16
Dunn, David Hastings, 144
Durch, William, 121

economic sanctions, 10
effects-based operation, 99
Egypt, 59, 93
82d Airborne Division, 95
Einstein, Albert, 82
Ekeus, Rolf, 110
El Baradei, Mohamed, 109
*Emergency Responders: Drastically
    Underfunded, Dangerously Unpre-
    pared,* 148–49
Eritrea, 93
Ethiopia, 93
European Union, 150
Evera, Stephen Van, 48

Falk, Richard, 43, 46–47, 51
Fedayeen, Saddam, 96–97, 106
Federated States of Micronesia, 93
Feith, Douglas, 22
Ferguson, Niall, 126
1st Armored Division, 95, 102
1st Cavalry, 102
1st Marine Expeditionary Force, 95
force protection, 137. *See also* troop
    shortages
Foreign Affairs, 55
foreign policy: changes to after 9/11,
    26–29; divisions within the Bush
    administration, 129–32; lack of
    American interest in, 126;

neoconservatives and, 19–20, 25–29,
    129–32; opposition to war in Iraq,
    86–87; of United States from 1989 to
    1993, 2
4th Mechanized Infantry Division, 102,
    104–5, 107
France, 86–87, 93, 138
Franks, Tommy, 100, 101, 103
Freedman, Lawrence, 6–7, 34
freedom, 18–19
Friedman, Thomas L., 118, 121
Frost, David, 8
Frum, David, 27, 30
Fukuyama, Francis, 152

Gaddis, John Lewis, 31
Galloway, Joseph L., 100
Garner, Jay, 130, 153
Gause, F. Gregory, 10
Gearty, Conor, 46
Gerecht, Reuel Marc, 20
Germany, 12, 86–87, 138
globalization, 143
global reach, 47–48
Gorbachev, Mikhail, 40
Gordon, Michael, 9, 98
Gordon, Philip, 24
Gore, Al, 26
Grant, Ulysses S., 65
Gray, Colin S., 16
Great Britain, 87, 127, 138
Guderian, Heinz, 90
guerra warfare, 62
guerrilla warfare, 134–37
Gulf Conflict, 1990–1991, 6–7
Gulf War (1991): aftermath of, 11–13;
    Bush administration and, 2–6; Bush
    doctrines rejection of, 66; deterrence
    and, 13–16; legacy of, 1; questions
    about United States performance,
    6–9; sanctions after, 9–11; United
    States foreign policy and, 1–2. *See
    also* Iraq War, 2003

Haass, Richard, 3, 36
Hagel, Chuck, 79
Halliday, Denis, 10
Hamas, 63
Hamza, Khidir, 15
Hanson, Victor David, 65–66
Haqqani, Husain, 135–36
Hart, Gary, 49, 53
Harvey, Robert, 50–51
Heisbourg, Francois, 43
Hendrickson, David C., 35, 39–40
heroin, 142
Hezbollah, 63
Hitchens, Christopher, 90
Hitler, Adolph, 12–13, 78–80, 81–82
Hoar, Joseph P., 103
homeland security, 148–49
Howard, Michael, 42
Hudson Institute, 19
Hussein, Qusay, 135
Hussein, Saddam: archives of, 114; case
    for preemption, 35–36; chemical
    weapons and, 15, 56; comparisons to
    Hitler, 78, 81–82; deterrence and, 13,
    16, 23, 32–33; as legacy of 1991
    Gulf War, 1; nuclear weapons and,
    15–16, 82–83; quick defeat of,
    105–7; survival of, 107–8; suspected
    link to al-Qaeda, 51–52, 59, 61–62,
    147–49; threat of, 141, 144–45;
    Vietnam analogy and, 83–84; view of
    Osama bin Laden, 50
Hussein, Uday, 135

Ignatieff, Michael, 83
Ikenberry, John, 41
INC. See Iraqi National Congress (INC)
India, 138
insurgency, in Iraq, 103–4, 120–21,
    133–37
International Atomic Energy Agency
    (IAEA), 60, 104, 109
International Institute for Strategic
    Studies, 27, 63

International Rescue Committee, 115
interrupted wars, 66
Iran: as axis of evil state, 50, 52; Iraq's
    desire for nuclear weapons and, 110;
    Iraq's oil interests and, 72;
    neoconservatives obsession with, 26;
    as rogue state, 38; United States
    infrastructure and, 132
Iraq: as axis of evil state, 50; complicity
    in 9/11, 52–54; debt of, 75; dissolu-
    tion of army, 139–40; government of
    after war, 116; infrastructure of, 127;
    insurgency in, 103–4, 120–21,
    133–37; lack of evidence of WMD,
    64; liberation of, 76–77, 95–97;
    neoconservatives obsession with, 26;
    oil interests in the Persian Gulf, 72;
    possibility of permanent bases in,
    131–32; possible alliance between
    loyalists and Islamists, 135; possible
    democratization of, 131–33;
    suspected link to al-Qaeda, 51–52;
    U.S reasons for war with, 52–60. See
    also analogies; Iraq War, 2003;
    preventive war
Iraqi National Congress (INC), 122,
    123–24
Iraq War, 2003: civil-military tensions,
    95–96, 98–100; coalition for, 93;
    conclusions about, 142–55; as
    demonstration of Bush doctrine, 68;
    force size in Iraq, 100–105; insur-
    gency after war, 103–4, 120–21,
    133–37; international dissension
    about, 93–95; main attack of, 94;
    military evacuation of Saudi Arabia
    and, 94; one-sidedness of, 90–93,
    105–7; outcome of specified war
    aims, 107–16; power vacuum created
    by, 104; public opinion of, 128; U.S.
    allies, 93; U.S. as liberator, 96–97;
    weapons of mass destruction and,
    108–14. See also analogies; preven-
    tive war; war aims
Islamic jihadists, 121

Islamist Justice and Development Party (JDP), 94–95
Israel, 18, 49
Italy, 93

Japan, 60, 85–89
Jayachandran, Seema, 75
Jervis, Robert, 146–47
Jiang Zemin, 40
Johnson, Lyndon, 65, 78
Jones, James L., 101
Joseph, Robert, 57
Jowitt, Ken, 43
Judt, Tony, 47

Kagan, Donald, 12, 20–21
Kagan, Frederick W., 12, 142, 154–55
Kagan, Robert, 18, 20, 61
Kamil, Husayn, 14
Kaplan, Lawrence F., 18, 22–23, 26–27, 57, 68
Karai, Hamid, 142
Karsh, Efraim, 6–7
Keegan, John, 90, 105
Keller, Bill, 23
Kennan, George F., 37, 57, 146
Kennedy, John F., 39, 53
Kennedy, Robert F., 39
Kenya, 63
Kerry, Bob, 113
Khafaji, Isam al-, 131
Khalilzad, Zalmay, 22
Khomeini, Ayatollah Ruhollah, 50, 57
Khrushchev, Nikita, 40
Kim Jong Il, 61, 145
Kissinger, Henry, 41, 150
Klare, Michael T., 72
Korea, 65
Kosovo, 66
Krauthammer, Charles, 18, 58, 104
Kremer, Michael, 75
Kristol, William: on appeasement, 79; on Bush and North Korea, 61; critique of George H. W. Bush and Clinton administrations, 22–23; on foreign policy based on military primacy, 20–21; influence as a neoconservative, 18, 19; on missile defense, 57; observations about George W. Bush, 26–27; Vietnam Syndrome and, 68
Kupchan, Charles, 150
Kurds, 5, 6–7, 97, 132–33
Kuwait, 3–4, 13, 93

LaFeber, Walter, 30–31
Laqueur, Walter, 45, 47
Lebanon, 68, 88
Lemann, Nicholas, 26
Levy, Jack S., 35
Libby, I. Lewis "Scooter", 19, 22
liberation of Iraq, 76–77, 95–97
Lieven, Anatol, 17, 136
Likud Party, 18
Lind, Michael, 146–47
Lindberg, Tod, 111
looting. s insurgency, in Iraq
Lugar, Richard G., 120

MacArthur, Douglas, 87
Mackey, Sandra, 10, 11, 80
Madison, James, 38
Mahnken, Thomas G., 8
Manhattan Project, 82
Mao Zedong, 40
Marine Corps, U.S., 101
Marshall, Joshua Micah, 70
Marshall Islands, 93
McCaffrey, Barry, 102–3
McCain, John, 96
McKiernan, David D., 106, 120
McNamara, Robert, 98–99
Mead, Walter Russell, 26
Mearsheimer, John J., 57–58
Meet the Press, 95–96
Mexico, 86
Middle East, 22–25, 69–70, 120, 122, 126. See also specific countries
Middle East Institute, 130
mission creep, 3

Mohammed, Khalid Sheikh, 59
Mongolia, 93
Morocco, 63, 93
Moussaoui, Zacarias, 54
Munich analogy, 78–83
Murphy, Richard, 97
Musharraf, Pervez, 145
Muslims, 135–36
Mustafa, Shuqri, 59
Myers, Richard B., 99–100, 103

narrow realism, 22–23
Nash, William C., 102
National Interest, 19, 79
National Journal, 146
National Security Strategy of the United States, The, 30–31, 34, 36, 42, 46, 134
National Strategy for Combating Terrorism, 48
nation-building: Bush's aversion to, 38, 117; democratization of Iraq, 131–33; Pentagon and, 118–20; political legitimacy of, 123–25; sustainability of, 125; troop shortages and, 120–21, 139–40; unsuitability of combat forces for, 121–22. *See also* reconstruction
NATO, 69, 110, 137–38, 150–52
neoconservatives: in the 1990s, 19–20; assumptions of, 125; critique of George H. W. Bush and Clinton administrations, 20–22; democracy in Iraq and, 131–33; embraced by Bush, 146–47; foreign policy of, 25–29; Munich analogy and, 79; nation-building and, 122; on regime change in Iraq, 124; rise to power, 22; view of America's role in Middle East, 22–25; view of America's role in world, 17–19; view of Iraqis as pro-American, 95–96; on war against Iraq, 58; war aims and, 69–70. *See also* Bush doctrine
New Republic, 19

Newsweek, 128
New York Times, 132
Ngo Dinh Diem, 124–25
Niger, 93
Nitze, Paul H., 146
Noriega, Manuel, 6
North Korea: as axis of evil state, 50; neoconservatives' obsession with, 26; nuclear weapons and, 144; as rogue state, 38; threat confusion of United States and, 60–61
Novak, Robert, 96
nuclear weapons: findings in Iraq after war, 108–14; as reason for war against Iraq, 2; rogue states and, 32, 143–44. *See also* weapons of mass destruction
Nye, Joseph S., Jr., 61, 126

occupation. *See* nation-building
Office of Reconstruction and Humanitarian Assistance (ORHA), 130
oil, 11, 71–73, 75–76, 104, 115–16
Oman, 93
Omar, Mohammed, 107
Operation Desert Storm, 5–6, 36
Operation Enduring Freedom, 143
Operation Iraqi Freedom: coalition for, 93; as demonstration of Bush doctrine, 68; military evacuation of Saudi Arabia and, 94. *See also* Iraq War, 2003

Pace, Peter, 135
Packer, George, 24–25
Paemen, Hugo, 152
Pakistan, 43, 52, 63, 93
Panama, 2, 6
peacekeeping. *See* nation-building; reconstruction
Pentagon: changes to force structure, 154; civil-military tensions in, 98–99; definition of terrorism, 46; nation-building and, 118–20. *See also* Department of Defense

Perle, Richard, 17, 20, 22, 24, 96
Philippines, 133
pipeline forces, 102
Poland, 138
political assassination, 47
Pollack, Kenneth, 9, 27, 52, 57, 112
polls, 128
Post, Jerrold, 55
Powell, Colin: appeasement and, 79; opposition to Rumsfeld-Wolfowitz option, 28; on preemption, 38; on Republican Guard, 4–5; on termination of 1991 Gulf War, 4
preemption strategy, 33–38, 69. *See also* preventive war
Present Dangers, Crisis and Opportunity in American Foreign and Defense Policy, 20
preventive war, 34–37, 39–40, 149–53. *See also* Iraq War, 2003
Project for a New American Century (PNAC), 19–20, 22, 118–19
public opinion, 128

Qatar, 93, 132
quagmire, 85, 135
Quandt, William, 9
Qutb, Sayyid, 59

Raines, Howell, 79
reconstruction: allies of United States, 137–38; cost of, 126–29; democratization of Iraq, 131–33; divisions within the Bush administration, 129–31; U.S. underestimation of, 153–55. *See also* nation-building
regime change: Bush administration and, 17; Bush doctrine and, 37–38; insurgency after war, 103–4, 120–21, 133–37; as means to topple Saddam Hussein, 10–11; probable consequences in Vietnam, 66–67; U.S. need for decisive defeat of enemies, 52; as war aim, 74. *See also* Bush doctrine

Report of the Quadrennial Defense Review, 37, 52
Republican Guard, 4–5, 92, 95, 100, 105
Rhodes, Edward, 18
Rice, Condoleezza, 24, 28, 33, 55, 108
Rieff, David, 10–11
Rodman, Peter, 22
rogue states, 31–32, 49–50, 61–62, 125, 143–44
Rommel, Erwin, 90
Roosevelt, Franklin D., 65, 82
Rubin, Trudy, 118
Rumsfeld, Donald: on Clinton administration, 98; on cost of postwar reconstruction, 127–28; focus on Iraq after 9/11, 27–28, 52, 112; force size in Iraq, 104–5; founding of PNAC, 19–20; Munich analogy and, 70–80; neoconservative wave and, 22; outcome of specified war aims, 107–16; on permanent bases in Iraq, 131–32; push for precision bombing in Iraq, 100; rejection of guerrilla warfare in Iraq, 134–35; on threat agents, 31; view of Iraqis as pro-American, 95–96; war aims stated by, 73–74; war plan of, 100–105
Rwanda, 93

sanctions, 9–11, 74–75, 115
Sandinistas, 47
Saudi Arabia: fear of preventive war, 43–44; Iraq as regional surrogate for, 116; Iraq's oil interests and, 72; Iraq War, 2003 and, 93–94; neoconservative view of, 23–24; terrorist attacks in, 63; U.S forces in, 13, 132
Scales, Robert, 99
Schmitt, Gary, 118–19
Schneider, William, 20
Schultz, George P., 129–30
Schwarzkopf, H. Norman, 4, 5, 8
Scowcroft, Brent: on aftermath of Gulf War, 3; departmental disputes and, 130;

Scowcroft, Brent (*continued*)
    on distinction between al-Qaeda and
        Iraq, 53–54; preventive war and, 41–42,
        79; on Saddam's hold on power, 5
Seib, Gerald F., 54
Senegal, 93
September 11th, 17, 52–54, 72–73
Serbia, 142
Sharon, Ariel, 46, 94
Shield of Achilles, 56
Shiites, 5, 7, 57, 97, 121, 123, 132–33,
        139–40
Shinseki, Eric K., 98, 118
shock and awe campaign, 95, 103, 107
Simon, Steven, 49
60 Minutes, 9–10
Snyder, Jack, 79
Somalia, 68, 88
Sorenson, Theodore, 39
Soviet Union, 18, 40, 44, 60, 65, 86
Spain, 86
Spanish-American War, 133
Special Operation Forces, 105
Stahl, Lesley, 9–10
State Department, U.S., 126, 129–31
Stern, Jessica, 115
Stimson Center, 121
Strait of Hormuz, 72
Strategic Survey 2002–2003, 126
Sunni Arab community, 123, 132–33,
        139–40
Syria, 52, 93, 132

Taliban, 97–98. *See also* Afghanistan
Tanenhaus, Sam, 112
Telhami, Shibley, 72
Terrill, W. Andrew, 136
terrorism and terrorist organizations,
        31–32, 45–48, 49–50, 114–15, 125
3d Infantry, 95
3d Mechanized Infantry Division, 102,
        119
threat exaggeration, 113–14
Trainor, Bernard, 9
troop shortages, 120–21, 139–40

Truman, Harry, 41, 44, 146
Tunisia, 63
Turkey, 86–87, 93–95, 132
Turner, Stansfield, 112
Tutwiler, Margaret, 13
Tuwaitha Nuclear Research Center, 103–4

unconditional surrender, 65
UNICEF, 10
United Arab Emirates, 93, 132
United Nations: after Iraq War, 2003, 115;
        result of sanctions against Iraq, 9–10;
        termination of 1991 Gulf War and, 3;
        U.S disdain of, 69, 137–38, 150;
        weapons inspectors, 109
United States: allies in Iraq War, 2003,
        93–94; federal deficit of, 128–29;
        lack of international participation in
        war, 127; moral legitimacy of, 152.
        See also foreign policy
UNSCOM, 110
UN Security Council, 86
U.S. Agency for International Develop-
        ment (USAID), 115, 126
Uzbekistan, 93

Van Evera, Stephen, 48
Versailles Treaty of 1919, 11–12
Vietnam, 54–55, 124–25
Vietnam analogy, 78, 80–81, 83–85
Vietnam Syndrome, 68, 98
Vietnam War, 66, 68
Von Sponeck, Hans, 10

Wallace, William, 102
Wall Street Journal, 54, 127
Walt, Stephen M., 57–58
Waltzer, Michael, 36
war aims: access to oil, 71–73; declared by
        Donald Rumsfeld, 73–74; democrati-
        zation of the Middle East, 69–70;
        demonstrating the ability to use force
        decisively, 68–69; discussion of,
        74–77; effect on possible allies, 93;
        preserving the balance of power, 67

War over Iraq: Saddam's Tyranny and America's Mission, The, 22, 57

Washington Times, 101

weak states, 31–32

weapons of mass destruction: effect of war upon, 149–50; findings in Iraq after war, 108–14; Hussein's perspective on, 11, 56; lack of evidence of in Iraq, 64; rogue states and, 32, 58–59, 143–44. *See also* chemical weapons; nuclear weapons

Webb, James, 88

Webster, Daniel, 35

Weekly Standard, 19, 79, 131

Weinberg, Gerhard, 81

Weinberger, Caspar W., 129–30

Weinberger-Powell doctrine, 68, 98, 125

White, Thomas, 98

white supremacists, 63

Wieseltier, Leon, 61

Will, George F., 113

Wolfowitz, Paul: 1992 Defense Planning Guidance and, 19; creation of PNAC, 19–20; dissent about termination of 1991 Gulf War, 3; focus on Iraq after 9/11, 27–28, 52; on imminent threat, 33; influence as a neoconservative, 22; on length of stay in Iraq, 135; on liberating Iraq, 76; on pre-war assumptions about Iraq, 118–19; on reasons for war, 112; view of Iraqis as pro-American, 95–96; writings of, 20, 21–22

Woodward, Bob, 27–28

World Vision, 115

Worley, D. Robert, 48, 62

Wurmser, Meyrav, 146

Yaphe, Judith, 96

Yemen, 63

Yugoslavia, 2

Zubaydah, Abu, 59

About the Author

Jeffrey Record is a well-known strategist and defense policy analyst with a doctorate from the Johns Hopkins School of Advanced International Studies. He is the author of six other books and a dozen monographs, including *Making War, Thinking History: Munich, Vietnam, and Presidential Uses of Force from Korea to Kosovo* and *The Wrong War: Why We Lost in Vietnam,* both published by the Naval Institute Press, and *Bounding the Global War on Terrorism.*

Dr. Record has extensive Capitol Hill experience, having served as a legislative assistant for national security affairs to senators Sam Nunn and Lloyd Bentsen and as a professional staff member of the Senate Armed Services Committee. During the Vietnam War he served as an assistant province adviser in the Mekong Delta and later was a Rockefeller Younger Scholar on the Brooking Institution's defense analysis staff and a senior fellow at the Institute for Foreign Policy Analysis, the Hudson Institute, and the BDM International Corporation. He lives in Atlanta, Georgia with his wife Leigh.

The Naval Institute Press is the book-publishing arm of the U.S. Naval Institute, a private, nonprofit, membership society for sea service professionals and others who share an interest in naval and maritime affairs. Established in 1873 at the U.S. Naval Academy in Annapolis, Maryland, where its offices remain today, the Naval Institute has members worldwide.

Members of the Naval Institute support the education programs of the society and receive the influential monthly magazine *Proceedings* and discounts on fine nautical prints and on ship and aircraft photos. They also have access to the transcripts of the Institute's Oral History Program and get discounted admission to any of the Institute-sponsored seminars offered around the country.

The Naval Institute also publishes *Naval History* magazine. This colorful bimonthly is filled with entertaining and thought-provoking articles, first-person reminiscences, and dramatic art and photography. Members receive a discount on *Naval History* subscriptions.

The Naval Institute's book-publishing program, begun in 1898 with basic guides to naval practices, has broadened its scope to include books of more general interest. Now the Naval Institute Press publishes about one hundred titles each year, ranging from how-to books on boating and navigation to battle histories, biographies, ship and aircraft guides, and novels. Institute members receive significant discounts on the Press's more than eight hundred books in print.

Full-time students are eligible for special half-price membership rates. Life memberships are also available.

For a free catalog describing Naval Institute Press books currently available, and for further information about subscribing to *Naval History* magazine or about joining the U.S. Naval Institute, please write to:

Membership Department
U.S. Naval Institute
291 Wood Road
Annapolis, MD 21402-5034
Telephone: (800) 233-8764
Fax: (410) 269-7940
Web address: www.navalinstitute.org